The
BEST VIEWS
from the
BOUNDARY

The
BEST VIEWS
from the
BOUNDARY

TEST MATCH SPECIAL'S
GREATEST INTERVIEWS

Compiled by
PETER BAXTER

CORINTHIAN BOOKS

Sold in the UK, Europe, South Africa and Asia
by Faber & Faber Ltd, Bloomsbury House,
74–77 Great Russell Street,
London WC1B 3DA or their agents

Distributed in the UK, Europe, South Africa and Asia
by TBS Ltd, TBS Distribution Centre, Colchester Road,
Frating Green, Colchester CO7 7DW

Published in Australia in 2010
by Allen & Unwin Pty Ltd,
PO Box 8500, 83 Alexander Street,
Crows Nest, NSW 2065

ISBN: 978-190685-021-0

Typeset in Minion by Marie Doherty

Printed and bound in the UK by
CPI Mackays, Chatham ME5 8TD

CONTENTS

Peter Baxter first worked on *Test Match Special* in 1966, and was the producer of the programme from 1973 to 2007. He co-ordinated the BBC's cricket coverage from every one of the Test-playing nations, and has also been part of the commentary team himself.

*Dedicated to the interviewers – Jonathan Agnew,
Henry Blofeld, Simon Mann, Jim Maxwell and the late
Ned Sherrin.*

*But especially to the memory of Brian Johnston, without
whose enthusiasm for the 'Views', they probably would not
still be going.*

INTRODUCTION

When I first took over the production of *Test Match Special* in 1973, the programme was on Radio 3. Although we had a fairly sympathetic network controller, most of his staff were not over-keen on the philistine invasion of cricket commentary. Thus, for intervals or when rain stopped play, my instruction was not to out-stay our welcome and to return the airwaves to serious music and speech as soon as possible.

In this period we only ever had occasional lunch intervals to fill from the cricket, which we did usually with recourse to listeners' letters. My predecessor used to say, 'Get them to explain the LBW law!'

'Your Letters Answered' was the title we gave these sessions, and I can remember sending a bag full of those not yet used on the air up to a Test Match at Trent Bridge and attaching to it a tag on which I frivolously wrote, 'Your Letters Unanswered', which John Arlott fell on as a great programme idea.

Towards the end of the seventies, however, it was discovered that Radio 3 could separate its FM and medium wave frequencies, so that music lovers need not be put out when the cricket was on. So, gradually, the network bosses became less enthusiastic about having some Radio 3 content in the intervals. This meant that I had to think of ideas to fill them myself.

One day during the winter of 1979/80 I heard an interview on the car radio with the playwright Ben Travers, who seemed more keen to talk about his love of cricket than about his famous Aldwych farces. He was telling how he had gone to Australia when his great friend, Percy Chapman, was captaining England on the 1928/29 Ashes tour. It seemed they had even shared a bath in the dressing room, to discuss the day's play.

Enjoying the interview as I did (the image of the bath dismissed), I started to speculate on other celebrities who had a great love of the game and quickly drew up an impressive mental list. I can't remember agonising long over the title. 'A View From the Boundary' came into my head as I walked from Broadcasting House to St Pancras station one evening. A programme idea was born.

I set the basic ground rule that our guests must have a love of the game, but no professional involvement with it. We would do the interviews 'live' in the commentary box – a rule that has been broken only five times in the 30 years of the feature, for HRH the Duke of Edinburgh, Paul Getty, Mick Jagger, Elton John and in 2010 for Colin Montgomerie.

At first my intention was to move the interviewing duties round the commentary team as appropriate to the subject, but very soon it became apparent that the role fell so well on Brian Johnston's shoulders that it became his spot. Apart from anything else, most of the interviewees just wanted to appear in order to be on with him.

After Brian's death in 1994 I again started sharing out the hosting job, but since 2007 Jonathan Agnew has been exclusively in the chair.

Around 180 guests have been grilled – not always on subjects remotely to do with cricket. Actors have been the best represented group (to Johnners' delight), but musicians, politicians (including three prime ministers) and representatives of other sports are close behind, along with a bishop and an archbishop, two former hostages and a pair of police chiefs. All human life is here!

Some have fascinated us, like Ben Travers with his memories of W.G. Grace. Some have been hugely impressive, like that former prisoner of Saddam Hussein, Ian Richter. Brian

Johnston persuaded some to sing with him, Jonathan Agnew persuaded Hugh Cornwell to sing to us, Henry Blofeld even got a line of song from the 'Beast of Bolsover', Dennis Skinner, and Max Boyce and Roy Hudd recited to us.

They range in age from Ben Travers, born in 1886, to Daniel Radcliffe, born in 1989. Some have set the interviewer a hard task, but most have been a joy, and this book is a selection of some of the best over the 30 years.

Peter Baxter

BEN TRAVERS

interviewed by Brian Johnston,
Lord's, 21 June 1980

Although hearing Ben Travers on the radio was the catalyst for 'A View From the Boundary', he was not the first victim. With the First Test of 1980 being at Trent Bridge, I lined up someone local for that – farmer and radio personality Ted Moult. Ben Travers was saved for Lord's, not too far from his Baker Street flat.

If I was anxious about his making the stairs up to our pavilion-top commentary box, I need not have been. Meeting him at the back door of the pavilion, I was impressed to see him make the six flights of stairs with scarcely a heavy breath.

The writer of the great Aldwych farces and 21 plays in all, as well as five novels, was a diminutive figure who was made a great fuss of when he arrived in the box by both John Arlott and Brian Johnston. We all proceeded to be astounded by his memory, which was unaided by any note or reference book. Bill Frindall checked several of his figures as he went along, to establish that his memory had hardly failed him.

There was a spin-off from this interview, when a publisher who had heard it invited Ben to write a book of his cricket memories and Brian to edit it. Although it was done without checking any facts, Brian had scarcely to correct anything. Sadly, though, Ben died just before its publication and the title had to be changed from its originally planned 94 Not Out *to* 94 Declared.

This interview was also deemed to have enough historical interest for E.W. Swanton to include it in the collection he made for the MCC tape, The Golden Age of Cricket.

Brian initially asked Ben when he had first seen a first-class cricket match.

*

BEN TRAVERS: Well, the first Test Match I saw – I think it was the first first-class match I saw – was at the Oval in 1896. I was nine years old and my father took me. They were three-day matches in those days, of course.

It started on a Thursday and it rained most of the first day. They didn't start until after tea and W.G. Grace and F.S. Jackson opened for England, followed by Ranjitsinhji. And it shows that crowds were still enthusiastic, because I remember that when Ranji came in to bat they started singing. I think he only made 7. It was a very low-scoring match. *[In fact Ranji made 8.]*

BRIAN JOHNSTON: And what did W.G. make, do you remember?

BT: Caught Trott, bowled Giffen for 24. And he was out first. Jackson played a very good knock. But England won eventually. It was a bowler's wicket. *[England 145 and 84; Australia 119 and 44. England won by 66 runs.]*

And then later I saw W.G. when he left Gloucester; he started London County at the Crystal Palace – a sort of club of his own. He used to get all the first-class cricketers to come and play for him on their days off – against the counties and that sort of opposition. And there I saw him make a hundred, with Ranji at the other end making another hundred – a very fine partnership. And then I saw him at the Hastings Festival. Oh, and I saw W.G. in one of only two matches in which he played with Jack Hobbs, or rather in which Jack Hobbs played with him. He used to take the London County team to the Oval right at the beginning of the season. It was Jack Hobbs' first appearance. He made 80-odd.

BJ: Ben, before we talk about Jack Hobbs and the rest, what was W.G. like as a man?

BT: Well, of course he was a great hulk of a chap. He was the great predominant figure of cricket in his time – more so than any other individual since. He had a rather odd stance in that he cocked his toe up. He had his left heel on the ground and he cocked his toe up. And he also awaited the ball, when the bowler was half-way through his run, with his bat off the ground. Some comments have been made in recent years about modern batsmen who have done that – Tony Greig, Dennis Amiss, Mike Brearley and Graham Gooch – but W.G. started it. Or at least he did it in his day. He was, I would think, a humorous chap. I don't think he was very sensible.

BJ: Did you hear him talk?

BT: Yes. Like another very large man, G.K. Chesterton, he had a curiously falsetto voice, coming out of so huge a frame. He was, incidentally, you know, a practising doctor. My mother was born and brought up in Clifton and W.G. Grace was their family doctor. None of them lived very long – except one. And she was a nun, so he couldn't get at her. But all the others died young.

BJ: Did you ever see him disagree with an umpire? He's got that reputation.

BT: Disagree! When I saw him make his hundred, he was caught at short leg by a pro. called Brockwell, a Surrey pro., off the bowling of Lockwood for 24 or so, and he made out that it was a bump ball. And he went towards Brockwell, flourishing his bat over his head as though he was going to fell him. So of course the umpire stood there utterly intimidated, gave him not out and he went on to make a hundred. Well, that was W.G.

BJ: And what about Gilbert Jessop? Would you tell me about him?

BT: There can't be many people about now who saw Jessop's classic 104 at the Oval in 1902. It was a wonderful occasion.

That was a very interesting Test Match. The Australians had already won the Ashes and that was the last Test. There was an Australian bowler there called Saunders. He was a brisk left-arm spinner. In the second innings England had to make 263 to win. The first four batsmen in the England side were A.C. McLaren, L.C.H. Palairet, J.T. Tyldsley and Tom Hayward, and Saunders got them all four out for respectively 2, 6, 0 and 7. F.S. Jackson then went in and stayed there. This was about the luncheon interval on the last day, with these four wickets all down to Saunders. Old Hugh Trumble was bowling at the other end. He'd had eight wickets for 65 runs in the first innings, so he was a menace. And I remember sitting on the right of the pavilion and seeing some of the elderly members leaving the ground disgruntled. They couldn't bear to see England so humiliated.

Well, Braund, who came in with Jackson after lunch, was immediately out to Trumble for 2 and in came G.L. Jessop. Jackson put up a wonderful performance – a most sensible innings. At the other end Jessop went absolutely crazy.

This menace, Saunders, who'd already dismissed all our stars – Jessop hit him for four fours in the square leg to long-on district. Hugh Trumble was bowling at the other end. Jessop hit him into the awning on the pavilion. The ball came back. He hit him there again next ball. And so he went on. The enthusiasm was tremendous.

England had utterly no chance of course – but hadn't they? This thing began to dawn – this faint hope, with this man going crazy. In those days the boater hat was the fashion. Everybody wore one and I remember when Jessop made his century staid citizens removed their boater hats and threw them like boomerangs into the air. Unlike boomerangs, they didn't return to their owners – a severe loss in those days. It was a great sacrifice. They must have cost at least three shillings a time. Oh, it was a wonderful sight!

And of course the most thrilling thing was the finish. Because when Jessop was out and Rhodes came in to join Hirst, they wanted fifteen runs from the last wicket. And there was the most canny piece of bowling from old Hugh Trumble. They made the runs gradually until the scores were tied. And Hugh Trumble from the Pavilion End – he'd bowled right through the innings – had a chap called Duff, a very good opening batsman, at deep long-on to the right of the pavilion in what became known as 'Sandham's Corner'. He served Wilfred Rhodes up a slow half-volley on the leg stump. Almost any batsman in the world would have said, 'Oh, here we are.' Crack, wallop – hit it into the air and get caught by Duff. Not a bit of it. Wilfred Rhodes gently tapped it past square leg and ran the one run. And that was that.

[This 1902 Test Match at the Oval gave rise to the legend that the two Yorkshiremen, George Hirst and Wilfred Rhodes, had said they'd 'get 'em in singles'. Australia 324 and 121; England 183 and 263 for 9. England won by one wicket.]

BJ: You've made a lot of tours of Australia, haven't you?

BT: Yes, I've been there several times. I was there, very luckily, in 1928/29 when I saw Bradman play his first innings for Australia against England in Brisbane.

It was a great tour. Of course England had a wonderful side. Percy Chapman was captain, with Jardine making his first tour and Farmer White – they were the three amateurs. Then there were Hobbs and Sutcliffe.

I must say, Brian, that the greatest Test innings I ever saw was played by Jack Hobbs at Melbourne in the first few days of 1929

– the Third Test Match – and he made 49. I think that 49 was the greatest innings I ever saw.

The wickets weren't covered in those days. They were at the mercy of the elements. They had a tremendous thunderstorm the night before and the sun came out the next morning and fairly baked the wicket. The Australians still had two or three wickets to lose in their second innings. Farmer White polished them off in a couple of overs. *[Setting England 332 to win.]* Jack Hobbs said, 'I'm afraid we shall be out by teatime.' And at teatime he and Sutcliffe were still there on what must have been the worst batting wicket anyone can conceive. I went and saw it at the close of play. It was like concrete with great lumps and holes in it. Utterly terrible. *[England won by three wickets – Herbert Sutcliffe making 135.]*

BJ: Have you ever worked out the best batsman and the best bowler you've ever seen?

BT: There are two kinds of batsmen, Brian, aren't there? There is the batsman who says, 'I'm going to slaughter you' and the batsman who says, 'You can't get me out'. I think the greatest 'slaughterer' I ever saw was undoubtedly Don Bradman. The greatest 'you-can't-get-me-outer' was Jack Hobbs and of course there were others like that. It's the approach to the game, not merely the execution – the mental approach to the game. I think the 'can't-get-me-outers' could play fast innings if the circumstances arose, but it's the sort of general attitude to it – Hutton, Woodfull, Lawry, Boycott.

And then, of course, of the 'slaughterers' there are many. Well, we saw one yesterday. *[The previous day Viv Richards had made 145 in this Lord's Test, reaching three figures in 125 balls and scoring 106 of his runs in boundaries.]* It's hard to believe, watching that innings yesterday, that there could ever be a better 'slaughterer' in cricket, but I think Don Bradman must be tops.

BJ: Did you see Victor Trumper?

BT: Oh yes.

BJ: How great was he?

BT: He was great. But he wasn't all that graceful. He was supposed to be, but he wasn't. He had the most extraordinary stance, with his knee bent in front of him. He was terrific. When I saw Bradman play at Melbourne in 1928, he made a glorious cover drive and an excited member in the stand jumped up and said, 'Trumper!' And he was damn nearly lynched. It was blasphemy.

BJ: Did you think then that Bradman was going to be a great player?

BT: Well, yes. We'd been told before the tour that there were two chaps who were up and coming cricketers – Archie Jackson and Don Bradman. Of course poor Archie Jackson would have been, I think, but he had consumption and died young. But, oh, Bradman, yes, he was terrific.

BJ: Do you like watching wicket keepers?

BT: I think Alan Knott is tremendous. In my young days Bertie Oldfield was supposed to be the best and then he was superseded by Evans and now by Alan Knott.
But there was a very strange wicket keeper – a marvellous wicket keeper in my younger days who's still going strong – although not still keeping wicket – called Howard Levett. He

used to stand up to fast bowling. Of course he couldn't do it today, unless he wore a pair of stilts. But that would rather handicap his wicket keeping, I should think. He was an amazing chap.

BJ: Just one more question, Ben. You wrote one farce about cricket, called *A Bit of a Test*.

BT: *A Bit of a Test*, yes. It wasn't expected to appeal to a very large public. It was after Douglas Jardine's tour with Larwood – the Bodyline row. And it was a sort of skit on that.

BJ: What was Ralph Lynn – captain of England?

BT: No, I'm afraid that was Robertson Hare.

BJ: Oh, purgatory and pandemonium!

BT: He went in first with Ralph.

BJ: And Tom Walls, what was he – the villain?

BT: No, Tom Walls merely produced. I think he kept out of it.

I used to have great fun with Robertson-Glasgow, dear old Crusoe. I remember picking a team from world history of those you'd like to see playing in a Test Match. I had a wonderful opening pair – Beethoven and John the Baptist, with Attila the Hun as fast bowler and Torquemada as the spinner. And marvellous umpires – Judge Jeffreys and Pontius Pilate.

BJ: We've had a wonderful 25 minutes and if it's ever raining at a Test here, may we ring you up to come and entertain us?

*

Ben Travers died on 18 December 1980 – sixth months after this interview – at the age of 94.

MICHAEL BENTINE

interviewed by Brian Johnston,
Lord's, 13 August 1983

I have often heard from people how they were made helpless with
laughter when they heard Brian Johnston and Jonathan Agnew in
hysterics over the notorious 'leg-over' remark and had to pull the
car into a lay-by or stop whatever else they were doing. Before that,
the TMS *session which seemed to have caused similar paralysis to*
the nation was this interview with the great television entertainer,
Michael Bentine.

Bentine started as a straight actor and then turned to comedy
after the war, co-founding The Goon Show *with Spike Milligan,*
Peter Sellers and Harry Secombe. While the other three carried on
with that, he turned to television where he created the Bumblies,
strange looking puppets after whom David 'Bumble' Lloyd gained
his nickname. His comedy programme It's a Square World *won a*
number of awards and introduced us to a wonderful imaginary
flea circus among other flights of anarchic fantasy.

Away from comedy, Michael Bentine was a scientist and expert
in parapsychology. He was also almost certainly the only holder
of the Peruvian Order of Merit to have been interviewed on Test
Match Special *– his father having had that nationality. Like Brian*
himself, Michael was educated at Eton, so there was a certain
amount of reminiscence of the old school, starting with Brian's first
question about whether at school he had been a cricketer or an
oarsman – or, in Eton language, a 'dry bob' or a 'wet bob' – before
we heard some of the tortured detail of his war service.

*

MICHAEL BENTINE: I was a dry bob – very much so. In fact,
when I was arrested for desertion … which was interesting,

because I wasn't in the RAF at the time, there was a very slight screw-up over the names and I was still waiting to go into the RAF. Because I volunteered many times, but they kept on saying things like, 'But you're of non-European descent.'

And I said, 'Well, even in this light I can almost pass for white.' Because in those days they were the most discriminating lot you've ever met in your life. And eventually this chap turned up with the RAF police uniform and he said, 'Mr Michael Bentine?'

And I said, 'Yes', thinking, 'At last! They've accepted me. I'm in!'

And he said, 'You're a deserter. Sixty-five days adrift.'

And I found myself here at Lord's in front of A.H.H. Gilligan, the captain of England, who was, of course, practically God. And he said, 'You can't be a deserter, you're an Etonian.'

And I said, 'I'm not only an Etonian, I'm a Peruvian – the only Peruvian ever born in Watford. They've arrested me and I haven't been in the RAF yet.'

And he said, 'I know, there's been the most terrible muck-up about the whole thing.' And then he said, 'When you were at Eton, were you a dry bob or a wet bob?'

And I said, 'I was a dry bob, sir.'

'Get your sixpenny?' [Sixpenny is the first cricket colour you can get at Eton.]

'Yes, sir,' I said.

'Play for your house?'

'Yes, sir.'

'Not a bowler, are you?'

'Yes, sir. Slow left arm.'

'Can't bowl a chinaman, can you?'

I said, 'Yes, I can bowl the chinaman.'

He said, 'Must have you in the RAF.'

I could have been Hitler's adopted son, so long as I could bowl the chinaman.

BRIAN JOHNSTON: You know you're talking about the chairman of selectors' – Peter May's – late father-in-law?

MB: Really? There were two Gilligans, weren't there?

BJ: Yes, A.E.R. was Arthur and this was Harold. So, you were a bowler, rather than a batter?

MB: I was an appalling batsman, because I suppose my eyes were beginning to go. By 1943 I think I was the only aircrew cadet who needed a Braille instrument panel. When they caught me trying to get the guide-dog into the front turret, there was murder. They put me into Intelligence, which I think shows how desperate they were in 1943. And all that happened here at Lord's. *[The Lord's pavilion was used during the Second World War for medical assessments and recruiting for the forces.]* And those were the days of Howard Marshall, with that lovely voice, 'A beautiful day here, with the tracery of clouds – a perfect setting.' He never told you about the cricket, but he told you everything else about the game. And the next time I saw him was on the beach-head in Normandy.

BJ: What were you doing there – Intelligence?

MB: Theoretically, but at the time I was praying. Unfortunately my truck had sunk. They'd opened the doors of the landing craft and I'd said, 'Forward!' And it went into about 80 feet of water and we sort of floated ashore with these life-jacket things on. And I spent about three days trying to find my unit, saying, 'Excuse me, old chap …'
'Get down, you're drawing fire!'

And this chap was in a shell hole and I heard this voice. He'd got this huge machine with him, which made recorded discs, and he said, 'It's a lovely day here on the beach-head and you can hear the sound of the shells going over. And earlier – of course you couldn't see them, but you could hear them – the gliders whistling through the air.'

And I thought, we can't possibly lose, because Howard Marshall's here. *[In the 1930s, Howard Marshall was the first man really to create the art of cricket commentary on the radio.]*

BJ: Now, you speak how many languages?

MB: I don't really. Everybody thinks I'm a linguist. I stagger along in several. I spoke French and Spanish, so the British put me with the Poles instantly.

BJ: You've been a bit shocked by the short-pitched bowling today.

MB: I was shattered by those bouncers coming in. 'Oh, yes he's hit him! Well done! Right on the side of the head! Fractured skull!' And they're all wearing crash helmets and body armour. It's like American football.

BJ: What did you do when you played?

MB: Ducked a lot. I didn't even wear a box in those days – I wasn't all that well developed.

BJ: You were one of the original cast of *The Goon Show*. How many of those did you do?

MB: Oh, Lord knows. I did an awful lot. *[For the record, it was 38 shows.]* I was one of the original four and I always felt that four was too many. Three's a magic number, four's not really a magic number. It was great fun doing it. I did it for about two years in the run-up to it and then I think I was with them for about two and a half years. And I'm still with them in spirit.

BJ: Is the humour of the Goons unique?

MB: I think it's the most magnificent rubbish ever written. It's absolute nonsense. We used to get away with murder. We had 'Singes Thing', the Irish arsonist, at a time when there was still the influence of Lord Reith, who was very Calvinistic.

BJ: But you were censored a bit on the Goons, weren't you?

MB: Well, they used to say things like, 'You can't say that. The inference is revolting.' And they didn't realise that we were using terrible tag-lines like, 'It's your turn next in the barrel.' But they hadn't been in the services and we were all ex-servicemen and we couldn't have cared less. They'd try to read into it all sorts of meanings and they were all old Army jokes, old Navy jokes or old RAF jokes.

BJ: Which voices were you?

MB: I was the original Henry Crun and I was Pure Heart, who was one of those idiots with lines like, 'Start up the engines of the mighty Brabazon.' And you would hear the sound of a steam train pulling out of a station and he'd say, 'Ask the chief engineer to step into my office.' It was all that insanity and people read into it as though it was some sort of intellectual exercise.

BJ: Now, I didn't see you on the halls, but didn't you have an act with a bit of a chair?

MB: I was desperate. I moved a lot. With an act like mine, you've got to keep moving. I did have this back of a chair, which I'd broken when I was with my brother and sister-in-law. It had fallen off and looked like a sub-machine gun and my brother had picked it up and said, 'I'll shoot you with it.' And I thought, 'What a marvellous idea', and I made things out of it and I did a lot of those things afterwards.

BJ: You did something with that thing you shove down a drain.

MB: A sink plunger. Yes, that became the last trolley bus in England and all sorts of strange things – Long John Silver, by shoving it on the knee – and I stuck it on my face. It nearly killed me – broke my nose, too.

BJ: Do you like working by yourself, then?

MB: Well, I've always been a loner essentially. I stammered so dreadfully until I was about sixteen, but at Eton a man called Burgess taught me to speak with 'a swing-and-a-rhythm-and-a-pause-and-a-run'. And the first thing I did was to walk into the Soc Shop, which of course is the tuck shop. And they all stopped as if I was the gunfighter who'd just come through the double doors. And I walked in and declaimed, 'N-may I have n-fish cake?'

And there was a dead silence and the lady said, 'What sort, dear? You want salmon or you want ordinary fish?'

I went, 'Well, er, er …' because I'd only learnt the first bit. And then I learnt to say, 'N-bangers and n-mash', so I lived off bangers and mash.

BJ: How did you cure your stammer?

MB: I slowly learnt the vocabulary. I got the food first and then I used to come into the shop to great choruses of, 'N-may he have n-fishcake!' Well, you know what a mad school it was.

BJ: And then you had this TV series, *It's a Square World*. This was your own thing, wasn't it?

MB: Oh yes. I've always written my own stuff. It was a sort of conglomerate-type mad news programme, which later became things like *Not the Nine O'Clock News* and *Monty Python* and generally got filthed up, whereas when I did it they were dead clean. But only because we weren't allowed to be anything else.

I once got hauled up for burning a brick, because I used to destroy Television Centre in pretty well every programme. I used to burn it up or send it into space or destroy it with a 'Gardening Club' giant man-eating orchid. And on this occasion I'd burnt a brick with a smoke machine. There was hell to pay. And they sent me this marvellous memo, which I have framed. 'Under no circumstances must the BBC Television Centre be used for the purposes of entertainment.'

One chap said to me, 'If it wasn't for you lot, this would be a good job.'

I said, 'If it wasn't for us lot, you wouldn't have a job.'

*

Michael Bentine died in 1996, aged 74.

RICHARD STILGOE &
PETER SKELLERN

interviewed by Brian Johnston,
The Oval, 27 August 1983

Early in 1983, Brian Johnston was the subject of This is Your Life, *back in the days when it was still Eamonn Andrews wielding the big red book. The ambush was pulled off with the considerable input of the Lord's Taverners, leading up to the moment when Eamonn appears, saying, 'You thought you were going to a Lord's Taverners event, but tonight, Brian Johnston, This is Your Life.'*

The actual show was done in the Kingsway theatre and I was fortunate enough to be included in the wonderful evening. At the reception afterwards I was approached by one of the Taverners who had been involved in setting Brian up – Richard Stilgoe. He told me that he'd really like to do 'A View From the Boundary' and, as I was never going to turn down a volunteer, I fixed a date then and there.

Johnners was a good friend of Richard's and an admirer of his ability as pianist, singer, lyricist, composer, humorist and – possibly closest to Brian's heart – punster. In Brian's estimation he was 'the best cabaret artist of the present day'. And that probably hasn't changed.

Nine years later Richard was to write and perform a poem for Brian Johnston's memorial service:

The cherubim and seraphim are starting to despair of him
They've never known a shade so entertaining.
He chats to total strangers, calls the Angel Gabriel 'Aingers'
And talks for even longer if it's raining.

Shortly before his appearance on the programme, Richard rang to ask if he could bring a friend – Peter Skellern, he of 'You're a Lady' fame. The two of them were involved together as singer/songwriter/ pianists in a cabaret act. Inevitably in the commentary box they were quickly 'Stillers and Skellers'.

*

BRIAN JOHNSTON: Let's start with Skellers. Are you a player of cricket or a watcher?

PETER SKELLERN: I'm a player. I play village cricket now and I played when I was at school. I was wicket keeper at cricket, goalkeeper at football and full back at rugby, which are all the 'hands' positions and great for a pianist.

BJ: Looking at your hands – for such a pianist, those are rather big mitts.

PS: You do need them, you know. People believe you're supposed to have long, elegant fingers to play the piano, but it's all wrong, really. You need big, meaty hands to do it properly. But I can play all sorts of music, except rock'n'roll, because it actually hurts my fingers to do that.

RICHARD STILGOE: This is, in fact, because he is protecting his wicket keeping skills all the time. I play rock'n'roll quite a lot, because I'm a slow bowler and it strengthens the spinning finger.

BJ: It's very brave of him, actually, as a pianist, to keep wicket, because you can get the odd knock on the finger.

PS: Well, I broke my finger once.

BJ: Did it affect your playing?

PS: Yes, it did for a year. I couldn't stretch the octave and I had to re-learn to stretch, and it still aches after a couple of hours.

BJ: Stillers, you play nowadays for the Taverners. Were you ever a very good player?

RS: No, I was appalling. I was absolutely dreadful.

PS: That's not what you said to me.

RS: It's very difficult, because, like everybody else who can't play cricket, I bowl slow leg breaks. Or I say they're slow leg breaks and we just happen to be unlucky and they're not turning today. I am in fact the natural successor to Underwood, but no batsman in the world knows this – so they hit me out of the ground.

BJ: How would you describe your occupation? Are you an entertainer?

RS: Well, partly an entertainer and partly a cricketer. I suppose a 'Tavaré artist' would be about the closest.

BJ: But you write all your own material and you're very good at producing a lyric at a moment's notice – about anything.

RS: Well, not at a moment's notice, if you're about to ask me to do one. It's my day off. I write songs about almost everything except cricket, because I'm terribly serious about cricket. I wouldn't dream of making jokes about it – it's far too important.

BJ: But your other great skill is making anagrams of people's names.

RS: I'm jolly lucky in that my name happens to rearrange itself into a lot of useful other names, like Sir Eric Goldhat, who is the richest man in the world. Then there's Dr Gloria Ethics, who you will seldom meet. And my favourite other one is Giscard O'Hitler, who is president of the whole of Europe.

BJ: Can you do anyone from the commentary box?

RS: You're rather a difficult lot. Your name, for instance, has got a 'J' in it. It's very difficult to hide a 'J'. I did once, years and years ago, work with an American group called the Tin Horn Banjos. And if you rearrange them you get ... Brian Johnston.

BJ: What about Sir Frederick Trueman, now? Is it possible to get one out of him?

RS: Usually, when you rearrange the name, you get something completely different from the character of the person, which is why, if you rearrange 'Fred Trueman' you get 'ruder fat men', which is obviously nothing like the character himself.

The longer names are, of course, harder. Christopher Martin-Jenkins – you get almost the whole of *War and Peace* if you rearrange that.

BJ: How long does it take you to write what are very much up-to-date lyrics?

RS: Like anybody in journalism, really, you do it at the last minute. And you rely on the adrenalin to get it done. It is easier to write a speech twenty minutes before you've got to make it than it is four weeks before, because terror gets it written for you.

BJ: Skellers, when did you start this mixture – you in the white tie and tails and then suddenly a brass band appears? It seems strange until you hear it and then it's an absolutely marvellous mixture.

PS: I was in the National Youth Brass Band when I was a boy. I played trombone. Being brought up in a Lancashire mill town, bands were all around you and that was the music that was made. The first hit song I did was 'You're a Lady' and it was about a northern girlfriend, so I decided to use a brass band rather than an orchestra. And it worked a treat. It surprised me too. It surprised everybody.

BJ: How long did that take you to write?

PS: A morning. I sound like Ernie Wise. Actually I wrote twelve songs in ten days, all of which were among my better songs, and all were used. It was just some brainstorm that I had. And that was one of them.

BJ: Does that happen with you, Stillers?

RS: Not always, but you do certainly get a week when you write some definitely second-division stuff – rather than the fourth-division stuff – and then four weeks when you can't write anything at all, however hard you try.

BJ: Do you keep bringing yourself up to date?

RS: You change the name of the prime minister whenever it's necessary, yes. It's been very difficult, actually, for all male performers having a lady prime minister. It brought Janet Brown to the fore and sent the rest of us rather into the background. I'm still working on my Neil Kinnock impression. *[Margaret Thatcher had at this time been prime minister for four years and Neil Kinnock had just become leader of the Labour opposition.]*

BJ: Have you got the Welsh lilt?

RS: Oh, no, it's mainly combing the hair across the top of the head that I'm working on.

BJ: You wrote a song about Lillee and Thomson. Were you the first to think about 'Lillian Thomson' as a woman?

RS: I think I originally thought of 'Lillian Skinner', because of the shoe shop. She became 'Lillian Massie' in the year when Massie got all those wickets at Lord's. And then, when Thomson took over, 'Lillian Thomson' started off and I did this song, which was then made hugely popular by Rachel Heyhoe, I think.

BJ: Can you give us the words?

RS: It's all about slips and covers and things and it's quite improper. I'm not sure if I can remember the words. I'm not sure if I should. It's mainly that in Lillian Thomson Australia have the world's best opening pair.

BJ: Oh, I see, it's that sort of song.

RS: Which is why I'm not going to sing it for you now.

> She's the fastest lady bowler the world has ever seen.
> Her bumper's awe-inspiring and her language far from
>   clean.

That's quite enough of that.

*

At that point, Johnners, as was his wont, persuaded his guests to launch into a version of one of Peter Skellern's hits, 'The Way You Look Tonight', in which Peter's singing was supported by a vocal brass section of Johnston, Stilgoe and Christopher Martin-Jenkins. It was relayed by the public address announcer to the crowd, who had previously been enjoying their lunch.

JOHN CLEESE

interviewed by Brian Johnston,
Headingley, 21 June 1986

'View From the Boundary' guests are always invited to spend as much – or as little – time in the commentary box as they want. One who arrived determined not to miss a ball of the morning session was John Cleese. He sat at the back of our poky, scruffy commentary box with a schoolboy's enthusiasm for the unfolding events and seemed surprised that we treated it – as it is for us – as another day at the office.

The star of Monty Python's Flying Circus *and* Fawlty Towers *and now so many more things revealed himself as a passionate follower of cricket.* A Fish Called Wanda *and his promotion to 'Q' in the James Bond films was still to come, but it was the cricket passion that was a good starting point for Brian.*

*

JOHN CLEESE: I wish I spent a bit more time watching it, because I do get very intrigued by it. It's a wonderful game and I lost contact with it a few years after I stopped playing. I really stopped playing after Cambridge and anyway I never played for anyone good at Cambridge – just my college.

BRIAN JOHNSTON [*an Oxford man*]: Is there anyone good at Cambridge?

JC: Oh, there were good ones at the time. It was Brearley's era, more or less. But I went off to America and I lost contact. It's funny, once you've been away from the game for two or three years, it takes a long time to get back in. I got back to England and didn't really get interested again until Somerset started winning matches. I grew up in the fifties, when I think they got the wooden spoon seven years in a row.

BJ: With people like C.C. Case and J.C.W. McBryan.

JC: That was before me. They were OK. But there was a time in the fifties when they used to win about one match a season and I used to trot down to Taunton or Weston-super-Mare to watch them and they were terrible, absolutely terrible.

BJ: You're a great analyser. The probing questions you were putting to us all earlier showed you were watching very carefully and trying to work things out.

JC: I find it fascinating – endlessly fascinating.

BJ: Can we go back to when you first played cricket. How tall were you as a boy at Clifton?

JC: Well, I was too tall too soon. I was six foot when I was twelve, at my prep school in Weston-super-Mare, where I was coached by Bill Andrews.

BJ: What a character!

JC: That's right. One of the difficulties of my cricket watching was that I grew up with that extraordinary Somerset team of the late forties, with people like Harold Gimblett and Arthur Wellard and dear Bertie Bewes.

BJ: Bertie Bewes – he had a pub later.

JC: Oh, he was wonderful, with that extraordinary little hop, skip and jump run-up. And tiny little Johnny Lawrence and Harold

Stephenson – I can't imagine a team so full of personalities. And anything after that has always seemed less colourful.

BJ: To me the sad thing is that their cricket was fun, although they might not have done so well. Now it's all 'You must win', and you get spectators who just want to see them win and don't really care about the characters or the type of cricket.

JC: But that's been a kind of continuing process as long as I can remember. Winning has become progressively more important and once that happens sport loses something, doesn't it? The great moments of sportsmanship do send a kind of thrill round the crowd, because they're a reminder that what is bringing us together is greater than the need to defeat each other.

That's why those great moments of sportsmanship are so touching and absolutely transform the atmosphere round the ground in a moment. But there's very little of that now because the idea that winning is more important than anything else has completely taken over.

BJ: Let's go back to a twelve-year-old six-footer. You could have been a demon fast bowler – the terror of the other schools.

JC: I was physically weak and fragile. I was incredibly thin, so I used to run up quite a long way and then bowl slow, which was a good trick for the first ball. Also it was only when I got to about the age of eighteen that I realised that I needed a long bat, because the moment I picked the bat up, I was literally overbalancing towards the off stump, having been at too great an angle to start with.

BJ: And when you went to Clifton, was the great Reg Sinfield coach?

JC: Yes, and a marvellous coach too. In fact, although I was fond of several of the masters at Clifton, I think I got more from Reg than I did from any of the others. He was a terrific coach, but he also had a wonderful kind of wry humour and wisdom about him.

He went on coaching at Clifton for years after I left and I remember him telling me that he was bowling fast to Bill Ponsford during the Australian tour of 1934.

BJ: And I saw him – it dates me – in 1926 with Dipper, who went in first for Gloucestershire.

JC: He bowled fast to start with and then off-spin.

BJ: Like Goddard.

JC: That's right. Sinfield one end and Goddard the other. [Reg Sinfield played for Gloucestershire from 1924 to 1939, scoring over 15,000 runs and taking over 1,100 first-class wickets. He played one Test for England in 1938.]

BJ: Did you have any other great players who you particularly followed – Compton?

JC: I suppose Denis Compton was one, but funnily enough it was more that old Somerset team that caught my imagination and I only began to lose interest after our fifth wooden spoon in a row. And then I seemed to get back into it, partly because the team of the late seventies actually started winning one or two trophies.

I can still remember sitting at Lord's in 1979 when we won our first Gillette Cup. We'd been in the final the year before and lost to Sussex and then we finally beat Northants. But it would never be the same. I actually sat there thinking, 'They've won something. They've actually won.' It was the first time they'd won anything in a hundred years and I felt it would never be the same again. The romance had gone out of it.

BJ: Did you ever captain a side?

JC: Yes, I captained my prep school team. I've got a photograph of myself walking off the field, because at that time I was already over six foot and of course all the others were about four foot. It's an extraordinary picture.

BJ: I hope you don't mind analysing yourself a bit. People think of you as irascible.

JC: Ah, but that's only since *Fawlty Towers*. What happens is that people form a kind of stereotyped image of you, depending on what was the last thing that you did. If you go back about twenty years to the time I started on the box with David Frost in 1966 – *The Frost Report* with Ronnie Barker, Ronnie Corbett, Julie Felix, Tom Lehrer – in those days I was very much Frostie's sidekick and people would expect me to be standing around by David Frost. Then shortly after that *Python* started and then I was regarded as a great kooky, zany, madcap.

BJ: Very often the establishment figure who was being mocked – in pinstriped suit and bowler hat.

JC: But that's not what people remembered so much, although actually that is what I did. People thought of me as just being wild and unpredictable. But unfortunately I've never achieved that.

BJ: In private life are you wild and unpredictable?

JC: No, I'm rather tame and predictable and boring, actually. Slightly introverted, which surprises people, but you often find that people who are slightly shy and introverted are able to explode into action when they're given a socially sanctioned opportunity to do so – like being on the stage and damn well having to be extrovert.

BJ: You did a pretty useful Hitler – an unlikely Hitler at six foot six or so.

JC: Yes, that Hitler sketch was one of my two or three favourites. I wrote it with Michael Palin.

BJ: I bet I know another one – the old dead parrot.

JC: The dead parrot I was fond of, and also the cheese shop.

BJ: Did you write those as well?

JC: Most of them. The Hitler one is the only one I think I ever wrote with Michael Palin, which was a great delight. But one of the disappointments of *Python* was that we always fell into patterns of writing with the same people. I think it would have been much more fun if we'd mixed the writing up.

BJ: Did you all sit round a table as a sort of soviet of writers?

JC: Well, we used to sit round for about three days at the beginning of a series and have lots of ideas and agree what we were going to write and then go off and write completely different things. I think that was because once someone had thought of the idea there was then no honour in writing it. The prestige comes with thinking of the idea and writing it. Then we used to get together each week and read each other's material out.

There was not a great deal of passion for cricket amongst the Python group. *[Although four years later Eric Idle did come on the programme.]*

BJ: But you used to do some sketches which took off me and Peter West once or twice. Who was the chap who put those in, because he obviously watched us closely and took off our mannerisms?

JC: I'm afraid that was me. I'd forgotten that sketch. I think I wrote that originally for the radio and then I think we re-wrote it, as far as I remember. And we also had 'Pasolini's Test Match', which had naked cricketers writhing on the ground.

BJ: Do you think that would improve cricket?

JC: No, I like it staid.

BJ: With the white flannels and all that. Let's hope they never wear shorts. Now at Cambridge you got into the Footlights. Had you ever done any acting before? Why did you join the Footlights?

JC: I don't really know. It's all very strange, because there's not a great deal of artistic activity in Weston-super-Mare and certainly no one in my family or anywhere near it had ever been in entertainment or on the stage or anything like that. But I think it was something to do with being so tall and also being an only child and therefore slightly reserved and capable of being on my own a lot without needing to seek out company. I think I found that when I first went to school I was a little bit of an outsider. And I think I discovered that by making people laugh I could get accepted and become more popular.

I discovered I could get laughs – I remember quite distinctly – in form 2A in Mr Sanger-Davies' English lesson. It was that particular moment that I started making jokes. And I remember that the class laughed. And I remember that it made me feel very good. It's actually a wonderful feeling to make people laugh. Everybody likes to tell jokes.

BJ: I've tried for years and I haven't had the feeling yet! Are you bored with being asked about *Fawlty Towers*? Do you mind people thinking of you as Basil Fawlty?

JC: I think there's always a bit of you that would rather the audience thought that the writing and acting was an exercise in craft of some kind. But it is a funny thing, because John Howard-Davies, who produced the first several *Fawlty Towers*, warned me in advance, when he realised the show was going to be a success.

He said, 'You realise that now everybody will think you are like Basil.'

And I said, 'Will they really?'

He said that it is always the case that straight actors are recognised as actors. Nobody thinks that Laurence Olivier is going to be terribly jealous because he played Othello. People are going to say his was a performance. But, he said that if you do a successful comic character, like an Alf Garnett or one of the Richard Briers or Leonard Rossiter characters, then they always think that's who you are. And I've noticed it's true, but it's only with comedy.

BJ: When you used to hit poor Manuel, was that a false clap, or did you actually strike him once or twice?

JC: There are ways of faking it, but on one occasion, I'm afraid, when I was hitting him with a saucepan, I didn't quite get the timing right and dear old Andrew Sachs was a little bit out to lunch for two days.

BJ: Now, you did twelve programmes.

JC: That's right, only twelve. And do you know how long ago they were? 1975 and 1979.

BJ: Any particular favourites? The one with the rat running loose?

JC: The rat I was enormously fond of. The special effects department produced that rat and I almost kissed them. We got about 60 seconds out of that rat sitting in the biscuit tin. I loved the dead body one and my favourite moment is in the one where he goes down to get the ducks from the restaurant. You remember he drops the first one, gets the second and he's only got the blancmange. The best bit is when he takes the lid off and puts it straight back on, as though it might help the blancmange to go away. But when he lifts it up again, he actually looks in the blancmange – puts his fingers down into it – just in case there's a duck underneath.

BJ: Is it a fact that you might be writing some more, or is it curtains?

JC: No, Connie and I wrote them together and after we'd done the twelve we definitely felt that if we wrote any more we knew what the audience would say. They'd say that they enjoyed it but that they weren't as good as the first two series. I don't think there was any way of getting round it. The second series was probably the best thing I'll ever do, which is why I don't come on television now, because if I do something that isn't as good, people will say, 'Ah, he's not as good any more.'

The only people who tell me they don't enjoy *Fawlty Towers* are hoteliers, who sit there for three minutes and suddenly they see what's going to happen. They see that the chef's going to get drunk, or there's going to be a dead body and from then on they sit there in the most appalling state of nerves. But I can get that watching England play cricket or football normally – particularly football – there's no enjoyment in it at all.

BJ: Well I hope you're going to spend the afternoon here with us.

JC: Oh yes. It's very nice to be asked and you do get the best view in England from this box. It's almost as good as television!

HRH THE DUKE
OF EDINBURGH

interviewed by Brian Johnston,
Lord's, 22 August 1987

In 1987 the Marylebone Cricket Club reached its bicentenary. Just a little ahead of Australia – the country, not the cricket team. Appropriately, the foremost cricket club in the world resolved to stage a celebratory match of such a quality that Test Match Special *could accord it nothing less than the full treatment, with ball-by-ball commentary.*

For such an occasion our 'View From the Boundary' would have to be taken by an appropriately significant guest. Who better than the only living person to have been President of MCC twice – His Royal Highness Prince Philip?

I tentatively put in our request for this special interview for a special occasion and was delighted when it was agreed. It would, however, have to be recorded (the first time we had done this for one of our 'Views') as the Royal Family would be at Balmoral at the time of the match.

Brian Johnston had met the Duke a few times before, so I was a little surprised to find him quite tense for this encounter, when we headed for our appointment at Buckingham Palace. He began the interview by asking what sort of a cricketer His Royal Highness had been in his youth.

*

Duke of Edinburgh: Well, I never was very good. I started at my prep school, Cheam. And then I had a bit of a break, because I went away to Germany for a year to school and then came back again to Scotland and played there until I joined the Navy.

BRIAN JOHNSTON: I rather cheated, I'm afraid, because I found a report of you at Cheam which said, 'An energetic all-rounder, highly unsympathetic to stonewalling.' A hard-hitting batsman?

D OF E: Well, I may have tried to hit it hard, but I don't think I really succeeded all that often.

BJ: And what about Gordonstoun? Did they take cricket seriously there?

D OF E: Fairly seriously, yes. But the only problem was that I was there right at the beginning and we didn't have a ground or a pitch. We used to go to the public park at Elgin and play there. But it was quite fun. We played all sorts of people, like the Army at Fort George and various schools.

BJ: And was there any cricket in the Navy?

D OF E: Very little, because I joined in the summer of 1939 and so was rather pitchforked into the war and there was really very little opportunity to play cricket. I did play once, though, just after the war, in Malta. And I had one ghastly match in Akaba. That's not a place to play cricket in my opinion. I know exactly what it feels like to run out of water in the desert. After I'd bowled three overs, my tongue swelled up to such a degree that I couldn't breathe.

I had a short period after the war when I played at Windsor. Do you remember the cartoonist, Jackie Broome?

BJ: Oh, yes.

D OF E: I remember one glorious occasion when I thought I'd bowl a googly. It came out of the back of my hand and when it hit the ground it actually used to go the wrong way, but this time it flew fairly high into the air and Jackie Broome saw this coming and ducked, whereupon it hit the wicket full toss. He then did a splendid cartoon of this ball arriving.

BJ: A thing like Spedegue's Dropper. *[The ball that was the fictional creation of Arthur Conan Doyle.]*

D OF E: That's right.

BJ: I'm told that you once took one for 12 against Hampshire.

D OF E: George Newman organised a series of matches for the National Playing Fields Association. The first one was at Bournemouth – the first time I'd ever played on a good pitch. I rather enjoyed it and of course playing with first-class cricketers. They had a marvellous way of organising the game.

BJ: They're pretty cunning, aren't they?

D OF E: Yes. Everybody was allowed to get off the mark, but there came a moment when it was considered that they'd had enough. Things got quite serious then. John Reid played in that match and I think he made the fastest 50 that anyone's ever made anywhere.

BJ: Not off your bowling, though?

D OF E: No, I think he was on my side. I thought I did rather well, though, making 25 runs. And at Arundel one thing I do remember is that I had Tom Graveney caught at short leg, which of course caused enormous hilarity all round.

BJ: What about the great moment in 1950, when you were approached by Martin Boddey and co. to become patron of the Lord's Taverners?

D OF E: I said 'patron' was a rather stuffy title for that sort of thing, so I suggested 'Twelfth Man'.

In the early days I suggested to them that, rather than go through all the business of making the donations and finding things to give the money to, their best bet would be to give it to the National Playing Fields Association, but with certain conditions. They should put one of their members onto the committee, because all the contacts were already there and they could distribute the money much more cheaply. That started them off and they were very successful.

BJ: And now they raise a million pounds a year.

In 1949 you became President of MCC. Was this unexpected?

D OF E: Totally, yes. I didn't know much about it, but I took some soundings and people said, 'Yes, go ahead'. So I accepted.

It was quite interesting, because it was at a time when cricket fixtures were growing at a tremendous rate and I could foresee that the demand on first-class cricketers' time would be so great that there would be no room for the amateur. I suggested then that they ought to have the county matches at the weekend, so that the amateurs could take part. And in mid-week there should be a professional league with groups of counties. Now the whole thing's become professional and squeezed out the gifted amateur. Which is a pity. *[The distinction between amateurs and professionals was abolished in 1963, when all first-class cricketers became 'players'.]*

BJ: Wasn't it rather awe-inspiring, when you had your first meeting there with all those august members?

D OF E: They're a very jolly lot, really. I've found the great thing in most sports is that provided you're interested in the sport, age or background make not the slightest difference. I was President of the International Equestrian Federation for years and I found exactly the same thing; people forget about everything else.

BJ: Then, unusually, you accepted to be MCC President for a second year in 1974.

D OF E: Well, I was asked and it seemed to me that it was something that would be quite amusing to have in the record books. Actually I discovered that there was a much more sinister reason for my being asked again and that was that the committee wanted to put up the subscriptions. So I walked into the Annual General Meeting to preside and was given the agenda which said they'd proposed the increases in the subscription. And I suddenly realised why I'd been asked back again.

BJ: But surely no one dared to boo you.

D OF E: Well, they did.

BJ: What about the role of the MCC today?

D OF E: I think the idea that one club can be the central club in England and also the governing body for the sport worldwide is nowadays very unreasonable. I think that the club has got the same responsibility that it always had, but inevitably it's got to share the responsibility for Test Matches and international cricket generally with a wider body. It's marvellous to say, 'Oh, this is the way it always used to be,' but the whole picture is different now. It isn't played the way it was 40 years ago and it's not organised that way any more either. There's so much more of it and there's so much more international cricket to oversee. [*At this time the ICC was still run by MCC and continued to be so until 1993, although they had yielded the administration of first-class cricket in England to the Test and County Cricket Board in 1968. That became the England and Wales Cricket Board in 1997.]*

BJ: What about the National Playing Fields Association? You're still very much involved as President of that.

D OF E: We ran into difficulties over the charity law, because, as the NPFA is a charity and originally helped out village clubs and anybody who wanted to play cricket, it is not allowed to give to an organisation that is not itself a charity. So now the main emphasis is on children's playgrounds and the whole range of children's play. The situation in that area is a bit confused at the moment, but there's plenty for the NPFA to do.

Local authorities do, of course, help a great deal, but they vary from one place to another. And of course with the provision of playing fields and play space, you've also got to get at the planning authorities, the new towns people and the development corporations who actually make provision for that space. We found that in the days of the new towns, for instance, we had the greatest difficulty in persuading them to leave room for playing fields.

BJ: And they are being encroached on more and more, aren't they? That's rather serious.

D OF E: That's another difficulty, you see, with the price of land so high. A lot of companies with their own playing fields wanted to expand, so they expanded onto those playing fields. One of the things we try very hard to do is to get employers in a town to gang together and provide playing fields on a community basis for everybody.

Now, of course, the difficulty is that even local authorities are beginning to get rid of playing fields, because they want to earn some money. Play space has had a pretty rough time in the last few years.

BJ: Do you regard team games and competitive sport as important?

D OF E: Well, I do, yes. The important thing about team games is that they're really a part of social education and it's the sort of education you don't get anywhere else. You learn to co-operate, you learn to sublimate your personality into the team, you have to learn to win and I think that's very good for people. Team games are, in a sense, not over-competitive unless you get into the professional end. In amateur sport, generally, people go and enjoy themselves. I go in for this carriage-driving and it's great fun.

BJ: Is that as dangerous as it looks? Have you been pulled off the box?

D OF E: Most people have turned over at some stage or another.

BJ: You make it sound very casual.

D OF E: It's not as bad as that.

BJ: It looks terrifying.

In contrast to all this, you have the Duke of Edinburgh Awards, which are very much for individuals, aren't they?

D OF E: That's the service section, which is individual, although you can do that through a group or an organisation. There's a skill section, which you can do in a group, perhaps in amateur theatricals or something of that sort. But those two sections can be done individually. Then there's a physical recreation section, which you can do individually or through team games. And then there's the expedition section where you have to go in a group of four, at least.

For a Gold Award one of the conditions is that you have to go away for a residential course for a weekend and of course for many young people that's the first time they've ever been away from home. They have to mix with other people, so it's a genuine community activity.

BJ: What made you start it?

D of E: It's rather a long story, but I remember a similar thing being started by my headmaster at Gordonstoun, Kurt Hahn. And he came to me in 1954 and said, 'My boy, I want you to start an award scheme.'

And I said, 'Well, you get a group together and I'll come and chair it.' And he did.

The aim of the exercise was to provide an introduction to the sort of activities that adults found interesting and rewarding, which in most cases were not included in formal education. They were the sort of things that took place at boarding schools, but not often in any other schools. It's now running in 40-odd countries, I think.

BJ: It's a very nice success story.

Can we just come back to cricket. Is there anything about modern cricket you'd like to see changed?

D of E: No. I don't think so. I only wish that sometimes some of their trousers fitted a bit better.

GARY LINEKER

interviewed by Brian Johnston,
Old Trafford, 2 July 1988

There was a time when county cricketers could play professional football in the winter. Chris Balderstone was among the last to manage it seriously, though you would have to go further back to find a double international. The pressures and length of season on both sides surely would make it impossible that it might happen again.

BBC Television's future principal football presenter was then still at the height of his playing career. Having started in the Leicester City first team in 1978, he had had one season with Everton and at the time of this interview was mid-way through his three-year stint with Barcelona. He was to leave Spain the following year for three years with Tottenham Hotspur. When he retired from the game in 1994, he was playing with the Japanese club, Nagoya Grampus Eight.

Gary Lineker won 80 caps for England and his 48 goals for his country is a record second only to Sir Bobby Charlton. But no other Englishman has matched his ten World Cup goals.

He was a natural to take a 'View From the Boundary', being no stranger to cricket grounds.

*

BRIAN JOHNSTON: Last year you qualified as a playing member of MCC. How many matches did you actually play?

GARY LINEKER: Well, you have to play five and I only had three weeks in England, because of living in Spain, so I had to cram a few games in. But with MCC having games all round the country on virtually every day of the summer, it was ideal for me.

BJ: I should explain to people that there's a waiting list of about 30,000 for MCC, but you can get in as a playing member if you're skilful at cricket.

So this is a great tribute to your cricket. Did you write and say you wanted to play, or did somebody put you up?

GL: You have to be nominated by a couple of people and then you have to prove your abilities as a cricketer in these five games and also prove to be a decent sort of chap.

BJ: Well, you'd pass that one easily enough. What about the cricket? How many did you make last year, do you remember?

GL: I had quite a good start at the Bank of England ground, where I got 69 or 70 or something like that. So that put me in good stead, being more of a batsman than anything else – although I kept wicket in a few games.

BJ: Oh, you enjoy wicket keeping as well?

GL: I'm a part-time wicket keeper, that's all.

BJ: Did you have any good players playing with you?

GL: I played that first game with Nick Pocock. *[Former Hampshire captain.]* That was nice, because I was a bit nervous for the first game. I never get nervous for football, but I was playing cricket. He settled me down.

BJ: Let's go back to the beginning. You're a Leicester boy?

GL: That's right. Born and bred.

BJ: And you played football for Leicester, but did you play cricket as a boy there?

GL: Yes, I played at all the representative levels until I left school at sixteen. I actually played with Russell Cobb right through school. I also played for Midland Schools, so cricket has always been a great love as well as football.

BJ: You had to choose between the two, did you?

GL: It wasn't really like that. I was offered an apprenticeship with Leicester City at sixteen and it was a chance that I didn't think I could refuse. Whether I would even have been good enough at cricket, I will never know, but I was certainly keen on it. I think it's difficult to say what sort of level you can achieve at that age.

BJ: And football clubs are apt to nab people early and offer a little bit of security in the way of money.

GL: Not a lot at that time. It was just the first opportunity that came along and I grabbed it. I've got no regrets.

BJ: You're only 27, might it not be possible for you to play enough cricket to make a go of it?

GL: I think you have to have extraordinary natural ability. I don't think I've got that. Obviously when I've finished playing football I shall endeavour to play as much as I can and, if I've got any ability, I'll reach the highest level I can. I think you should always want to play at the highest level that you can possibly achieve.

BJ: And one of your great assets is your speed. You're a bit of a sprinter?

GL: I'm just an all-round sportsman. I think I've always had a bit of an eye for a ball and a bit of pace. I'm a sportaholic as well.

I love all sports – golf, cricket, snooker, football – you name it, I'll have a go.

BJ: What was your best time for the hundred metres?

GL: When I was a bit younger – I don't think I'd manage it now with all the kicks and bruises I've had – I think I ran 10.5 seconds. Natural speed has always been one of my great assets. I'm not one of the most naturally gifted footballers, like Glenn Hoddle or Maradona. I can get on the end of things in the box by using a bit of pace.

BJ: You pounce on it rather. What's your normal weight?

GL: About twelve and a half stone.

BJ: Because inevitably you get knocked about and shoved off the ball and treated roughly. Have you had any bad injuries?

GL: I've been very, very fortunate, touch wood. I just pray that it will continue. If it happens, it happens. You keep your fingers crossed, but there's no way you can stay out of trouble on the pitch, thinking, 'I don't want to get injured.' But I've been lucky so far.

BJ: How long did you play for Leicester?

GL: I was at Leicester for eight years, from starting as an apprentice to leaving.

BJ: And were you always in the centre forward position? Can we call it centre forward nowadays?

GL: I still call it centre forward myself. And I've always played in that position ever since I can remember playing, except the first few games I actually played for Leicester, when they stuck me out on the wing. I made my debut there, replacing an old favourite, Keith Weller. And I was awful, to be quite honest. I didn't really know what I was doing.

BJ: You must have dashed down the wing at great pace, though.

GL: Yes, but I was never the sort of player that can get the ball and go past a player with it. I was more likely to receive a pass behind the defence and sprint after it, so I certainly was not a natural winger.

BJ: Has the centre forward position changed? Do you wander more than the old centre forwards used to? I mean Dixie Dean didn't wander much. He was up there, waiting.

GL: I can't remember Dixie Dean! *[Dixie Dean's career ended with the outbreak of the Second World War. He scored a record 100 goals in the 1927/28 season, so it is unlikely that Gary would have remembered him!]* I think in the old days they used to play with two wingers and the defenders didn't really get anything like as tight and hard as they are now. So it was quite easy for the wingers to beat a man and nip a centre in for the big centre forward to nod in. There were far more goals then. It was probably more entertaining for the crowd, but football's far more physical now.

BJ: You have to go and get the ball a lot now, do you? You can't expect people to drop it at your feet.

GL: It's nicer if they do. But on the Continent, if you want to get involved in the game, you do have to go and look for the ball. The great thing is to get on the end of chances, not to worry about missing them. And if you can get to the greater percentage, then the more goals you'll get.

BJ: I know you've had an interest in snooker. How good are you?

GL: I've played at club level. I'm a great friend of Willie Thorne – he's a keen cricketer too – and of course I learned a lot from him and got to a reasonable level without any natural ability at all.

BJ: Would you enjoy being on the snooker circuit?

GL: To be honest, I prefer team sports. I think that snooker and golf are lonely games. I like the association of being involved with a team, like cricket or football.

BJ: Cricket has a great asset, unlike football, in that it is a team game, but you are your own man while you're out there and it's all up to you.

GL: I think all team games have that aspect to them, even football. If you're through and you've got the goalkeeper to beat, then it's down to you and nobody else. I think all team games need individualism, but in the end it is the strength of the whole team that will see you through.

BJ: And when you were at Leicester, did you follow Leicestershire cricket? Who were your heroes?

GL: Well, he won't thank me for saying this, because he's now a very good friend of mine, but David Gower was my hero. He's only a few years older than me, but I used to go down to see him every game, especially in the summer holidays when I was fourteen and fifteen and David was just starting. I think I saw his debut. I believe it was in a Sunday League game. But before that there was Brian Davison who I used to love to watch, who hit the ball very hard – and Ray Illingworth as well.

BJ: Illy was captain then.

GL: That's right. And he brought the most successful times Leicestershire have ever had. I think it was 1975 when we won the Championship and the Benson and Hedges Cup.

BJ: Have you ever aspired to be a bowler?

GL: In my early days I bowled a few leggies – very badly. I got hit around a little bit. I used to buy a few wickets just tossing them up.

BJ: Gosh, we could do with a leg break bowler today. I should concentrate a bit on that when you retire from football if I were you. Keep batting as well and then we shall have another double international. That would be great, wouldn't it?

GL: I think that it's impossible now, with the length of the soccer season, to get to the level of an international cricket player. Our season lasts eleven months of the year, with training to get fit for it.

BJ: It's got too long, hasn't it?

GL: It is, really, especially if you're involved in the international scene, where at the end of the season there is either a European Championship, the World Cup or a tour of God knows where. The cricket season, of course, is the same as it was. But it would be impossible to be a double international again.

BJ: You miss a lot of the cricket season by being in Spain.

GL: People ask me what I miss and I can honestly say the only thing I really do miss – except for my family and friends of course, and we see quite a bit of them – is cricket. Fortunately I can pick up the World Service and I can listen to the *Test Match Special* commentary.

BJ: I don't suppose the Spanish evening papers have the cricket scores.

GL: No they don't. It is incredible how difficult it is to explain cricket in Spanish. They all say, 'Yes, we know, the one where you knock it through the hoop.' They all think it's croquet.

BJ: Now, what about the wicket keeping?

GL: I didn't really start until I was fifteen or sixteen. I tended to get a little bored fielding all the time and I like to be involved. And I think one day we were struggling for a keeper and I said, 'Well, I'll give it a go.' And I enjoyed it. Obviously at first I found it a lot easier standing back, but gradually I moved up.

BJ: It's nice standing up, isn't it?

GL: It's more fun. You need a little bit of experience, though, because standing up at the wicket is the art of wicket keeping.

BJ: And first of all you need a few spinners to get you going. Pity you can't bowl your leg breaks to your own wicket keeping, you might stump someone off your own bowling if you did.

GL: I never got it past the bat. I used to get them caught on the boundary.

BJ: Denis Compton always used to say that a day playing cricket was far more tiring than 90 minutes of a soccer match. Do you believe that?

GL: Yes, in a different sort of way. A long day on the legs, especially fielding, does tire you a bit. It's a different sort of thing, though. You probably get more whacks in football and when you walk off you're limping. You've got a few knocks that clear up in a day or so, whereas in cricket you have another go next day. It's a different sort of tiredness.

BJ: How do crowds affect you? Do you find you play better in front of a big crowd, or would you be just as good playing – as some cricketers have to – in front of three men and a dog?

GL: All good professionals like to think they're as good in front of a small crowd as a big crowd, but I think it really does get the adrenalin flowing when you've got a massive crowd behind you, all cheering you on. Subconsciously or not, I do think it makes you give that little bit extra.

BJ: You've mentioned snooker and running. Do you play golf as well?

GL: I'll have a go at anything. Living out in Spain, I'm not actually a member anywhere, but I play off about twenty. I'm an occasional sort of golfer. I used to play a lot when I was younger and then stopped playing for quite a time and snooker took over. When I got out to Spain, I found that the weather makes golf the perfect pastime. So I've stopped playing snooker now and golf's taken over.

BJ: Well, Gary, let's hope when you retire from football, we'll be talking to a double international.

DAVID ESSEX

interviewed by Brian Johnston,
Lord's, 24 June 1989

These days on Test Match Special, *the producer is very lucky to have Shilpa Patel working her magic to persuade guests to appear on 'A View From the Boundary'. They usually find it hard to resist her and I always reckoned that if I asked her to get the Pope on, within half an hour he'd be walking through the commentary box door.*

But even Shilpa finds it easier if you can by-pass the agents. As far as our programme is concerned, they are often more of an obstruction than a help.

Early in 1989 I rang an agent to try to get David Essex, who I'd heard was keen on the game, onto the programme. I was in the process of getting the usual, 'Oh, I don't think he'd be available for anything like that' brush-off, when the agent I was speaking to said, 'Just a minute.'

The phone was obviously passed to another hand and a voice said, 'Who is this?' And I realised that I was speaking to David Essex himself. I put my case. 'I'm taking the family to France on holiday on that day,' he said, 'but I'll delay it for this.'

Although he had been in the music business for some years before, David Essex's big break was his role in the musical Godspell, *which led to his being cast as Che in the original production of* Evita. *In the meantime he had had number one hits with 'Gonna Make you a Star' and 'Hold Me Close'.*

He was about to add an unexpected singing role to his repertoire. Brian's favourite moment from the early years when he did 'In Town Tonight' was having wheeled a piano up to the stage door of the Victoria Palace theatre to perform live with Bud Flanagan. Maybe it was the fact that this was Johnners' 77th birthday that gave rise to his wanting to do the same with David Essex – with-out the piano. Perhaps, too, it was a sign of those times that Brian asked him first about his earring.

*

DAVID ESSEX: I have it because on my mother's side there's a kind of gypsy background, and it was put into my ear at a very early age by a relative and it caused a few problems at school.

BRIAN JOHNSTON: And is it the same one you've always had?

DE: No, I tend to lose them. I take them out when I wash my hair and they disappear.

BJ: Let's talk about your cricket. I hear glowing reports of you from Tim Rice. You play for his Heartaches team, don't you?

DE: Well, yes. But he's obviously a liar. I am a lousy cricketer. I am a lousy all-rounder. I enjoy cricket very much. I play some club cricket and I play for Tim, as you said, and I also play for the Eric Clapton XI. In fact we played most of the Australian team and we won. It was at Northampton for charity. They were terrific, because they'd played all day against Northants and at six o'clock we had a match for a children's charity.

BJ: And how did D. Essex fare?

DE: I did all right. I came in to bowl to Steve Waugh and I bowled what I thought was a pretty excellent ball, Yorker length, bit of movement in the air and of course it went for six, which I thought was a bit much.

But my fondest memory is that my son, Danny, who's twelve, played. And Dennis Waterman was at the other end and Danny came in for the last over and they put Merv Hughes on to bowl.

BJ: Had he got a helmet on?

DE: No helmet, big pads. Seven slips they set. Merv Hughes came running in from the sight screen. Danny lifted his bat. Merv floated down this lovely ball and Danny hit it for four. The crowd went nuts. Merv waved his fist – it was really lovely.

BJ: Any chance of seeing Danny Essex playing for Essex or England?

DE: Well, he's very keen. He loves the game and the main thing is he enjoys it. I don't know how much ability he will eventually have. Only time will tell. But he does love it – and I love it, too.

BJ: What sort of pace have you got when you bowl?

DE: It's medium club class, which is very slow at Test level.

BJ: Do you have to bat high up the order, because you're always going off to some concert?

DE: Well, I like to say that. That's my excuse, because I can't stand going in at ten and trying to bash around for runs. I like to go in around four or five, really. But the batting's come on, because I started really as a bowler.

The story of me and cricket is quite strange, really, because I captained the school cricket team, but it was never a passion. Football was always the passion. Cricket really only came about because of my son, Danny. A couple of years ago he kept saying, 'Dad, come and bowl at me.' So he brought me back into the game.

And for the last two years I really could have been a professional amateur cricketer. I've been playing more or less every day in all these teams that I moonlight in. It's great fun.

BJ: I think I read somewhere that you failed deliberately in your exams, so that you could go to a school that played soccer rather than rugger. Is that right? You would have had to play rugby in a grammar school.

DE: Yes, I drew Popeye on the exam paper.

BJ: How many marks did they give you for that?

DE: The drawing wasn't very good, so I don't think I got many marks for it. It was a maths exam.

BJ: Where did you go to school, then?

DE: In east London. They've pulled the school down now. It was a lousy school. It was the kind of school that had a terrible reputation and therefore attracted not quite good enough teachers. It was like a vicious circle. The sport was good. The football was very good and we played cricket, which was something. It was a state school.

BJ: Was it organised cricket, or just rough stuff?

DE: There wasn't any coaching. We played on matting on an asphalt base.

BJ: You must have got the ball to move a bit there.

DE: Well, it was a sort of big, pudding ball. If you could get it to the next wicket it was an achievement.

BJ: So you were born in the East End?

DE: Yes, I was born in Plaistow.

BJ: And Essex is an assumed name.

DE: The trouble was that when I wanted to join Equity, there was an actor called David Cook, which is my real name. And you cannot join the union with the same name as an existing member. I was living in Essex and it seemed a pleasant name. I'm glad it wasn't Middlesex.

BJ: That might have been taken wrong, I think. So when did you begin to take an interest in music?

DE: I used to go on adventures into Soho from about the age of thirteen. The East End was great. It was a great playground, because it was bombed a lot in the Second World War and that left us kids with lots of bomb craters and air raid shelters and bits of houses to run in and out of. So it was lovely.

But to catch the bus up to the West End, where all the music and the clubs and the bright lights were, that was real adventure. And I was strolling along Wardour Street one day and I just heard some music coming out of a basement and I went down with a friend of mine – who I think became a milkman – and I was besotted by the music. I was thirteen and I just knew I had to be a musician.

BJ: Would it have been my sort of music?

DE: Yes, though it wasn't Flanagan and Allen.

BJ: Well, I'm more of an Ivor Novello man, you see.

DE: Then it wouldn't have been. This was R and B music – which is short for rhythm and blues.

BJ: That's all right, I like that, too. So then did you try to learn an instrument?

DE: Well, it seemed to me, because I didn't have a lot of patience – I've got more now – that if you hit a drum it answered immediately back. So it seemed sensible to learn the drums. Later I played guitar very badly and I write on the keyboards. So I've branched out since the drums, but they were the first thing.

BJ: When did the voice come?

DE: That was all fluke and luck really, because all I ever wanted to be was a jazz drummer. And I was playing the drums and the lead guitarist turned round one day and said, 'Look, man, I can't play lead guitar and sing at the same time, so someone else has got to sing,' and they all pointed at me.

So I started singing these strange urban Chicago blues songs and that was it. It went downhill from there, Brian.

BJ: You've got a very recognisable voice. It's quite different from anyone else's. Did you have any lessons?

DE: Not really. I did a lot of work in repertory and so I was able to make major mistakes in front of small audiences, so it didn't matter too much.

BJ: So you did some straight acting?

DE: Yes, I've played Byron for the Young Vic.

BJ: Did he win?

DE: No, he definitely lost. It was very interesting, but I always feel like a musician that acts, rather than an actor who sings.

BJ: I first saw you in *Godspell*.

DE: That was a marvellous show.

BJ: I thought it was and I remember you were carried out through the auditorium.

DE: The strange thing about *Godspell* was that we rehearsed and rehearsed and the theatre that we were supposed to open in suddenly cancelled. They'd seen ten hippies running round and they thought, 'No, this is rubbish.' So the only place that we could open was at the Roundhouse. And it opened and there were queues round the block. It was phenomenal. It was a terrific cast, with Jeremy Irons as John the Baptist and Marti Webb and Julie Covington. And, although I was playing Jesus, there wasn't really a star. It was very much an ensemble type of show.

BJ: It preceded *Jesus Christ Superstar*, didn't it? I don't know if that gave them the idea.

DE: I don't know. Sometimes these things are in the air. Ideas seem to come at the same time. It was a very different show.

BJ: Was *Godspell* a moving thing to play?

DE: It was, yes. I used to hear people crying and sobbing. It was something special. I did it for two years and the strangest thing was the interval, where the audience would come up and have a glass of wine.

BJ: That's right, it was all very friendly, but it didn't give you much rest in the interval, did it?

DE: What was extraordinary was people's reaction to me playing Jesus. They really were awestruck. So you felt you had this tremendous responsibility for people's innermost faith. It was a great show. It's probably the show I've enjoyed most.

BJ: And two years – do you mind the routine of a long run?

DE: I do, actually, yes. The incredible thing is that, although the monotony of the routine does get you down and change your life, really, every night is different and the inter-relationship between the actors and audience is always different. So that gives you a stimulus.

BJ: Did you enjoy doing *Evita*?

DE: I did. The great thing about *Evita* was that it was under an intense spotlight. Everyone was very interested in the show, it was very difficult to get tickets and it was a big success. But the overriding thing for me was that I was able to do it for just six months, which was brilliant.

BJ: What was that thing you sang at the start?

DE: 'Oh What a Circus'.

BJ: What about the Tim Rice lyrics? He's your captain in the Heartaches, so you'd better be careful.

DE: Oh, what a marvellous cricketer!

BJ: I asked about his lyrics. I know he's a great slow left-arm bowler.

DE: I think Tim's lyrics are very good. I think one of the songs in *Evita* – 'High Flying Adored' – is probably one of the finest popular lyrics written in the last 30 years. He has this knack of directness and of using unusual words in a direct context.

BJ: So when did you start composing? You've had two number one hits in this country, haven't you?

DE: Yes, and 23 top thirties.

BJ: Not bad.

DE: The writing came about because it just seemed more honest to sing things that had come from you, lyrically and musically.

BJ: You're a clever boy, but how do you sit down and write a tune?

DE: I sit down using keyboards – mainly the piano. But it's a strange process. I've got a new album out called *Touching the Ghost* and the title song outlines how intangible song-writing is and how difficult it is to tell where the creative spark comes from.

BJ: Where do you get your spark? In the bath, or walking about, or in the middle of a big innings?

DE: Never in the middle of a big innings. I once made up a song in Antigua during a session in the outfield spent waiting for another West Indian to hit a big six. It's called 'Look at the Sun', because I was looking into the sun and I thought, 'Well, all these balls are just going over my head. I'll make a song up.' That's the only one.

Generally I think I store pictures and images. I'm very much an observer. As an only child, I think you spend more time by yourself. So I watch and store things and then when the commitment is there to write I'll sit at the piano and do it. But I only really write out of panic. 'We're in the studio on Monday, have you written the songs?' sort of thing.

BJ: What do you think is your public? Is it basically young people, or are you amongst the oldies as well?

DE: I think it's a fair mixture now, because I've been at it a fair while.

BJ: Now, I did sing 'Underneath the Arches' with Bud Flanagan. It would give me great pleasure to sing it with you. Do you know the words?

DE: I don't really. We'll kind of wing it. Are you Ches or Bud?

BJ: I'm Bud really. You can do the Ches thing.

*

And they did, with David Essex encouraging Brian at the end with a muttered, 'Big finish, big finish.' It must have been good, because Radio 4's Pick of the Week *used it, and then it was even included in* Pick of the Year.

JOHN MAJOR

interviewed by Brian Johnston,
Lord's, 28 July 1990

Some years ago a thoughtful listener, moved by all the references to celebrated people dropping into the commentary box, sent the TMS team a visitors' book. Years later it makes very interesting reading. And one of the things one can do is to chart the senior political career of that great cricket lover, Sir John Major, with his changing office addresses.

When he first visited us he was Chief Secretary to the Treasury, then it was as Foreign Secretary, and when he came to take his 'View' he was Chancellor of the Exchequer. Four months after this interview he was Prime Minister in succession to Margaret Thatcher and happily that didn't stop him dropping in on us occasionally, when security considerations permitted.

It is well documented that on the day in 1997 that he lost the election to Tony Blair and New Labour, he went to the Oval to watch his beloved Surrey play. Indeed, on Desert Island Discs *he chose the Oval as his luxury. Later he was even to become President of Surrey and in 2007 he brought out an acclaimed history of the early days of cricket –* More Than a Game.

Brian started by asking when his interest in cricket had started, noting that, born in Merton, he was qualified for Surrey.

*

JOHN MAJOR: I was qualified for Surrey in everything but talent. It really started when my family moved to Brixton when I was about ten. I was within walking distance of the Oval and that was at the time when Surrey were beating everyone, generally within two days – that marvellous team that won the championship from '52 to '58 inclusive. It was, I think, the best county side I ever expect to see. They were truly magnificent and I watched them whenever I could.

BRIAN JOHNSTON: Where did you sit at the Oval – under the gasometer?

JM: No, I sat on the other side. I sat at square leg with the batsman at the pavilion end in the popular seats there, and by pure habit I used to go there for years after as well.

BJ: What chances did you yourself get of playing cricket? Were you coached?

JM: I played a bit at school. We had quite a good cricket team at school. I played for them and I played a bit of cricket after school as well. I played a bit in Nigeria when I first went there at about twenty, to do some banking. But my cricketing days came to an end after a motor car accident in Nigeria when I was twenty or so and I haven't played since. *[A year after this interview, Mr Major opened the batting with the then Australian Prime Minister, Bob Hawke, in a match to mark the meeting of Commonwealth Prime Ministers in Zimbabwe.]*

BJ: So we were robbed of – what? A fast bowler, or what would England have had if you'd been fit?

JM: You were robbed of an extremely mediocre medium-paced bowler.

BJ: Banking in Nigeria sounds an interesting job.

JM: Yes, it was. It was certainly that. The greatest enthusiasm that people had there was for the weekly cricket match. They had their priorities absolutely right.

BJ: It does happen all round the world.

So when you watched that Surrey side, were there any special favourites you picked out? Was it the bowlers you liked – Bedser, Laker or Lock?

JM: Oh, they were tremendous. It was such a superb team and they were so varied. I always thought Alec Bedser bowling was like a galleon in full sail coming up to the wicket. Last evening Brian Rix said to me that he'd been batting a few years ago against Alec Bedser in a charity match. And he'd said to Alec, 'Let me have an easy one to get off the mark.' And he said Alec couldn't do it. He just couldn't bowl the bad ball. And I can well believe it.

But the rest of the team were superb. I used to time, with an old stopwatch I had, how long it took the ball from leaving Peter May's bat to hitting the boundary. It wasn't long.

BJ: Ah, those famous on-drives.

JM: And I think that Tony Lock was the most aggressive-looking bowler I ever saw – and fielder.

BJ: And a little lesson in leadership, too. Because old Stuey Surridge was a tremendous leader. He was a very forceful leader, too.

JM: He was. I met Stuart Surridge for the first time about six weeks ago. I remember thinking as a boy, when I watched him standing there round the wicket, where he fielded absolutely magnificently, that he was one of the few men I've ever seen who could scratch his toes while standing upright. He had these amazingly long arms and he just caught everything – truly wonderful.

BJ: Very brave he was, but then they all were – Micky Stewart and Locky, walking in when he was fielding at backward short leg, which not many short legs do.

JM: Some of Lock's catches are still unbelievable, even in retrospect. You just didn't know how he got there and how he held it.

BJ: But when did you see your first Test Match, do you remember that?

JM: Well, I remember the first Test Match I listened to seriously. It was an Indian Test Match and it was in 1952, when India were nought for four in the second innings.

BJ: We had a certain gentleman – Fred Trueman – in here just now, who was not unconcerned with that.

JM: He took three of the four wickets. It was an astonishing scorecard.

BJ: But have you been able to go to Test Matches much?

JM: I've been to quite a few. A good deal fewer than I would wish to have gone to, but, yes, I've been to quite a few over the years. I saw a bit of the last Test Match in 1953, when the Ashes came back, and I saw some of the '56 series.

BJ: I wonder, when you have all these conferences, are you ever brought in notes with the latest score?

JM: Certainly in the period I was Chief Secretary and we had great negotiations with colleagues over spending matters, the meetings did used to break up for critical parts of the Test Match, to watch it. My then secretary, who was a Surrey member and a fanatical cricketer, used to send in notes to say the Test Match had reached a critical stage and we used to break up and watch it. Nigel Lawson is also a great cricket supporter – a great Leicestershire fan – and we used to sit there, with Nigel in the chair, his fellow ministers, lots of extremely important mandarins and others at the other side of the table and a piece of paper would come in that would be passed gravely round the table. It was the Test score, it wasn't the markets, I promise you.

BJ: Did you just nod as though it was important financial news?

JM: Well, over the last couple of years, some of it was very grave.

BJ: Are quite a few members of the Cabinet keen followers?

JM: The best cricket player in the Cabinet is probably Tom King. He's a good cricketer. *[At this time Tom King was Secretary of State for Defence. In 2001 he became Lord King of Bridgwater.]*

BJ: He also keeps wicket, I think.

JM: He keeps wicket as well. Peter Brooke is a walking *Wisden* and knows a great deal about cricket.

BJ: We could put him against the Bearded Wonder and he'd stump him, d'you think? *[Peter Brooke was Secretary of State for Northern Ireland at this stage, while the Bearded Wonder was, of course, the late Bill Frindall.]*

JM: I think, as a non-gambling man, I might put my money on the Bearded Wonder, but not by much. Peter Brooke knows a great deal about it. And there are a number of others.

BJ: I suppose, because you were injured, you haven't been able to play for the Lords and Commons.

JM: No, I'm afraid that motor accident ended my playing days. I wouldn't run too well now, otherwise I would love to play.

BJ: They play some very good cricket. It mingles up the parties, too. They don't seem to bother about the politics.

JM: Indeed not. Bob Cryer, the Labour MP, is a very fine left-arm slow bowler. There are some good cricketers right across the Commons.

BJ: What's the first thing you read in the papers in the morning?

JM: I do read the sports pages every day. I tend to read Matthew Engel when he writes cricket. That is the first thing I turn to in that particular newspaper. *['That particular newspaper' was the* Guardian. *Matthew Engel went on to be editor of the* Wisden Almanack *between 1992 and 2007.]* I much miss the fact that Jim Swanton doesn't write quite as regularly as once he did. I thought he was supremely good. And I much enjoy reading Tony Lewis. But I do turn to the sports pages at an early stage in the morning.

BJ: Are you great on the literature of cricket? Have you got a big library of cricket books?

JM: Quite big, yes. I do read a lot of cricket. I've been trying to get hold of a book on cricket that Richard Daft wrote a long time ago – way back in the 1870s or 1880s. Richard Daft's great grandson, incidentally, is the Cabinet Secretary, Robin Butler – another fine cricketer. The Civil Service has some extremely good cricketers. But I haven't been able to find that book in old bookshops. Robert Atkins has a copy which he jealously guards and lends to me occasionally. *[As a result of this broadcast, Mr Major received a copy of the Richard Daft book.]*

BJ: What other great cricket writers in the newspapers do you remember especially?

JM: In the evening papers, when one used to go out and see how Surrey were doing and whether the game would go into a third day, I remember reading E.M. Wellings a lot.

BJ: He wrote a lot of very good sense – and played for Surrey, too.

JM: And of course in terms of literature, like everybody, I've read a lot of Cardus.

BJ: Which is absolutely marvellous stuff. He and Arlott and Swanton – and Robertson Glasgow – did you ever read him?

JM: I've not read a lot of him.

BJ: If you can get any of his little vignettes about players, they were absolutely brilliant. He was the chap who said, 'Hammond, like a ship in full sail', which was a perfect description of Hammond going to the wicket.

JM: I wish I'd seen him bat, too.

BJ: But I suppose you don't get a lot of time to read, do you?

JM: Well, I do, actually. Whatever time I go to bed, I tend to pick up a book for half an hour or 45 minutes, just to wash away the rest of the day. And it is often a cricket book.

BJ: I hope that doesn't send you to sleep.

JM: I go to sleep, but it's not the book.

BJ: Young James, your son, is he a good cricketer?

JM: He's a better footballer – and for the reason that there isn't as much cricket at schools as there ought to be. The point about cricket in schools is that it takes such a long time-span. That's the real difficulty. And whereas I think the staff are willingly prepared to give up an afternoon for a football match – to get the pupils there, play the game and get them back – it's a good deal longer for a cricket match.

BJ: Are you a quick learner? I mean you had to switch suddenly to the Foreign Office. How did you brief yourself in that short time? Because you appeared terribly knowledgeable when you went to conferences immediately afterwards.

JM: You're very kind to say so. You read a lot and hopefully recall. It's really a problem of total immersion. It's the same in cricket in many ways. I'm sorry to name-drop, but I bumped into Arthur Morris today – a very great player – and he remembered hitting Wilf Wooler for four fours off the first four balls of a game down in Glamorgan. And I said, 'That was a bit extravagant.' And he said, 'Not as extravagant as the field that had been set,' which he then described to me. So I think these things just stick in the mind. He, 40 years on, remembers the field placing.

BJ: If you ask Fred Trueman about any of the wickets he took, or the innings he played, he'd tell you. He's got a marvellous memory.

JM: Yes, it's a great gift.

BJ: Are you great on music?

JM: I like music very much and I go whenever I can, which isn't as often as I would wish, with Norma. She's forgotten more about music than I'll ever know.

BJ: And besides cricket, any particular hobby?

JM: Well, I read a lot. I'm very fond of the theatre. I go and watch a fair bit of football and athletics if I can – most sport.

BJ: You're a cricket fanatic and a man after our own hearts and I hope you'll continue to listen to us.

JM: Brian, I will. I wouldn't miss it for the world.

*

In 1994, as Prime Minister, John Major spoke movingly in his address at Brian Johnston's memorial service at Westminster Abbey.

MAX BOYCE

interviewed by Brian Johnston,
Trent Bridge, 6 July 1991

*Back in 1987 we had that great Welsh rugby fly-half, Barry John,
on to take his 'View' at Edgbaston. As he was leaving, he said, 'Oh,
by the way, the bloke who drove me here would love to do it one
day, too.'*

'Why, who is he?' I asked.

'Max Boyce,' he said.

*It took four more years, but at last we got that splendid Welsh
entertainer along. He had joined us the night before at our favourite hotel, Langar Hall, and with the heavy overnight rain, we told
him he wouldn't be missing much if he delayed his arrival at the
ground on Saturday. But the clearing up operations were so successful that it was decided that a start could be made after an
early lunch. And those words 'early lunch' sent me scurrying to the
phone to get Max moving. He made it.*

*Although his passion for Welsh rugby is at the heart of many of
his songs and poems, he loves his cricket, too.*

*

MAX BOYCE: I was listening this morning on my way here and I
heard David Lloyd say something about Wales having done terribly well. I thought, 'Oh good, Wales have done well in Australia.'
But he meant the whales – the water-sucking machines drying
the ground.

BRIAN JOHNSTON: Have you ever seen Wales play in Australia?

MB: Yes, I was out there thirteen years ago. I went on the 1978
tour and I followed them. It was a wonderful tour, because it

was the grand slam side, but of course they didn't do terribly well out there.

There was a wonderful woman from Llanelli out there and she asked me where the Welsh team were staying, because, she said, 'I've made 30 warm Welsh faggots for the team.'

She went round to the hotel with these and Clive Rowlands, who was the team manager, accepted them and said, 'The boys will have them for breakfast.'

Well, Wales played the Test and lost and the next morning the first person I saw was this woman in a Welsh costume, with tears running down her cheeks. 'Don't be upset,' I said, 'It's only a game.'

'Oh, Max,' she said, 'Do you think it was the faggots?'

I was telling the story on Australian television and of course a faggot in Australia has got a totally different connotation. They were falling about in the studio when I said that Wales had lost because someone had given them 30 warm Welsh faggots.

BJ: What about the cricket side of your life?

MB: It was my great love when I was younger and I played from about sixteen in school and then in the South Wales League. Every side had a pro., so it was a good standard of cricket.

BJ: And what sort of a cricketer were you?

MB: Alan Jones, the former Glamorgan opening bat, described me as having the finest temperament of any fast bowler he'd seen. My line and length lacked a bit, but I had a fine temperament. I was a fiery opening bowler. I liked it very much.

BJ: Did you base yourself on Fred Trueman?

MB: Yes, I used to pretend to be Fred.

BJ: You are Welsh through-and-through. Where were you born?

MB: I was born in a little mining village called Glyn Neath in the Glyn Neath valley, which is about sixteen miles from Swansea.

BJ: Was that a mining area?

MB: We had six pits there and there aren't any at all now. The last one closed during the last miners' strike. Very much a pit village – a very pretty village now.

BJ: Was your father a miner?

MB: Yes. My father was killed in a mine explosion a month before I was born, in fact.

BJ: But that didn't put you off, because you went into the mines.

MB: I suppose, coming from an area like that, you didn't think of it as being dangerous and hazardous, because all your friends did it and all your family did it. People who've never lived in a mining area would say, 'Why did you go down the pit?' – exactly as you've just said. But you didn't think of it, because it was part of the lifestyle of that particular community. There was nowhere else to work. There were no factories. Everyone worked underground.

BJ: But did you gradually find that you were able to make people laugh?

MB: I never intended to be an entertainer. I started out as a sort of folk singer. I spent ten years underground and five years in engineering and then I bought a guitar and started singing in the local folk clubs. Just upstairs in a pub and you'd invite professional folk singers down and then the local people would get up and sing a couple of songs.

I wasn't doing terribly well and then I started writing my own things. It was the time when Julie Felix was singing about Vietnam. Well, I couldn't sing about Vietnam with any credence, so I sang about the things I knew about, like shift work and the fact that the colliery was being closed. And it struck a chord with people. People could identify with the things I wrote about.

Then gradually the introductions became longer and it became a bit of story-telling. The songs became more infrequent and now I'll sing maybe only 20 per cent of the time in a performance of an hour and a half.

BJ: When did your career really take off – in the early seventies?

MB: I was known in Wales from about 1970, 71, but in Britain nationally in about 1973. I cut an album in Treorchy Rugby Club. We couldn't sell the tickets – it was 50 pence – because I was completely unknown. So people went into the streets and said, 'There's a lad cutting a record. Will you come in, because without an audience it will be impossible.' And they formed the audience and that record went on to sell over half a million.

BJ: That was your first big hit.

MB: First national success.

BJ: I remember all these marvellous descriptions of rugby matches – 'I was there'.

MB: That 'I was there' came about actually in a cricket dinner in St Helen's where I was asked to perform for Glamorgan, and I'd never performed in an after-dinner context before. And I thought, 'How can I put these stories together?' And the thing that linked them all was the fact that I was there. From there it became a bit of a catchphrase, so I incorporated it in the stage act.

I heard someone talking about Botham's match at Headingley in 1981 and he said, 'As Max Boyce would say, I was there.'

BJ: Having mentioned him, what about Ian Botham, the famous pantomime king? He performed with you in Bradford – a very successful pantomime season. He's a big figure off stage, what's he like on stage? *[Botham had performed in* Jack and the Beanstalk *the previous winter.]*

MB: He was wonderful. I think he'd say himself he struggled for the first week.

BJ: Well, he would do.

MB: I think if I had to open the batting or come in at number six, I'd struggle as well. What I will say about him, he was tremendously disciplined. We'd been friends a long time and I said, 'No, I won't have you,' because I was afraid it might destroy our friendship. I thought he'd be terribly bored, but he absolutely loved it. He was never late and he went round all the local hospitals and signed autographs.

BJ: Did he sing?

MB: No, he didn't sing. It's not a big part, but the main fact was that it was him.

BJ: A few mentions of cricket.

MB: England were in Australia and whenever Gower was mentioned we'd have the sound effect of an aeroplane. He'd go, 'Hello, David.' *[During the previous winter's tour of Australia, a disaffected David Gower, along with John Morris, had flown low over the ground in a hired Tiger Moth during the game against Queensland at Carrara and been fined for his effort.]* What I was most concerned about was I didn't want to ridicule him. I didn't want him to go with some arty director in another show, who'd make him do stupid things and decry him as a person. So, because I have great admiration for him as a man and as one of the greatest players the world has ever seen, I protected him in that way and I didn't give him any line that would have made him look silly. And he became this very strong king and people could relate to him.

BJ: Well, I've never known there was a king in *Jack and the Beanstalk*. Was he up with the ogre?

MB: Some people thought he was the giant.
   I saw the nasty side of the press – 'the fibre-tipped assassins'. I think somebody wrote after the opening night, which went sensationally well, 'The only thing more wooden than Ian Botham was the beanstalk.' But he himself stuck it on the dressing room door to remind himself. He was measurably better by the end.

BJ: What about Glamorgan cricket? Have you followed that always?

MB: All my life.

BJ: Who were your special heroes?

MB: Well, at the moment Hugh Morris is on everybody's lips. I wonder, if he'd have come from Essex or Middlesex, would he have played more? *[Funnily enough, Hugh Morris was to play in the Test Match following this interview. His three-Test career covered the last three Tests in England in 1991. He was later to become Managing Director of England cricket.]*

BJ: There's the old Welsh thing. But you've got some very influential people there, Tony Lewis and Ossie Wheatley, for instance. What about the others? Do you ever see Don Shepherd?

MB: Yes, I play a lot of golf with Don. I used to pretend to be Don. Owen Phillips' garage became the pavilion end and we used to draw white lines on the wall with chalk. And I remember Owen Phillips was the best opening bat in all West Glamorgan. He was in once for 23 weeks. And when I finally got him out he'd say, 'Not out!'
  'Why's that?'
  'There's no chalk on the ball.'
  So when I see the action replays and cameras in stumps, I think it was a far better day when the reason why you were out or not depended on whether there was chalk on the ball.

BJ: Twenty-three weeks! I think that's one for Bill Frindall's record books. You go round the world literally, don't you?

MB: I can really only go where there is huge British involvement, like Canada, New Zealand, Australia or Hong Kong. It's not just Welsh. When people are away from home they flock to see you. If the truth be told, you don't have to be terribly good in Australia, because people go there, they drag their Australian friends along and they laugh at everything. So I've had some great tours of Australia.

BJ: Can you give us one of your poems? I've been asked to ask you for 'The Incredible Plan'.

MB: I'd never be able to remember it and it's about twelve minutes long. But this is a similar poem I wrote about when Llanelli beat the All Blacks in 1973. Again an occasion when I'm glad to say I was there.

'Twas on a dark and dismal day
In a week that had seen rain,
When all roads led to Stradey Park
With the All Blacks there again.

They poured in from the valleys,
They came from far and wide.
There were twenty thousand in the ground –
And me and Dai outside.

The shops were closed like Sunday
And the streets were silent still
And those who chose to stay away
Were either dead or ill.

But those who went to Stradey
Will remember till they die
How New Zealand were defeated
And how the pubs ran dry.

Aye the beer flowed at Stradey,
Piped down from Felinfoel
And the hands that held the glasses high
Were strong from steel and coal.

And the air was filled with singing
And I saw a grown man cry
Not because they beat the All Blacks,

But because the pubs ran dry.

Then dawned the morning after
On empty factories,
For we were shtill at Shtradey –
Bloodshot absentees.

But we all had doctors' papers,
Not one of us in pain.
And Harry Morgan buried
His granny once again.

And when I'm old and my hair turns grey
And they put me in a chair,
I'll tell my great grandchildren
That their grandfather was there.

BJ: That is great – well done!

MB: I've always been an avid listener to the ball-by-ball. We used to set out on concert tours, with my old friend, Philip Whitehead, who plays up in the Saddleworth League, when there were Test Matches on, leaving at ten to eleven, before the ball-by-ball started. And we used to look at maps, because we'd hate to miss a ball and the great problem was – tunnels. In the Dartford Tunnel especially you'd miss maybe three overs. So you'd draw out a route plan where there were no tunnels and you'd listen to Brian Johnston. It took us five hours for a short journey once – we went the no tunnel route!

BJ: You sing and then talk – a mixture?

MB: Yes, a sort of pot pourri of story-telling with a few songs wedged in between, but they're all true stories that I've embroidered and coloured and added to and they've become routines as such. But they're all born of truth.

Some of the most amazing stories are absolutely true. For instance, I was coming back from recording an album in London and I went to find a seat on the train on my own, because I was shattered. I'd been up all night. And who gets on the train but Stuart Burrows, the tenor. And I said, 'Oh, Stuart, I've had too much red wine last night, do you mind if we don't chat till we get to Newport?'

And he said, 'I've just finished a week of opera myself. I feel the same way.'

The train pulls out of Paddington and when we get to Royal Oak a soldier comes into the carriage. The Royal Welch Fusiliers have just come home from Belfast. 'Max! How's it going, Max? Hey, Max, give us a song! "Sospan Fach"! Hang on, I'll go and get the boys.'

Fifteen soldiers come in now. 'Max, Max, we've brought you some Newcastle Brown!' And they've got a big crate. 'Max, give us a song! We're on a train – it's first class, come on, lads!' He takes off his hat, with the three Welsh feathers. 'If you won't sing for the beer, sing for this.'

So I'm under pressure now. 'Oh lads, I can't sing.'

And then Stuart Burrows – arguably the greatest lyrical tenor in the world – says, 'He is not singing.'

This soldier says, 'Who are you? His manager, is it?'

Stuart says, 'Yes, I'm his manager and he's not singing.'

'Come on, Max, give us a song.'

Stuart says, 'He's not singing, but I'll sing instead.'

'We don't want you to sing, we want Max to sing.' Finally they relented and said to Stuart, 'OK, you sing.'

Stuart Burrows got up on that 125 train from Paddington and sang 'Waft of Angels through the Skies', this wonderful voice ringing through this compartment. And all these commuters were waking up and saying, 'I say, the sandwiches are stale, but the cabaret is awfully good.'

And this soldier turns to Stuart at the end and he says, 'Listen, pal, I don't know much about singing, but as far as I'm concerned you're wasting your time managing him.' True story. You couldn't invent that.

BJ: If you'd been feeling fine, what song would you have chosen?

MB: Strangely enough, when anyone's asked for a party piece, mine has always been 'The Road and the Miles to Dundee', a Scottish folk song. I don't know why. I suppose I can remember it.

BJ [*with studied innocence*]: How does it go, Max?
[*And Max, after a chuckle to acknowledge that he'd been reeled in by a master, sang a verse of the haunting song.*]

BJ: Do you like all sorts of music?

MB: I like lyrics, perhaps, more than music. And I was thinking of a cricket link for today and I thought of Dylan Thomas and his wonderful gift of painting pictures with words.

The only thing that I know of Dylan Thomas writing of cricket was so vivid a picture that he painted of young kids playing on the beach by St Helen's, and another kid, who's got nobody to play with and he's stuck, hoping that the family who are playing cricket will ask him to join in. And Dylan Thomas called it 'The Friendless Fielder'.

The loneliness of the friendless fielder
Standing on the edge of family cricket,
Uninvited to tea or bat.

I wish I'd written that.

BJ: I didn't know he was into cricket.

MB: He just wrote about anything. He went to St Helen's and he lived near there. He just looked at things and wrote of them. This wonderful descriptive ability. The fattest woman in Neath Fair was described as, 'Her eyes like blackcurrants in blancmange'. It's a wonderful vision. And his grandfather was so wild he was 'Like a buffalo in an airing cupboard'.

BJ: I wish he'd written about cricket, he could have described some cricketers, too. Have you written about a Test Match?

MB: No, the only cricket I've written about is when I played for a side called Ponteddfechan in the South Wales League and unfortunately, back in about 1970, they drove the extension on the Heads of the Valleys motorway right through our cricket ground and that was the end.

It was village cricket at its best and about five years ago we had a reunion match and all the people who ever played for this little village played again. We cut the wicket with a tractor and a five-gang mower and all the old lads came back. Of course you couldn't bowl fast, because it was really wild and because of the motorway, one boundary was about 75 feet. And there were houses, so you could be 'out in gardens'.

This guy Alan Wicks played and the next day he was playing for a fairly good side at Arundel. And his captain said, 'Tell me, Wicks, are you playing much these days?'

'Yes,' he said.

'I don't know where to put you in. Are you playing well? Did you play yesterday?'

'Yes, I did.'

'How many runs did you get?'
'I got 70.'
'How did you get out?'
'I was "out in gardens".'
So he stuck him in at number eleven.

BJ: We'll have to make that the eleventh way of getting out.

MB: But it was a sad occasion.

BJ: Yes, awful, losing the cricket ground.

MB: And they'd played there for a hundred years. So I wrote a parody of Tom Jones' 'Green, Green Grass of Home'. And it got to the speaking bit –

And as I bat and look around me
At the four short legs that surround me
I realise that surveyor wasn't joking.
'Cause they'll bring that ugly concrete highway
And take away what once was my way.
I can't believe my green, green field of home.

BJ: Do you still play a bit of charity cricket?

MB: Yes, I play for the Taverners whenever I can.

BJ: What length of run nowadays?

MB: Oh, it's just as long, but I have a packed lunch half way now.

BJ: What's your favourite ground?

MB: Obviously St Helen's. I used to go to watch touring sides and my mother used to make me banana sandwiches. And

I remember the days when we used to beat Essex before the bananas went black.

BJ: What about your rugby? Who were the greatest rugby players you enjoyed in Wales?

MB: Probably Gerald Davies and then Gareth Edwards. And Barry John was probably the finest outside half. And there's a wonderful story about when we played golf in a big tournament at the Royal Glyn Neath Golf Club and there was the greatest rainfall for 87 years. After twelve holes it was abandoned because the greens were completely under water. We only had three showers and because everybody came off the course together there was chaos in the changing rooms.

So this lad said, 'I only live a hundred yards from here. Come down to my house for a bath, Mr John.'

'Call me Barry,' he said.

So they go down to his house and Barry's in the bath, having a glass of home-made ale and this lad's on the phone to his father. 'You'll never guess who I've got in the bath! I've got Barry John!'

'Good God!' he said. 'Whatever you do, don't let the water out. We'll bottle it!'

BJ: Now, when you leave here, I hope you've mapped out your course so that there are no tunnels on the way, because I hope you'll be listening to us.

MB: I've checked the tunnel route and there's only one – in Monmouth. So I'm going to wait until the end of the over and then hurtle through the tunnel at Monmouth, so that I won't miss a ball.

PETER O'TOOLE

interviewed by Brian Johnston,
The Oval, 10 August 1991

It was Paul Getty who introduced Brian to Peter O'Toole and such was the actor's enthusiasm for the game that it didn't take long for him to agree to come and be our guest at the Oval. That enthusiasm extended to his getting a coaching qualification and putting it to good use regularly at Brondesbury Cricket Club in north London.

His list of film credits is impressive, including Becket, The Lion in Winter, What's New, Pussycat?, Goodbye, Mr Chips, Troy *and* Venus, *but he is still perhaps best known for one of his earliest films – Lawrence of Arabia. For that he received the first of eight Oscar nominations for best actor. It is a record number of nominations without winning.*

The day he made his way up to our rooftop commentary box at the Oval was significant. The previous evening had been the infamous occasion when Jonathan Agnew had suggested, in his summary of the day's play, that Ian Botham 'couldn't quite get his leg over', and Johnners had been quite unable to control his giggles. On this Saturday morning the incident had been replayed by various radio stations and seemed to be the talk of the nation.

The Test Match in progress was significant, too. The West Indies went in to it leading the series 2-1, having won every rubber with England since 1974. By the time of this third day lunch interval, England were in a strong position. Phil Tufnell had just taken the first two of his spell of 6 for 25, which would see the West Indies following on, on their way to a five-wicket defeat.

The drama of the match was heightened by the retirements of Viv Richards, Malcolm Marshall and Jeffrey Dujon. Such a powerful scene could be appreciated by an actor.

PETER O'TOOLE: I'm often asked why cricket means so much to me. And it's this high drama. Tufnell comes on – takes a wicket. Botham returns – takes a wicket. Viv Richards, the great king, delays his entrance. Delays and delays and delays. Finally he comes on with a couple of balls to play before lunch to a standing ovation. And of course he could have been out first ball.

BRIAN JOHNSTON: Have you ever had an ovation like that? It lasted the time it took him to get to the wicket.

PO'T: And I believe he was deeply moved – and who wouldn't be?

BJ: Well, Bradman says he wouldn't be, because when I asked him whether he had tears in his eyes when there were three cheers when he went out in his last Test, he said, 'No, no.' But I bet there were really.

PO'T: I saw Bradman play at Headingley in 1948 and he scored 33, having threatened to score a century in the evening before. And as he walked back to the pavilion there were no tears. He looked extraordinarily grumpy and very, very thoughtful – in a huge cap and walking very slowly indeed. *[Bradman did make a century – a match-winning 173 not out – in the second innings of that Test Match.]*

BJ: Before we go on with the cricket, I'm colour blind, but I gather those are green socks.

PO'T: They are green socks.

BJ: Now, why do you always wear green socks?

PO'T: Because my daddy was very, very superstitious and wouldn't allow me to wear anything green on a racetrack, so my way of being disobedient was to wear something green which he couldn't see.

BJ: He was not unconnected with the bookmaking business.

PO'T: He was a bookie.

BJ: Were you a runner?

PO'T: I was a runner, but not exactly an official one.

BJ: When did you first start playing cricket?

PO'T: I was reared in the north of England, so cricket for me began in Yorkshire – where else? I remember the first real turn-on for cricket for me was being taken to the news cinema over and over again to watch Hutton's 364, here at the Oval in 1938, when I was six. And the great joy and cheers in the cinema are very clear to me. Then, towards the end of the war, I remember in Roundhay Park Sir Learie Constantine and Arthur Wood.

BJ: Great wicket keeper.

PO'T: They put together Sunday sides and there was an Australian team and we little boys could be chosen as ball boys to stand on the boundary, and one of my great moments – in fact my greatest moment still in cricket, even though I wasn't playing – was when I was standing at long off. Constantine scored 50 in eighteen deliveries and he whacked the ball over the ropes and it fell into my hands. I remember this huge man just beaming and waving his bat. It was a lovely moment.

BJ: Now, what about the talent? We're never modest. If one goes to the Lord's indoor school during the winter, you can be seen there.

PO'T: True. I love to turn up and play. I love to be with cricketers. I'm not any good any more. My hope – wish – nowadays is to be involved in a stand. If I can plug up one end and let somebody else do the scoring and occasionally pop in a little single and charge up and down the wicket.

BJ: Have you got the Trevor Bailey forward defensive?

PO'T: Yes, I've got that, much to the amusement of all my chums. When I say 'play' it's an overstatement. What I do is creak out to the square and hope to plonk a little timber on the ball. I hope to turn my arm over and get a maiden or perhaps a wicket.

BJ: Leg tweakers or anything?

PO'T: I have a delivery which is really, really special. It does absolutely nothing.

BJ: That's very good.

PO'T: From leaving the hand to pitching – nothing at all. This confuses many batsmen.

BJ: But you go into the indoor school. Who do you play with there? You go once a week, roughly.

PO'T: I usually go with young chums whose delight is to try to knock my head off. They love it. They see this silly old fool turning up and padding up and they love to fling down the leather and try to take my head off.

BJ: I saw someone I know who is a member at Brondesbury and he says that every Friday night you go and coach the boys there.

PO'T: Well, that's a delight for me. I'm with my standard – under nines. I love to – less coach, than encourage.

BJ: Do you give them a demonstration of your strokes?

PO'T: No, I'm the bowling machine and the umpire.

BJ: This is great, because we've got to get the young, haven't we?

PO'T: This is why Brondesbury is such an extraordinary club. If you go there on a Friday night, it's one of the most delightful sights in cricket. The entire field is filled with little boys. The nets are filled. There are something like a hundred little things in white there and it's a lovely sight. Cricket is in the hands of the young.

BJ: Do you play with odd actors and people still?

PO'T: I play for a club called Lazarusians.

BJ: I don't really know that one.

PO'T: Well, you may. We're not doing too badly.

BJ: What sort of people do you play?

PO'T: We play some high-class stuff. We've played Northamptonshire professional coaches and drew with them and we won against Sandbach.

BJ: And where does O'Toole bat?

PO'T: He opens.

BJ: Against all the hostile fast bowling. What do you look like in a helmet?

PO'T: Well, we were playing in Northamptonshire and a distinguished pro., who was in the other side, insisted that we all wear helmets because the pitch was bouncing. So I went into the pavilion and was given a helmet and I couldn't find my way out of the pavilion. I stumbled around and I couldn't see where the door was. I'm sure I looked like a Dalek, so I took it off.

BJ: And you can't hear in one, either. What about the bowling then? Do you get any wickets?

PO'T: Sometimes I get a wicket or two. I get a few maidens. For me one run is now what six runs meant when I was a boy. One wicket now means a five-wicket haul. If I do a decent piece of fielding I'm very happy. If I take a catch I'm delirious and as long as I don't become a passenger with the team, I'll keep on playing.

BJ: Are you good at sprinting round the boundary?

PO'T: Oh, that's a great sight. I'm greatly encouraged by my team, who say, 'Go on! Go on! Off he goes!' and I puff and pant.

BJ: I think we last met in a box at Lord's, watching a Test Match. Do you go quite a bit?

PO'T: I always do watch as much cricket as I possibly can wherever I go in the world, be it in the West Indies or Australia. I was in Australia for Christmas, watching. Which brings me to the subject of David Gower. I have the solution. David will go to live in the West Indies until he qualifies as a resident and then he will play for the West Indies and come back here at the age of 37 and tonk everybody round the park. *[Gower had been dropped for this series after a tour of Australia which had included the celebrated flight in the Tiger Moth. He was to play three more Test Matches the following year against Pakistan.]*

BJ: I think he'd have to live there a bit longer after having played for another country. He's obviously a hero of yours. Who are the past heroes you've had?

PO'T: Hutton was my god, until along came a tall, handsome man called Flying Officer Miller and to this day he's my cricketing god. I met him in Sydney about a decade ago and we had a long, long chat about the old days.

I remember watching him play a long innings – I don't know where or when, but I remember his back foot like a stanchion. He was moving out to everything. He was everything I wanted to be as a boy. *[The great Australian all-rounder, Keith Miller, was a romantic figure who emerged from his wartime service with the RAAF based in England, to bring a joie de vivre to post-war cricket fields.]*

BJ: When he played slow bowling sometimes, he nearly did the splits, because his back foot was static at the crease and he stretched forward.

Can we talk a little bit about yourself, because you don't appear to have come from an acting family. How did you get into acting?

PO'T: Looking back on it now, there seems to have been an inevitable logic to it all, but there really wasn't. I stumbled into it from one thing to another. Somebody got ill in an amateur production and I took over. And then someone said, 'You ought to do it professionally.' Then I thought, 'Shall I try this?' Then I got a scholarship to RADA and it went from there.

BJ: And you got the scholarship, so I'm told, for rather sort of barging in and making a nuisance of yourself.

PO'T: It's not quite true. But what is true is that I'd spent the night in Stratford-on-Avon, watching Michael Redgrave play King Lear. Then, looking for somewhere to sleep – I had no money – I slept in a field with a chum. And we'd covered ourselves with what we thought was straw, but it was indeed merely the cosy to a dung pile. So, when we'd thumbed a lift to London, we weren't exactly fragrant. But the lorry driver dropped us at Euston station.

BJ: Very quickly, I should think.

PO'T: Even that was a bit terrifying. It was a lorry carrying beer barrels and we were standing on the barrels. We got off at Euston, aiming for a men's hostel where we had booked a bed, and I passed the Royal Academy of Dramatic Art. I popped in and started talking to the commissionaire at the door. We were looking at a bust of Bernard Shaw and the commissionaire and I were telling stories about Bernard Shaw, when Sir Kenneth Barnes came along and joined in the story-telling. And one of my stories may have intrigued him. *[Sir Kenneth Barnes was director of RADA from 1909 to 1955.]*

BJ: I should think the smell did.

PO'T: Well, my companion had said, 'You will be removed from there, O'Toole, by a person with a clothes peg on his nose.'

BJ: They tell me your bagpipes played a big part in the first film part you ever got, in *Kidnapped*. Is that right?

PO'T: That's right.

BJ: Did you actually have to play them in the film?

PO'T: I did. It was my friend, Peter Finch, who was in it. There was a part for Rob Roy McGregor's son, who had a bagpipe competition with the part that Peter was playing. And Finchy had said, 'There's only one actor I know who plays the —— bagpipes.'

BJ: Well, this is useful. For promising people who want to go on the stage, go and learn the bagpipes. You might get a part from it.

Now – *Lawrence of Arabia*. One or two others turned the part down.

PO'T: Did they?

BJ: Weren't you told? You snapped it up as soon as it came along.

PO'T: I felt I was in the slips and the ball came my way. I thought, 'I'll have that one.'

BJ: You were on a pretty sandy wicket for a long time.

PO'T: Very – and with Omar Sharif, another good cricketer.

BJ: Did you have any games of cricket?

PO'T: We did. In the middle of the desert in 120 degrees, to the astonishment of the Bedouin, who hadn't the foggiest what was going on.

BJ: Did they field for you?

PO'T: No, they didn't, but they looked at the ball with great suspicion. Then one of them picked it up and thought, 'This is a wonderful weapon', and they were flinging it about.

BJ: Did it take an awful long time to do?

PO'T: It took a couple of years. It became my life. It was more than just a film – it was a huge adventure.

It was everything that a young 28-year-old man could wish for. I was out in the desert in the Holy Land, working with a genius – David Lean – with a superb company of actors.

BJ: Quite a few in the cast, to say the least – thousands.

PO'T: I need a scoresheet, or I'll leave someone out. I was like a young matador – another bull would come in.

'Who's this morning?'

'Anthony Quinn.'

'Who's today?'

'Alec Guinness.'

'Who's today?'

'Anthony Quayle.'

'Who's today?'

'Donald Wolfitt.'

'Who's today?'

'Claude Rains.'

'Who's today?'

'Arthur Kennedy.'

'Who's today?'

'José Ferrer.' It was astonishing.

BJ: Not a bad team, that.

Isn't it extraordinary how many actors love playing cricket?

PO'T: There is an affinity between this game and ours. Well, think of C. Aubrey Smith, who captained his country.

BJ: That's right. Only one Test Match he played and he captained England. *[Charles Aubrey Smith captained England in South Africa's inaugural Test Match in 1889 in Port Elizabeth. He caught a fever which prevented him from playing in the other Test of the series. Much later he became an actor.]* Did you ever play in Hollywood?

PO'T: No, but Hollywood, as you know, has a cricket team. And lots and lots of West Indians are going to live in California. Down in the Valley they're setting up cricket matches. So it may take on. In America, you know, they call cricket 'baseball on Valium'.

BJ: Jonathan Agnew and I disgraced ourselves yesterday by corpsing. Are you a corpser?

PO'T: Hopeless – pathological.

BJ: Have you had any experiences on the stage or in a film where you simply couldn't go on?

PO'T: Oh yes. Twice I've been in productions where the curtain has been pulled slowly down. One of my favourite moments was in Brighton in a play which was not very successful and was not going to have a long life. It was a complicated play, set on a strand, with the corner of a little beach-side cottage and the back of the set was the sea. Lots and lots of gauzes and lights and complicated things, to make it look like the sea. And, indeed, I entered from the sea with Sylvia Syms in our bathing costumes.

On the beach was a lovely man called Nicholas Meredith – no longer with us – a great giggler. And his first line was, 'Good morning Roger.' I was Roger. Then he had to erect a deckchair, which is never easy. It's a tricky old business. Your fingers get trapped. And I remember the line very clearly, because I heard it for seven or eight weeks. 'Good morning, Roger. There's something about a deckchair – austerity, poise and comfort. The austerity is an illusion, the comfort is achieved only with difficulty and the poise we leave to Pamela.'

Well, he would do that line erecting a deckchair and not once did he get the deckchair up. Nick had a habit of twisting his hair into little spikes. This meant, 'I am not giggling.' Then, when he coughed, this meant 'I am certainly not giggling.' So there was Nick, twisting these huge spikes on his head and coughing away and after an agonisingly long time of not getting the deckchair up, he left behind this crumpled mass of timber and canvas and said, 'I'm going to post a letter,' and walked into the sea.

The only thing I could think of was, 'I did not do this. This is not me.' So I hid behind a palm tree.

Nick was floundering around, looking for a letter box in the sea amongst the gauze and electricity at which point everything went potty – sparks and flashes. And onto the beach came a fireman in a brass helmet with an axe.

And of course the curtain came down very, very slowly. The producer immediately looked at me and wagged his finger. But it wasn't me.

BJ: You've done a fair bit of Shakespeare – *Hamlet*, for instance.

PO'T: That was funny too. I came on stage at the Old Vic to play Hamlet and I'd been down below with a stage hand, trying to pick a winner. I walked onto the stage and I knew that Noël Coward was out front and he was sitting in the front row with his friends. And I said, 'To be or not to be, that is the question.' I heard a snigger. 'Whether it is nobler in the mind ...' – snigger – '... to suffer the slings and arrows ...' – snigger. I thought, 'What am I doing?' and I had a quick glance down to see if my fly was open.

Finally there was real proper laughter throughout the entire audience and I didn't know why. At which point, Rosemary Harris came on as Ophelia and I put my hand to my forehead and realised I was wearing 20th-century horn-rimmed spectacles. How should I get rid of them? So I said to Rosemary, 'There should be no more marriages!' and I flung the specs at her.

BJ: That's great. And your Macbeth got a few laughs. Was it meant to?

PO'T: Not really. Again the chief cause was this awful sense of the ridiculous. As Banquo appeared, drenched from head to foot with blood, down the Waterloo Road came an ambulance and you could hear the siren clearly. I caught Brian Blessed's eye and I'm afraid we were both giggling.

BJ: The great thing is you've had fun all the time.

PO'T: All the time. And I hope it continues.

BRIAN JOHNSTON

interviewed by Ned Sherrin,
Lord's, 21 June 1992

To mark Brian's 80th birthday I thought it would be fun to turn the tables on him and make him the surprise 'victim'. To deceive such an arch practical joker as Johnners, though, took quite a bit of thought.

First I had to get someone to do the interview who he would believe was a real guest, but who could do the job perfectly. A number of names went through my mind, to be dismissed as either not believable in cricketing terms, or someone we'd had before. Then a brainwave struck. Ned Sherrin.

Brian knew that Ned was on our 'hit list'. He was doing a regular Saturday morning programme on Radio 4, Loose Ends, *which put him in London on those days and should leave him available, but only for Lord's and the Oval. That should be fine. The actual birthday was 24 June, two days after the Lord's Test with Pakistan.*

Ned liked the idea, when I called him, though he said, 'I hope that doesn't mean I would miss my chance to be a guest on the programme one day.' I promised him it wouldn't, but then he threw a small spanner in the works by revealing that Loose Ends *that day was due to come from the north. He wouldn't be able to make it. 'I could do Sunday,' he offered.*

I decided to leave it billed in the Radio Times *for the Saturday, so that Brian wouldn't smell a rat and just make a late – and apparently emergency – swap.*

Ned arrived with his battered briefcase and indicated to me the notes he had left in the top, asking that I hand them to him as he was starting. In those days the news was always read at the start of the interval and then the studio presenter would hand back to 'Brian Johnston to introduce his guest taking "A View From the

Boundary"'. I briefed Bill Rennells in the studio carefully and his handback, to Brian's uncomprehending astonishment, was: 'And now, to introduce his guest, taking "A View From the Boundary", here's Ned Sherrin.'

*

NED SHERRIN: We're turning the tables on you today, Brian. Today, this is your boundary.

BRIAN JOHNSTON: What are you doing to me?

NS: You're being interviewed; I'm not.

BJ: I don't believe this.

NS: Absolutely true. Aren't you going to be 80 on Wednesday? Haven't we heard about it all week?

How do I fill half an hour talking to you? Because you've done 46 years. You must have counted up the number of hours that you've rambled on up here.

BJ: Rambled is the right word, but of course I didn't ramble quite so much in the early years, because I started on the telly and one was meant only to speak when you could add to the picture. And if you watched very closely, you didn't speak at all, really. That was the first thing we were told about television commentary.

NS: Your first cricket team was Temple Grove *[prep school]*, where you played with Douglas Bader.

BJ: He was very popular, because he was a brilliant cricketer and every Saturday he used to get a hundred against another school and we used to get off prep every time he got a hundred. And he was a marvellous rugby player. He'd have played for England at both, I'm sure. *[Douglas Bader was the Second World War fighter pilot who famously continued to fly after the loss of both legs.]*

NS: Then there was the terrible injustice of your Eton career – not being crowned with keeping wicket for the first team.

BJ: I don't know about injustice, but a chap did stay on a little bit longer. He was nineteen and a half I think. But I captained the second XI and as usual, I think, I had more fun doing that. The trouble was that when they came to Lord's, we had two fast bowlers called Page and Hanbury and when you look at the records, he let 35 byes. Well, goodness knows how many I'd have let, but I had a quiet chuckle. But he was a nice chap and we were friends.

NS: And you had the sympathy of a great cricketer at the time, George Hirst, didn't you?

BJ: George Hirst was the coach there and one of the most lovable characters you could ever think of. He took me under his wing – partly because just previous to the Lord's match I'd stumped someone down the leg side off him.

He was a little round ball of a man then. He used to bowl left-arm round the wicket inswingers and I casually whipped off the furnitures, so he rather liked me and took me all round Lord's when I came up here. He took me up to the scoreboard and introduced me to everyone. He was a lovely man.

NS: The early hero was Patsy Hendren, wasn't it?

BJ: Patsy became a hero of mine when my brother threw me a cricket bat when I was about ten and said, 'You're Patsy Hendren and I'm Jack Hearne.' And I worshipped him from that moment.

I used to get *The Times* before my father could get it and look at all the cricket scores. I then read in an advertisement one day, 'Why not take Wincarnis wine like E. Patsy Hendren of 26 Cairn Avenue, Ealing, London W5'. Well, who would give an address like that nowadays? Imagine Ian Botham doing it!

Anyhow he did and I wrote to him and said, 'Please Mr Hendren, can I have your autograph?' And he wrote back with three little autographs. And the thing about that that has affected my life is that in 'Patsy' he never crossed the 't', and when he wrote 'Hendren' underneath the final 'n' there were two little lines. When I sign my autograph now, it's 'Johnston' without a crossed 't' and two little lines. So he had a great effect. He was a lovable man.

NS: One of your earliest doubtful jokes, too – the heckler on the Hill in Sydney.

BJ: I used to go up when he was scoring for Middlesex and he used to tell me all these stories, and he said that in 1924, when he was fielding in front of the Hill on Arthur Gilligan's tour, Tommy Andrews skied a ball up to him. Patsy was hovering underneath and a voice shouted out, 'Patsy, if you miss this ball, you can sleep with my sister.'

So I said, 'What happened, Patsy?'

He said, 'Well, as I hadn't seen his sister, I caught the catch.' Which is a typical Hendren remark.

NS: How many times have you had to tell that one on *Test Match Special*?

BJ: I don't think I've ever told it on *Test Match Special*.

NS: An original Johnston joke on *Test Match Special*.

BJ: There are not many of those.

But he was very funny and he had this marvellous story of when he was sitting in a railway carriage and there was a very ashen, grey person sitting in the far corner, with a white silk scarf round his neck, looking in a terrible state, and Patsy tried to cheer him up. He said, 'How are you?'

The chap said, 'I'm miserable. Our side only wanted one wicket to win the other day and I got an easy catch at mid-on and I put it down and the other side won. I feel absolutely dreadful.'

And Patsy, joking, said, 'If I'd done that I'd have cut my throat.'

And the chap said, 'I have.'

NS: What about this trick that has never been done on radio before, I gather. The ability to tuck your right ear in.

BJ: I'll take the headphones off. I used to be able to tuck both in, but I think only one stays in now. I have done this on Derek Nimmo's show and on *Parkinson*.

NS: The top part of the lobe is going in. We've still got to get the bottom part in …

BJ: In hot weather it stays in rather longer. Then I can flip it out by going … like that!

NS: Beautiful!

BJ: First time it's been tucked in on the air.

NS: Now I hadn't realised that you'd had a distinguished career by political association. You and Neville Chamberlain were god-fathers to the same child.

BJ: That's right. Alec Douglas Home made me and Neville Chamberlain joint godfathers of his daughter, Meriel. And I went to see him off when he went with Chamberlain to Munich. He was short of a shirt and he was suddenly told he was going and he came round to William, his brother, who I shared a house with, and said, 'Has anybody got a spare shirt? I've got to go to Munich to see Hitler.' So we lent him a shirt and we went down to Heston to see him off. They got into a tiny little aeroplane, the sort of thing you see at a display of Moths – all strapped up. They got into this and went off to Munich. *[This was Prime Minister Neville Chamberlain's meeting with Hitler in September 1938, after which he claimed to believe he had won 'peace for our time'. Alec Douglas Home, Lord Dunglass, later to be Prime Minister himself, was Chamberlain's Parliamentary Private Secretary.]*

NS: Is there one fragrant pre-war memory? You were shipped off to broke coffee in Brazil for a time. Were you captain of the Brazilian national side?

BJ: I went to study the coffee bean. I didn't learn much about it. There are an awful lot of coffee beans in Brazil. But I did play cricket out there on the mat, and my only real triumph was when an American cruiser came in and we took them on at softball, which is the equivalent to baseball, but I think the ball is slightly bigger, and I scored a home run. They have no mid-off at baseball and I hit the ball through mid-off and I got a home run.

NS: Back at home after the war, it was 1946 when you joined the BBC. Was that a chapter of accidents, or a chapter of luck?

BJ: A chapter of luck, because when I was in the Grenadiers during the war, Wynford Vaughan-Thomas and Stuart McPherson came down to brush up on their war reporting in Norfolk before they went across to Normandy. They came and had supper in a wood with us and I got to know them and I thought no more about it.

After the war I happened to meet them at a dinner party and they said, 'We're short of people at the BBC, come and do a test.' They stuck me out in Oxford Street and they said, 'You ask passers-by what they think of the butter ration.' And if you ask silly questions, you get silly answers. So they said, 'Not very good, but at least you kept talking. Come and join us.'

So I said, 'Well, I really want to go into the theatre somewhere.'

And they said, 'Come and join us for three months.' And I stayed until 1972, when I had to retire.

NS: The television box had three distinguished names alongside yours early on – P.G.H. Fender, Aidan Crawley and Crusoe – Robertson-Glasgow, the best cricket writer ever.

BJ: Absolutely. And a great humorist. It didn't quite come over on the telly. He had a very sepulchral voice and when the producer said, 'Give the score', he'd say, 'For those who weren't listening when I gave it two balls ago.'

And Percy Fender, indignant because he had a nose even bigger than mine and a chap up the line said, 'Will you please hold the microphone nearer to you, we can't hear you.' And nothing happened. So they said, 'No, we still can't hear you. Will you hold it so it's touching your nose.' And he said, 'I am!' And of course it was miles away from his mouth. He got indignant.

He was talking about Hayward and how he used to wear a panama hat when he was playing for Surrey, and this was in the middle of a rather exciting hat-trick, I think. So the producer said, 'Stick to the cricket, Percy.' And he put down his micro-phone and said, 'Well, if he's so bloody clever, let him do it himself.' They were a bit irregular in those days.

NS: And poor Pauline – you postponed your wedding because there was a Test Match.

BJ: Well, we had to get married a little bit earlier. It was rather a good thing, actually, because I had to be sure of being here for the Test Match. The colonel, her father, wasn't too pleased, because I proposed to her after a week and she gave me an answer after a month and we decided to get married before the cricket season started. So we were married within three months. But it seems to have worked.

NS: Where are those tattoos that she disapproves of so much?

BJ: I've only got one, just on my left arm here, which is of two crossed cricket bats. I had it done when I was doing *In Town Tonight*. We went down to the Ship Builders' Union or some-thing, down in the East End, and this chap with the little elec-tric needle was so nervous as I was interviewing him that the bats don't look anything like bats and the little ball doesn't look anything like a ball. But it's on my left forearm and I can be recognised by that.

NS: We'd better examine, I suppose, the question of the gaffes. The famous one, I suppose, is 'the bowler's Holding ...'

BJ: That is the only one I didn't know I'd done. I got a letter from a lady who said, 'Mr Johnston, we do enjoy your com-mentaries very much, but you must be more careful. We have a lot of young people listening. Do you realise what you said the other day when Michael Holding was bowling to Peter Willey?

You said, "The bowler's Holding – the batsman's Willey."' No one told me about it at the time.

NS: And then you got into trouble with the leg-over.

BJ: Well, this is Aggers' fault. It was the Friday of the Oval Test Match last season at the close of play. The producer, who bullies us like mad, said, 'Go through the scorecard.'

So we went through the scorecard until we got to Ian Botham, who'd been out hit wicket. And Aggers made a very long explanation of why he did it. And in the end he said, 'He just couldn't get his leg over.'

And I said, 'Couldn't get …' I got as far as that and then I was more professional than I think I've ever been, because I went on reading the scorecard for about 30 seconds without going. But then I had to and I went wheezing away with laughter.

But what didn't help us was Peter Baxter, stupid ass, said to Aggers, 'Say something.'

Well, Aggers was hysterical and all he could get out was, 'Lawrence …' And he broke down after saying that.

But the interesting thing in those giggles – and we've had lots in the box – we've always had a professional like Trevor Bailey or Richie Benaud who would take over.

NS: Someone with no sense of humour you mean.

BJ: No, someone disciplined. And we had Tony Cozier this time, who just sat silent, listening to it all. He should have taken over and said, 'Well, I'll go on with the scorecard.' So we were made to look rather stupid.

NS: Has Mrs Rex Alston forgiven you yet?

BJ: 'Now from Southampton to Edgbaston, where they're play-ing till seven o'clock. So over for some more balls from Rex Alston.' She didn't forgive me for a long time about that.

NS: Is it apocryphal, the one about Princess Diana going up the steps into the pavilion?

BJ: No, that was right. I was on Queen Anne's statue outside St Paul's for the Royal Wedding and I saw the carriage with the outriders and I said, 'Here's Lady Diana, and her carriage will draw up below me. She'll be met by her father, Earl Spencer, and they'll walk up the steps into the pavilion … I mean the cathedral.'

NS: Then there was the funeral of George VI.

BJ: That was unfortunate. I was doing that for television with Richard Dimbleby. He was in St James's Street and I was at Hyde Park Corner. I thought, 'I must get this right,' and I wrote it down and read it every night before I went to sleep. 'Here comes the procession now, led by five Metropolitan policemen mounted' – and they'd told me they'd be on white horses – 'on white horses.'

When the day came, I heard Richard Dimbleby say, 'Over to Brian Johnston at Hyde Park Corner.'

And Keith Rogers, my producer, said, 'Go ahead, Brian. Good luck.'

And I said, 'Here comes the procession now, led by five Metropolitan policemen mounted …' – and they came round the bend and they were on black horses. So all I said was, 'mounted … on horseback.'

And Keith Rogers, on this very serious occasion, said, 'What do you think they're mounted on – camels?' And there was I, trying to be very serious.

And we had this awful business – which is always recalled at state occasions – of, when the cortege came by, having to stop myself saying, 'Here comes the main body of the procession', which would have been disastrous.

NS: Wasn't there a time when you were suddenly commenting on a close-up of Yardley?

BJ: This was at Trent Bridge, the first time we went there for television, when Weekes and Worrell put on 280-odd and at about four o'clock I remember saying, 'Well, obviously Norman Yardley's got to do something about this. I wonder what he's thinking?' And as we put the camera on him in close-up, he was scratching himself in a very unfortunate place. So I said, 'Well, obviously a very ticklish problem.' But his wife gave him the most terrible rocket when he got home. Poor Norman. What a lovely chap he was.

NS: You were a sort of precursor of Jeremy Beadle in your radio career, weren't you? There were all sorts of practical jokes you used to play on people. There was the restaurant gag with Cliff Michelmore and two other commentators.

BJ: It was rather extraordinary to see what people's reactions were. Cliff Michelmore was the host at a table and I was disguised as a waiter and we did things like giving everyone a nice bit of Dover sole except the chap whose leg we were pulling. He just got the backbone with the head and the tail on. Michelmore said, 'Are you happy with your fish?' and this chap said, 'Oh yes, very good, very good,' and never reacted at all.

Another thing was at Victoria station, when I had a mask on like a wolf, to see people's reactions. And I heard people say, 'Oh there's a wolf there – must go and catch my train.'

We put out the announcement, 'Will the people who have taken the 8:18 train from platform six, please return it. It's needed first thing in the morning.'

NS: It gives one faith in the imperturbability of the British character.

BJ: Just outside Victoria station Kenneth Horne and I tried to give money away. He was saying something about his old aunt having died and left him money and he wanted to distribute it, but people just wouldn't take it at all.

NS: Did you enjoy tremendously the change from commentary on the television to commentary on the radio?

BJ: Well, radio is a more natural medium and it's easier, because you have to keep on editing yourself on television – or you should do. On television, if you're very technically up on the game, you don't want to be told about the technicalities, because you understand it. And if you don't understand it, you don't understand the technicalities. So a television commentator's in a very difficult position.

NS: How did you enjoy your first trip to Australia? Because it was quite late in life when you penetrated the colonies.

BJ: I got a thing called 'grace leave' when I'd done ten years in the BBC, when they used to let you go off for three months. And I decided to go to Australia. And the Beeb very kindly said, 'We'll use you while you're there.' And I went out – very posh – first class in a Britannia and arrived 24 hours before the

Test Match started in Melbourne. I went there and there was a chap commentating and they said, 'You've got to go on second; Alan McGilvray's aeroplane's late.' And when I started England were seven for three, which wasn't a very good start, and at that moment a pigeon dropped something from the rafters in that big stand at Melbourne. That was my christening in Australia. *[This was the 1958/59 tour, when Peter May was captain of England. He made 113 himself after this terrible start in the Second Test, but Australia won by eight wickets and took the series, for which England had been favourites, 4–0.]*

NS: This was the time when Benaud was captain and there were three who you accused of chucking.

BJ: I never accused them at all, but the umpires should have. There was Meckiff and I remember seeing Slater, the off-spinner, who was bowling in the nets and I said, 'What a good idea, because people so often bowl in the nets. Much better to chuck, because you can be so much more accurate.'

And this chap said, 'He is bowling.'

Slater – we didn't mind about him, but Meckiff was a bit dangerous.

NS: How many tours have you done since then?

BJ: Well, I did altogether ten tours, and one I was very proud of was when I was the neutral commentator for the last Test Matches that South Africa played for so many years, when Australia went there. *[In 1969/70.]* I was with Charles Fortune and Alan McGilvray.

NS: There's a very nice story of one of your favourite interviews with Uffa Fox, when you had a problem understanding how he, who spoke no French, could manage with his wife, who spoke no English.

BJ: That's right. I was interviewing him on telly and I said, 'How does it work?'

And he said, 'My dear fellow, there are only three things in life worth doing – eating, drinking and making love – and if you speak during any of those, you're wasting your time.' Which is a good philosophy. He was a lovely chap.

NS: How about umpires? I like the story very much of the Duke of Norfolk's umpire at Arundel.

BJ: Well, that's an old classic, really.

NS: That's never stopped you before, Brian.

BJ: He was playing a match against the Sussex Martlets. Eleven o'clock start. At a quarter to eleven they were an umpire short, so the Duke drove down to the castle to get his butler, Meadows. He found him polishing the silver. 'Meadows, get your apron off. You're umpiring.'

It was one of those days with a bit of drizzle. Not enough to bring them off, just making it slippery. The Duke came in to bat at number ten and he was at the non-striker's end. The chap batting thought he'd better let him have the bowling, so he pushed one and said, 'Come on, your Grace, come one.'

His Grace set off and he slipped and landed slap on his face in the middle of the pitch. Cover point picked up the ball, threw it to the wicket keeper, who whipped the bails off, turned to the square leg umpire and said, 'How's that?'

The square leg umpire – inevitably – was Meadows the but-ler. What was he to do? He drew himself up and said, 'His Grace is not in.'

NS: Is it equally shop-soiled, the Bradman one, when he was defending Australian umpires?

BJ: A friend of mine, called Tom Crawford, was arguing with Don during Peter May's tour. There had been a very good umpire on the previous tour called McInnes, but he was not quite so good on this tour. Tom Crawford was saying what we often say about our umpires at home – it doesn't quite apply now – that they're all Test cricketers and they know what goes on in the middle. He said to Don, 'The trouble with your people is they learn all the laws, but they've never actually played first-class cricket.'

And Don said, 'What about McInnes? He played for South Australia until his eyesight went.' Then he realised what he'd said.

NS: There's the Reeves and Robins one, too.

BJ: Robins was a bit fiery-tempered and he'd bowled very badly for Middlesex, and he said to the umpire, Reeves, 'Take my ——— sweater and you know what you can do with it.'

And Reeves said, 'What, sir, swords and all?'

NS: Can you pick out a special Lord's memory?

BJ: Well, I suppose the best one was in 1969, when Alan Ward of Derbyshire was bowling in his first Test Match. Off the fifth ball of an over to Glenn Turner of New Zealand, he hit him very hard in the box. He collapsed in the crease and the cameras panned in. He was lying there and you pretend he's been hit anywhere except where he has. Suddenly he got up, so I said, 'He's looking a bit pale, but he's very plucky, he's going on batting. One ball left!'

NS: I was hoping for an epic cricket moment, Brian. I wasn't hoping for another bit of sleaze.

BJ: The epic was undoubtedly 1963. One of the great Test Matches, when Colin Cowdrey came out at number eleven, with his wrist in plaster, to join David Allen, with two balls left and six runs to win. Just before the start of this last over, my producer suddenly said, 'Right, hand back to the news at Alexandra Palace.'

Luckily Kenneth Adam was then Managing Director of television. He was mad on cricket and he was watching at home and got on the phone to the news and said, 'Go back to Lord's at once.'

So in the middle of saying something about President Kennedy, they said, 'We've got to go back to Lord's.' And we got back in time for the last over with David Allen playing defensively at the last two remaining balls.

NS: Well, many happy returns of Wednesday, Brian.

IAN RICHTER

interviewed by Brian Johnston,
Old Trafford, 2 July 1992

Among the piles of letters we used to receive in the commentary box before the advent of e-mail reduced that to a trickle, there was always a bulging BBC internal envelope from Bush House, the home of the World Service. For years there were a couple of periods during the day when the main stream of the World Service would join the commentary, prompting the familiar 'And we welcome World Service listeners with the news that ...' from the commentator in action at the time. Certain parts of the globe were also treated to the 'Special Overseas Cricket Transmission' for the duration of Test Matches.

After receiving one of these bags of letters at the start of the last Test Match of 1991 against the West Indies at the Oval, I also got a call from the World Service sports producer, Geoff Parker, drawing my attention to one airmail letter that he had set apart from the rest. It was, he felt, a particularly interesting one.

It came from Baghdad and I read it with a growing feeling of amazement as I realised that the sender was actually inside Abu Ghraib prison.

'I'm confined out here and have been for some time. One of my great comforts is listening to the ball-by-ball commentary and I have been delighted to hear England's win at Headingley, after a long twenty-two-year wait.' It was signed by Ian Richter and I realised that I had been reading about him and his incarceration in Saddam Hussein's Iraq.

I handed it to Johnners as he was going on the air for a commentary stint which would include our time on the World Service. My briefing was of necessity slightly rushed – and of course whispered – and I realised that he had not fully taken it on board when

I heard him express the view that it must be lovely in Baghdad at this time of year.

The first Gulf War, prompted by Iraq's invasion of Kuwait, was begun and ended during the five and a half years of Ian Richter's imprisonment.

Happily, thanks largely to the persistence of his wife, Shirley, in November 1991 Ian was released, and in the publicity of his return I thought that the following season, when the dust had settled, it would be wonderful to let him take a 'View From the Boundary'. And so we were delighted to welcome him to a wet day at Old Trafford.

*

IAN RICHTER: It's wonderful to be here, even in this weather. I've had enough sun in the last few years. I could do with a bit of rain, but I don't like it interfering with my cricket.

BRIAN JOHNSTON: I've had a report from the Naval and Air Force Attaché from the British embassy in Baghdad. *[He had rung the BBC that morning, when he heard that Ian was going to be on the programme.]* A chap called John Marriott, who said you were a very fine cricketer and that you were a wicket keeper who opened the batting. So you're a sort of Alec Stewart. He said you were also a fine squash and hockey player. Is all that right?

IR: In my younger days I did play hockey for South Africa and played cricket for South African Universities and Western Province once. I have two first-class matches to my credit. Not a lot, but I've always had a deep love for the game and it did help me enormously during my early days of solitary confinement – getting into little exercises like picking world cricket teams.

BJ: That was mental exercise. What about playing out there before you were arrested? What sort of cricket did you have?

IR: Very little in Baghdad – but fun cricket. We used to play for the embassy side against various nationals. We played an Indian side or a Pakistan side every now and then. And occasionally we'd come across a side from a company with a very large contract – one that had enough players to put together a team. The Indians and Pakistanis used to bring one or two surprises from time to time and it was a variable pitch.

BJ: What sort of pitches were they? Matting?

IR: No, we had a grass pitch. The British embassy in Baghdad is delightfully set right on the River Tigris and I think the Iraqis have been trying to move them out for several years now, but been resisted. It's a glorious setting with many trees and it's a grass wicket of variable bounce.

BJ: Did you ever hit a six into the River Tigris?

IR: Yes, I did manage one, for which I had to forfeit several beers.

BJ: Since coming back here have you had any cricket?

IR: I was kindly invited by the Free Foresters to play against my son's school at Ampleforth. It was a wonderful arrangement and we had a glorious day during the festival weekend. It was quite glorious to be playing cricket again. I was so impressed with the way Don Wilson looks after the boys there. He doesn't push them too hard, doesn't destroy their natural talent and at the same time he guides and keeps them going. *[Don Wilson, the former Yorkshire left-arm spinner, had been MCC's head coach for several years, before taking up the post of coach at Ampleforth in 1991.]*

BJ: Can you remember the final world XI that you selected over the five and a half years?

IR: Well, I found it so difficult defining periods. Originally I started with the post-war period, then narrowed it down to people I'd either seen or heard of. There were two or three sides. I could never actually settle on one, but I guess it would be something like: Greenidge and Barry Richards opening the batting. At three we could have had Kanhai or Greg Chappell or Vivian Richards. I would have looked at Graeme Pollock possibly at four, having a slight South African background. Clive Lloyd at five, maybe. I had great difficulty in choosing the all-rounder – Procter, Botham?

BJ: What about your bowlers?

IR: So many – Wes Hall, Charlie Griffith, Ray Lindwall, Keith Miller – four wonderful bowlers – Fred Trueman.

BJ: You had to include him, though he's not in the box.

IR: And Geoff Boycott was first reserve, if Richards and Greenidge hadn't got a hundred by lunch.

BJ: So you're going to get him to bring out the drinks. He wouldn't like that.

IR: Wicket keeper, too, was a difficult choice. Knotty possibly.

BJ: You say you received the ball-by-ball. How did you actually get it?

IR: For the first three years I was in solitary, so I had virtually nothing. But eventually I got a radio and I started playing with it. And I managed to get a copy of *London Calling [the World Service magazine of programme timings]*, which announced that they were having a ball-by-ball service and I tuned in quite fruitlessly one morning. I then, quite by chance, discovered that if I listened to a certain frequency, once it finished shortly after lunch UK time, if I twiddled the knob a little further to the left, I would pick up the South Eastern wavelength, where it was being beamed to. It was rather faint, but if I cocked an ear to one side and told every one to shut up – I was quite fierce about that – I would have four or five hours' cricket. So it was wonderful.

BJ: Let's just work back a bit. How did you gain a set?

IR: Well, it took a bit of pushing. As you can imagine, it was not something the Iraqis were terribly keen on doing. I think my wife got hold of three. The third one got to me after various people had intervened along the way and that made a huge difference to my quality of life.

BJ: And did your Iraqi guard put on headphones and listen to the commentary?

IR: Er – no. They're not the keenest of cricketers.

BJ: Let's go back to the beginning. First of all, you are South African.

IR: Yes, born there and came over to Britain in '72 after I got my MSc in chemical engineering. And I've been here ever since.

BJ: So, why did you go out to Iraq?

IR: We had sold a large water treatment plant to them – drinking water – and the requirement was that we had to set up an office there within twelve months of signing the contract. So it was a career move, really. I wasn't an expatriate as such. It seemed a good step forward to move out of engineering into management and so I accepted the chance and went out for three years. I was asked to stay another year and asked to stay yet another year and then, actually on my departure to come back, the grey faces arrived.

BJ: Were you on your way to the airport?

IR: I was at the airport.

BJ: With the plane outside, waiting to take you back to the old country. What did they do?

IR: It was frightening, really. They came up to me and they said, 'Your passport's out of order.'

I said, 'I don't think it is.'

And they said, 'Well, come with us to the old airport.' And I thought something was wrong when five goons jumped into a Mercedes with me, because not many people have Mercedes in Baghdad, apart from privileged people.

We drove well past the old airport, and I was refused access to my wife and I said, 'Where are we going?'

They drove me to a piece of wasteland and said, 'Lie down on the floor.' That was terrifying. I thought I was going to be executed then. You hear these stories. In fact all they were doing was preventing me seeing where they were taking me, but I didn't know that.

Then I arrived at the great Majabrat headquarters. I guess it's like the KGB headquarters in Moscow. It's a sort of dark place.

BJ: And were you then questioned?

IR: I was questioned for three days. They tried to associate me with one person, failed to – and then a second, then a third.

BJ: What were they accusing you of?

IR: Various things. One was bribery. Second was espionage and as they kept on trying, the more desperate they got.

BJ: Without offending any of them, I would have thought bribery was rather a normal thing.

IR: It's strictly forbidden out there. As I was not a director, I had no ability to sign foreign currency cheques, so it was fairly far-fetched.

BJ: Who were you accused of bribing?

IR: The Mayor of Baghdad, who was not our client at the time. Our client was something to do with the Ministry of Housing, which was nothing to do with him.

They quickly found out that he was nothing to do with me, and I think all-in-all I had been held as a hostage for this chap who's over here who had assassinated an Iraqi Prime Minister some years ago.

BJ: Did you have any sort of trial?

IR: They left me alone after the three days for roughly nine months. That was a challenging period, too. Day after day in the darkness.

BJ: Were you in solitary?

IR: Yes. That was a difficult period.

BJ: In the dark. Take us through a day. One just can't imagine it. Do they shove food through at you?

IR: A cup of tea in the morning – a cup of tea in the evening. I went on hunger strike for the first two weeks and refused to eat what they were giving me. I'll never know, if I'd had the courage to keep going, whether they'd have let me go on. But eventually they called me in and they were very upset. They said, 'You've got to eat something. We're going to bring you a roll from out-side. Will you eat that?'

I said, 'Well, I'll see what the roll is.' And eventually hunger got the better of me and I started eating the roll.

But the first two or three months were difficult, because I didn't know what was happening. I kept thinking that help was at hand any moment. But then I realised that you had to get on with life by yourself.

BJ: Were you visited at all? Did the Ambassador come and see you?

IR: They were trying desperately to get access to me, but it wasn't permitted. I had the pillar of using my mind – and that was either developing a mathematical equation or picking a cricket team.

BJ: What things did you have? Pencil and paper?

IR: No, absolutely nothing. No light. It was just a blank cell. I slept on the floor.

BJ: Absolutely unbelievable. What do you think of all day? Choosing your world XI?

IR: Yes. You invent a business. You see how it would do in Britain, or how it would do in Saudi Arabia. It was very important to keep the mind going.

BJ: Did you get any sense of time?

IR: I had no watch and couldn't detect time through the light. The only way I kept track of the days was through the tea in the morning and the tea in the evening. I had a passion to keep track of the days. It was a real thing with me.

BJ: And no news from outside whatever?

IR: No. After about three months I was shown to the British Chargé d'Affaires, but I wasn't allowed to speak to him and he wasn't allowed to speak to me. It wasn't easy for a year and a half to two years, but then things got slightly better.

BJ: You're throwing that away. It wouldn't be easy for a week or a day. What were the Iraqi guards like?

IR: At first they were fierce. It was a difficult situation. I don't think they have much regard for human life and they were desperate to extract information from people they held, so they used various techniques in so doing. After that, when I was transferred to the main gaol, I think I was discriminated against for some while, but eventually my discipline and daily routine appealed to them, I think. And we gradually made friends. They weren't the people who had arrested me, they were just normal prison guards.

BJ: Did they talk to you?

IR: At first they were terrified, because Iraqis are really discouraged from speaking to foreigners, but gradually they plucked up courage and saw that I had two arms and two legs and two eyes and went running every now and then – 'The mad Englishman who likes this, but he doesn't like that.'

BJ: Where were you allowed to run, though?

IR: Well, that again took about three years, but eventually I persevered and I said, 'I want to run round that dusty football pitch you've got out there.'

And they said, 'But no one runs here.'

So I said, 'Well, I want to.' It was wonderful, running, because it took me away from the maelstrom of Egyptians and Sudanese and the cigarettes and the spitting and it was just a bit of peace.

BJ: But how were you physically? Your legs must have been completely weak to start with.

IR: They weren't too bad, because in solitary after two months I realised that no one was going to get me out of this and I had to survive myself, and I got stuck into the exercises then. So I used to leap about, doing star jumps and press ups and occasionally I'd get a knock on the door, saying, 'What the hell are you doing in there?' But generally that kept me going and I did find physical exercise important mentally, too. The two seemed to go together.

BJ: Now what about the Gulf War? Did you know when it had started?

IR: Yes.

BJ: Did their attitude change?

IR: It didn't. They were surprisingly good to me during the war. Whether that was because I'd built up a relationship and a respect before that, or whether they were just hedging their bets on how the war was going to go, I don't know, but they were very good to me during the war.

The war itself was difficult to handle, because there was a desperate shortage of food and water, so we really had to struggle to survive.

BJ: Were you bombed at any time by our planes?

IR: Yes. Funnily enough, there was a strike of lightning and thunder the night before the war started and we all thought, 'Oh, God, this is it.' But they came the next night and there was an army camp round us, which got plastered. But for the first day or two you get frightened of bombs and then you get used to the noise. You get a bit blasé about it and get this feeling that it's not going to happen to you.

BJ: Did they try the propaganda and say how great Saddam Hussein was? Presumably they worshipped him.

IR: Well they had to worship him, but gradually, after the war, when there was this insurrection, I was amazed how many people came to me and said, 'This man has ruined our country.' That took a lot of saying to a foreigner. It could never have happened before the war.

BJ: And you were made more comfortable, were you? Did you have a better cell with other people?

IR: It was very crowded when I first left solitary and was brought to the main prison. I was in a hall about 40 metres by 60 metres, with about 60 people in it. So it was very crowded. A bit like a goldfish bowl. After five years I was given a cell of my own and that was marvellous. I put up a big sign saying, 'ENGLISHMEN ONLY. PICCADILLY CIRCUS. KEEP OUT.'

BJ: What a relief! And your wife went out to visit you regularly?

IR: Yes. Shirley had come back to Britain after six or nine months, having been refused permission for a while, and then led this marvellous campaign. She was absolutely wonderful. She came regularly until the invasion of Kuwait, when, of course, we didn't see each other for a year.

Then she came out with ITV and there was this most extraordinary interview. I thought she was coming out, but I'd no idea of the time and I walked into this room and there were all these cameras and Jeffrey Archer was there. So it was a sign that things were going well, but I'd been through so many disappointments, I didn't take it as a sign at the time. But the fact that they did allow a TV crew in was good.

BJ: And how did you actually hear the news that you were going to be released?

IR: The Russian Ambassador came to see me three days before I was released and he said, 'Ian, I'm terribly sorry, relations between Britain and Iraq are particularly bad at the moment. Sadruddin Aga Khan's coming out, but I really wouldn't bank on him. He's going to try, but things are just terribly bad at the moment.'

So I said, 'Oh well, thanks for that.' He was a super chap. The Russians were marvellous to me after the war. They found me and helped me.

So then three days passed and nothing happened. And I went out and ran a half-marathon, to get rid of my pent-up fury at not being released. And I had a shower, which was a bucket of water and a ladle. And a guy came to me and said, 'You've got five minutes to leave.'

And I said, 'As I've spent five years as your guest, you can give me a bit longer.'

He said, 'No, there is a press conference. We've got to be there.' I think Saddam Hussein would have killed him if he hadn't got me there in five minutes. So I grabbed a shirt, borrowed a tie and unfortunately lost all my letters, but I preserved my books – particularly the cricketing books which people had sent me. Towards the end I got most of the *Wisdens*.

BJ: I suppose you had to catch up, didn't you? Those years when you were in solitary and didn't get the cricket news.

IR: I missed '86 to '89, basically. So I missed a period when we lost a few.

BJ: And you read of the successes of various new people. That must have been fascinating – a new breed of cricketers.

IR: It was. Lamb had come and gone and come back again and, yes, a whole new breed had come through.

BJ: And as soon as you were released, where did you go?

IR: I went to a hotel and I had 24 hours with Prince Sadruddin and his team and then flew back with his plane.

BJ: He did a good job. Did he?

IR: Marvellous guy. Shirley met him during her visit to Iraq three or four months before I was released. She went to see him and he promised to help. And many people who said that helped in their own ways, but Prince Sadruddin kept in telephone and fax contact with her weekly thereafter.

BJ: Would you ever go back there?

IR: I don't think so. I think I've probably donated enough of my life.

BJ: And now you're starting a cricket tour. You said you were playing for the Free Foresters. How many did you make? How many stumpings?

IR: Twenty-six, one stumping and two catches. And the next match I got one and dropped two catches.

BJ: That's roughly the way cricket goes. So who are you going to be playing for now?

IR: Well, I have Emeriti in a week's time.

BJ: That's the club formed by the Catholic schools, roughly – Downside, Ampleforth?

IR: And they had to include St Aidan's in Grahamstown, where I was brought up – a Jesuit school. I'll be playing for a number of sides and Don Wilson wants me to play over the bank holiday.

BJ: It would be nice keeping wicket to him. You'd get a few stumpings.

IR: When I came back I spent the winter up in Yorkshire and he allowed me to play with the first team squad at their indoor nets. And he bowled to me and he's a wonderful bowler. He just twiddled it over and stretched me forward and a little bit more forward each ball – lovely to see.

BJ: It sounds to me that if we were all put into solitary confinement, we'd all become better cricketers. How did you pick it all up after five or six years – picking up a bat again, or putting on the gauntlets?

IR: I think a moving ball game is instinct – squash or tennis, that's all come back to me, too. But I can't hit a bloody golf ball.

BJ: But did it affect your eyes? There you were in darkness. What happened when you suddenly saw the light?

IR: I was worried about that, but it seems fine.

BJ: So you can still see the ball. The other thing – having trained running round that football field, you've now run in the London Marathon here. You must be mad. What was your time?

IR: Four hours 30 minutes, less ten minutes to get to the start, so I claim four hours twenty. When we came back we were interviewed by a lot of people and after one day we said, 'Right, that's it.' Somebody from a running magazine rang up and said she wanted to do an interview. I said, 'Sorry, those times have passed now.'

And she said, 'But I'll get you into the London Marathon and I'll get you kit.'

The kit disappeared towards my children rapidly, but she got me into the London Marathon and the Red Cross, who'd helped Shirley a lot while I was away, asked me to run for them.

BJ: So you got some money for the Red Cross. How did you feel when you crossed the line?

IR: I felt pretty grim at about 23 miles, when we got to Tower Bridge for the second time, but, as luck would have it, I bumped into Shirley, who'd spent three hours looking for me, and that sort of raised me for the last three miles. Yes, it was fun to finish.

JOHN PAUL GETTY JR.

interviewed by Brian Johnston,
Headingley, 24 July 1993

Once famously reclusive and shy, Paul Getty became only the second of our 'Views' to be recorded, when he asked that his great friend, Brian, should come to his flat overlooking London's Green Park.

His father, John Paul Getty, another great anglophile, had been reckoned to be the richest living American in the 1950s, the family money coming originally from oil. Paul Getty himself hit the headlines in 1973, when his eldest son was kidnapped in Italy and had an ear cut off before a ransom was paid.

Having discovered a love of cricket, Getty became a great benefactor of MCC at Lord's and his substantial financial contribution to the building of the Mound Stand earned him membership and a box in the stand, where many famous names were entertained during Test Matches. In 1986 he was rewarded for his philanthropy with an honorary knighthood. When he eventually became a British citizen, he could assume the title. Although that had not yet happened, he endearingly referred to England as 'we'.

He created his own cricket ground on his estate on the edge of the Chilterns, where he invited Brian to be his match manager. The recording of this interview followed the day after one of these games. Johnners started at the beginning, by asking him where he was born.

*

PAUL GETTY: I was born on a boat in the Mediterranean.

BRIAN JOHNSTON: A boat!

PG: Yes, I was born on a boat, but I was brought up mostly in California – originally in Los Angeles and then in San Francisco. And that's where I had all of my schooling.

BJ: And you've been an American all your life and still are an American.

PG: Still am – yes. *[But only for another four years, as he took British citizenship in 1997.]*

BJ: And what sort of sport did you play as a young chap?

PG: I swam for the school team and I was pretty good at swimming – breast stroke. And I played baseball, but not in an organised fashion. I played baseball in scratch games.

BJ: Did you follow it closely?

PG: Oh, absolutely. I used to listen to the broadcasts of the San Francisco Seals.

BJ: They have marvellous names, don't they?

PG: Joe DiMaggio had come from the San Francisco Seals.

BJ: Oh, I've heard of him.

PG: He was the sort of Denis Compton of his day.

BJ: He hit the home runs out of the ground, did he?

PG: He was a very great batsman.

BJ: What were you, the pitcher or the catcher?

PG: Whatever they'd let me be.

BJ: Is it fun to play – baseball?

PG: It certainly is, yes. I expect like any other game.

BJ: Americans always claim that cricket's so slow and baseball's so fast. Is it a quick game?

PG: Well, I had an American friend with me yesterday at the match and she said the one thing in common with the two games is that you can turn away and talk for a long time.

BJ: Typical woman's remark. That is, I suppose, true.
So, baseball was what you followed for a long time.

PG: Baseball and American football, yes.

BJ: Are you an expert on that? All those huddles? Do you know what it's all about?

PG: I did in those days, yes. It's changed a lot. Then when I discovered cricket it was a whole new world for me.

BJ: Well, you say 'discovered cricket'; how did you discover it?

PG: Well, Mick Jagger, who lived near me at the time, used to come by my house and he would want to watch the cricket when it was on and I would have to watch it too. And I would ask questions. I'd heard about this game and I'd seen cricket bats and I'd always thought, how can you fail to hit the ball with a bat as big as that? It fascinated me. It's a very complicated game. It was a challenge to try to understand it.

BJ: How did you set about it? Have you read a lot of books? I know you've got a lot of books on it.

PG: I started to read in the press about the matches and I very much admired the style of writing of the cricket journalists.

BJ: Yes, we've been lucky with our cricket writers on the whole, haven't we? People like John Woodcock and Jim Swanton. *[John Woodcock was for many years cricket correspondent of* The Times *and E.W. Swanton of the* Daily Telegraph.*]*

PG: And then as I became more interested, I started to read the books.

BJ: And the videos. Now, have you got every video that's ever been made about cricket?

PG: I have quite a few of them, Brian.

BJ: And you look at them.

PG: I do, yes. Especially in the close season.

BJ: So you spend your winter watching cricket.
And the other thing you do – if there's a Test Match abroad, which starts at 3.20 in the morning our time, you watch it.

PG: I'll be up at 3.20am, yes. I might nod off, but yes, I'll be watching it.

BJ: I think that's great. And with the Tests in this country, you've got a huge television screen, so you watch that.

PG: I can hardly take my eyes away from it.

BJ: But I think you sometimes listen to us.

PG: I always listen to you. It's my invariable style. As much as I admire Richie Benaud as a television commentator – I think he's the very best – I turn the sound down on the television and put on *Test Match Special*.

BJ: Have you got any heroes you can pick out that you like looking at on the videos?

PG: There are so many. I don't want to forget anyone and lose a friend. But of course there's Compton and all those people. I love them all.

BJ: We're talking the day after your cricket match. *[At Wormsley.]* You had surrounding you then some wonderful cricketers.

PG: Well, there was an Australian team there – none of them less than 70 years old – who could beat our team today any day.

BJ: Well, there was Keith Miller and you were talking to him – or he was talking to you – for at least half an hour non-stop. He's still very good.

PG: Nothing wrong with Keith. Ray Lindwall was there, Alan Davidson, Bill Brown.

BJ: Have you seen him on the video?

PG: I haven't seen him on film, no.

BJ: He was a very good opening bat.

PG: Yes, I've read about him and it was a thrill to meet him.

BJ: And there were one or two English people.

PG: Oh, Compton was there and Godders was there in full flow.

[The last referred to was Godfrey Evans, who, with Denis Compton, played against the great Australians, Keith Miller and Ray Lindwall, in, among others, the 1948 Ashes series. Bill Brown played his last Test in that series and Alan Davidson didn't make his Test debut until 1953. Lindwall died in 1996, Compton in 1997, Evans 1999, Miller 2004, and Brown 2008.]

BJ: Are we wrong, people like you and me who love cricket, in thinking that cricketers are perhaps nicer than other games players and certainly that there are more characters?

PG: I think that's so, Brian, I do. I love the company of cricketers.

BJ: If I may say, you're rather like a schoolboy when the cricketers are around you.

PG: I come alive, don't I?

BJ: I expect you to ask for their autographs.

PG: I do – on bats that they sign for me.

BJ: In your box at Lord's you often have dear old Bob Wyatt sitting there. Has he helped you understand cricket? *[The former England captain, Bob Wyatt, played 40 Tests between the wars. He died in 1995.]*

PG: It's always fascinating talking to him about his days in cricket and then about cricket in general and about how cricket should be played. But it was Gubby Allen, probably, who taught me more about what I understand cricket to be.

BJ: Did you used to sit with him in the pavilion at Lord's?

PG: In the pavilion originally, yes. And then he used to come up to my box in the Mound Stand. He was a great man.

BJ: Yes, he was the sort of king of cricket at Lord's, really.

PG: He certainly was. The king of all he surveyed from his window in the committee room.

BJ: The special Allen chair.

PG: The Allen chair and the Allen window.
[Sir George 'Gubby' Allen captained England, was chairman of selectors, on the MCC committee from the age of 33, was President of the club and its Treasurer for twelve years. He died in 1989.]

BJ: I'm just wondering if he'd approve of some of the things that go on today. What do you dislike about international cricket as you watch it?

PG: Well, I dislike the commercialism and I dislike a lot that I see.

BJ: Coloured clothing?

PG: Coloured clothing is against everything that Gubby and I would stand for indeed, yes.

BJ: Have you been to a one-dayer? Have you seen the black sight-screens and white ball yet?

PG: I haven't. Nor do I intend to. *[The first World Cup to be played in coloured clothing had happened only the year before this interview.]*

BJ: Are we old-fashioned, do you think? Because I'm against it, too.

PG: I think I probably am very old-fashioned. And I think that younger chaps would say I am and the players themselves would think I am. But I proudly proclaim that I am old-fashioned.

BJ: Yes, I do, too. It's a pity to me that people don't smile more.

PG: And we won't mention any names, will we?

BJ: One or two very gloomy faces on the field. And I think that to lead you've got to have a cheerful smile.

PG: I would have thought. Just to encourage your chaps to get moving you'd want to flash a smile once in a while. *[Graham Gooch was the England captain in 1993.]*

BJ: And the dissent with the umpires. That's not very good.

PG: That's not very good. Swanton was reading a letter from Keith Miller, saying that he'd never heard the Don *[Bradman]* complain about being given out. He might have felt that it was an unfair call, but he'd never heard the Don complain.

BJ: He tucked his bat under his arm and walked off. Mind you, he wasn't given out so often.

PG: He didn't get out too often, no, but Miller had taken the trouble to write to Swanton about the dissent these days.

BJ: We were talking about your box at Lord's. The great thing is you have all these cricketers past and present, but you have a lot of people from the professions and the arts – actors and things.

PG: Actors seem to like cricket. Like Peter O'Toole …

BJ: And he plays it.

PG: Yes, he does. He has a coaching certificate. He has a son that he's coaching.

BJ: Who he thinks will play for England. We've all thought that our sons will play for England. Not many of them do. But he's going to play in your eleven at Wormsley before the end of the season. And Albert Finney comes round. He's devoted to cricket.

PG: Yes, it's widely appreciated in the acting fraternity.

BJ: Your box is in the Mound Stand. Now, you mustn't be modest about this – you contributed quite a lot towards that, didn't you?

PG: I did. It's a very great building and it was very important that it should be built, I felt.

BJ: Did you have any say in the architecture of it?

PG: None at all. Nor would I ever ask to. I think the committee responsible chose very well. Prince Charles approves of it.

BJ: Oh well, that must be all right.

And then also for Lord's you contributed to the Denis Compton and Bill Edrich stands at the Nursery End very generously.

PG: I was able to and it was my pleasure to be able to help.

BJ: You made a stipulation about that, though. You said that at least 4,000 of the seats had to be available to the ordinary paying public.

PG: That's right. And Gubby had a stipulation too, which was that it couldn't block off the view of the trees.

BJ: And the trees are still there. I suppose it's true to say that you could probably get another 10,000 people in if you raised the stand up and hid all the trees.

PG: But that's the kind of thing that was important to Gubby.

BJ: You're a member of MCC. Are you a member of other cricket clubs as well?

PG: I Zingari I'm very proud to be a member of. And Swanton wouldn't want me to forget that I'm a member of the Arabs.

BJ: The Arabs being Swanton's own team. And for the listeners' benefit, there's a great rivalry between Paul's side and the Arabs and we've had two matches so far. The Arabs won the first one and the one this season was a draw. I think an honourable one for us, don't you?

PG: I think it was. I think if we'd had a little more time we might well have won it.

BJ: I don't think Jim would agree about that.

PG: He certainly wouldn't. I wouldn't argue it with him, either.

BJ: You've achieved something that all of us would love if we could – to have your own cricket ground. Now, first of all, you bought Wormsley, this lovely estate. Is it in Oxfordshire or Buckinghamshire?

PG: Actually the line runs through the estate.

BJ: And did you buy it with the purpose of building a cricket ground, or did it suddenly occur to you?

PG: This was an after-stroke of genius. It was a corn field originally and I took on more than I realised when I decided to have cricket there. I thought you only had to shave the field off, plant some stumps and play cricket on it. It's a good deal more than that. This is our second season and the square was laid the year before the first season. It'll take a few more years to get it ticking.

BJ: Well, I think everybody who's played on it says the pitch is absolutely perfect. The outfield will get better and better.

PG: I hope so.

BJ: Who designed the pavilion – which has got a lovely thatched roof? It's a marvellous rustic pavilion.

PG: I specified what I wanted about the thatched roof and the bails and stumps in the railings round the balcony.

BJ: You're a bit of a man for thatch. There's even thatch on the scoreboard. So, what do you feel when you sit out as you did yesterday in the sunshine watching there?

PG: I love it, Brian. I definitely feel that I'm master of all I survey. It's really wonderful.

BJ: We've got this background of all the trees, some of which you lost. The cows are there and the sheep.

PG: And the deer come down to watch the cricket, actually.

BJ: Now, you've got lots of interests, but there is one I very much enjoy, when you kindly invite me here and we see old films. You show me a film and will tell me every single person in the cast. So how many films have you got? It's a tremendous collection.

PG: Oh, I suppose about 5,000 on video and a few hundred on sixteen millimetre.

BJ: As a boy did you go regularly to the cinema?

PG: I did, as all boys of my age did, go to the cinema at least once a week. And I used to go to Twentieth Century Fox as a little boy, with my friend. And to keep us out of trouble they used to park us in a projection room and show old films to us.

BJ: And the other thing that we have in common, which is ridiculous, is *Neighbours*. I don't understand why we watch it every day – and you ring up if something's happened.

PG: I'm afraid I'd have to say about that that it makes me laugh. They have about three plot lines. They have to re-use the sets, don't they?

BJ: I think we're due for another accident, we haven't seen the hospital set recently.

I must mention your books. You've got a most marvellous library down at Wormsley. Have you collected those yourself?

PG: I have indeed. They're the books that I've loved and collected over the last 35 to 40 years.

BJ: The contents are important to you and the binding obviously as well, because they're beautifully bound.

PG: My major interest is I suppose the beauty of the book. The binding, the printing and its historical importance.

BJ: This is not a cricket library, we must establish.

PG: No, there isn't a single book about cricket in it. The cricket books I have – which are quite a few – are elsewhere in the house.

BJ: And the other thing I would love to have done is to own *Wisden*, which you've just bought.

PG: I don't know how that happened, to tell you the truth. It just sort of overwhelmed me and there it was.

BJ: Well, it's probably the best book in the world, when it arrives every spring.

PG: What would spring be without that yellow cover? No changes are planned. *Wisden* will remain as it is.

BJ: It surprises me that you've never been to Australia.

PG: I fully intend to go the next time that we're playing there. I've promised myself and you, Brian.

BJ: Let's hope that you'll be able to meet Mr Harold Larwood.

PG: Oh, that would be a very great honour, Brian.

BJ: And you genuinely feel when you meet a cricketer that it is an honour.

PG: Well, these are people I've admired and read about over the years and they are heroes to me.

BJ: We're back to the schoolboy in you. Long may you remain that.

*

Sir Paul Getty died on 17 April 2003, aged 70.

ROY HUDD

interviewed by Brian Johnston,
The Oval, 21 August 1993

This 'View' is poignant, because it is the last one that Brian Johnston did. But if he had known that fact, he would probably have picked this last subject, because it brought him to his other great love – music hall. He had as happy a session with Roy Hudd as in any of the fourteen seasons that he did 'A View From the Boundary'.

At this time Roy Hudd was entertaining radio audiences with the weekly comedy satire show The News Huddlines *and was already regarded as the great authority on music hall. Away from comedy, he has made frequent straight acting appearances.*

*

BRIAN JOHNSTON: He's the last bastion – if I may use the word – of music hall.

ROY HUDD: Pardon – what was that?

BJ: But also he loves cricket. Roy Hudd – Hudders to me – let's deal with your cricket first. Were you ever a player?

RH: I was never really a player, Brian. I did play two years ago for our team at the open air theatre in Regent's Park. And I'm sending for that tie. Out first ball, I was!

BJ: The Primary Club. *[It being a Test Match Saturday, Johnners was wearing the Primary Club tie for TMS's favourite charity, which assists the blind.]*

RH: I wore the outfit that I had as Bottom in *A Midsummer Night's Dream* batting. We were playing the Regent's Park police and they didn't think it was particularly funny, so the first ball came whistling down – out! Thank you very much.

BJ: But you have supported and watched cricket for many years.

RH: It's many years since I've been to the Oval. Because this is my team – Surrey. But I got here this morning and what a wonderful surprise. The first person I saw when I walked in was the man we used to call the question mark. It was Raman Subba Row. He looked exactly like a question mark when he walked out. [*Subba Row played for Surrey in 1953 and '54, before moving to Northamptonshire and later becoming chairman of Surrey and the Test and County Cricket Board.*]

BJ: So you supported Surrey when they were winning, winning, winning.

RH: They were terrific in those days, weren't they?

BJ: Any particular heroes of that Surrey side?

RH: Well, Stuart Surridge, of course.

BJ: A great figure – a leader.

RH: Absolutely. And we saw lots of good games here. My hero of all time was Godfrey Evans, though. Wonderful character, looked marvellous and couldn't he keep wicket and couldn't he thump 'em about a bit?

BJ: He'd have been great on the stage.

RH: He was a Dickensian character.

BJ: What do you think of cricket today?

RH: I've enjoyed this morning like mad. This has been our finest hour. *[Although Australia had come to the Oval 4–0 up, England had just taken a first innings lead and were in the process of building on it. They eventually won by 161 runs.]*

BJ: 1936 you were born. You didn't start in show business till you were 21 – at Butters – Butlins.

RH: Yes, I was a redcoat at Butlins. I did lots of shows at the boys' club and then in the RAF I did lots of shows and then I went to Butlins as a redcoat. I thought I was going to be a comic and they said, 'Well, actually you're redcoat "entertainers".' Eight quid a week we got and it meant you did all the shows as well as taking all the kids to the fair and dancing with all the sort of duff crumpet. You had to do all that as well.

It was an incredible way to start in the business – a summer season there. In the next chalet to me was a chap called Dave O'Mahoney, who was a very funny guy as a redcoat and he eventually changed his name to Dave Allen. And in the next one was the one who used to pull all the birds, which used to drive us mad – a fellow called Harry Webb. And he became Cliff Richard. So it wasn't a bad season.

BJ: What sort of thing did you do?

RH: I did a double act with another chap, but most of the time it was running about doing all the jobs.

BJ: I read that at one time – before you were a redcoat – you were a sugar shoveller.

RH: I'm glad you said that right, Brian.

BJ: I took care. What is a sugar shoveller?

RH: It was at Paynes chocolate factory in Croydon. It was really just shovelling the sugar into the things to make the Paynes Poppets. I did that – I did all sorts of things. I was a commercial artist – I was a lettering artist, basically. But when I went into the RAF, between my going in and coming out, some swine invented Letraset, so that was the end of my career as a commercial artist.

BJ: Did you ever go and do a stand-up straight comic act in the music halls? They were slipping away by then – there weren't many around.

RH: I think I'm quite well known for closing down more variety theatres than anybody else in the history of show business. I came into the business proper as half of a double act in the late fifties, when all the variety theatres and music halls were closing, which was a very sad time. We used to play them on Saturday night and on Sunday they used to put the padlocks on the doors. It really was the end of variety.

BJ: Which of the great ones did you see?

RH: I saw quite a few, because my gran used to take me to the Croydon Empire just after the war when I was a little boy. So I saw lots of people there and it was an interesting time to go to variety, just after the war, because you still saw G.H. Elliot, Randolph Sutton and Hetty King and people like this. They were all coming to the ends of their careers, but there were lots of young performers who were just starting – Harry Secombe, Max Bygraves, Bruce Forsyth.

BJ: Frankie Howerd.

RH: That's right. All those people were just beginning, so it was a terrific period to be introduced to the variety theatre.

BJ: I'm not so keen on the old-time variety – I'm for the thirties people.

RH: Well, you are, Brian, because you're much younger than I am.

BJ: Thank you. I was lucky to see the Millers and the Flanagans and Allens and all those people.

RH: I saw quite a few of those, because they did carry on until well into the fifties, particularly Bud Flanagan of course and the Crazy Gang. My gran always used to take me to the Victoria Palace, because it was on the train from Croydon. Just walk across the road and we used to see them.

And people used to say to my gran, 'It's dreadful you taking him to see all those dirty old men running about, doing sketches, chasing women.'

And she used to say, 'Well the great secret is they never catch them.' She was absolutely correct.

BJ: Did you ever actually meet them?

RH: I met Bud quite a lot, because I'd just joined the Grand Order of Water Rats and Bud was still very much an important part of it. And I remember going to see Bud at the Victoria Palace in what would have been their last show and going backstage to see him. And he said, 'Do you want a souvenir?'

And I said, 'Yes, I'd love one.'

He said, 'Here you are,' and he took his straw hat off his head and gave it to me.

I said, 'What are you going to do for the second half, Mr Flanagan?' And he opened a case and he had about 500 hats in there.

BJ: Like Dickie Bird's white cap. You took part in the stage show *Underneath the Arches* and you do this marvellous impersonation of Bud. Is that the original straw hat you wear?

RH: That is the one I wore all through the West End when we did *Underneath the Arches*. I've got a lot of spares, but I keep that one he gave me.

BJ: What do you think was so great about Bud, because he was my particular hero, too.

RH: I think he was the Master of the Revels as far as that Crazy Gang was concerned. I don't think he was particularly the funniest. Everyone thought Monsewer Eddie Gray was the funniest and the best, but Bud had that wonderful voice. He had an aura about him.

BJ: He had a heart.

RH: That's right. And the others didn't. They were all anarchists. Monsewer Eddie Gray was the great hero. I worked on *Underneath the Arches* with Chesney Allen, who was still with us at that time, and he used to tell us smashing stories. He always thought that Monsewer was the funniest.

During the war, when they were going round entertaining the troops, they got to one isolated RAF camp somewhere in two cars. And the policeman on the gate stopped them and said, 'Who are you?'

And Bud said, 'We're the Crazy Gang.'

'Oh, really. Let's see your papers.'

And while all this was going on, Eddie wound down the window of the next car and said, 'Ve haf com here for ze plans of ze Blenheim bomber.'

So the fellow said, 'They're the Crazy Gang – let them in.'

My favourite story of his was when it was almost his last season and he did a summer season with Tommy Trinder. He was getting very old and he said to Trinder, 'Look, it would be a great help to my act if you came on in it and just did a gag. You're a big star, Tom, and it would be a great boost to my act if you came on.'

He said, 'Of course, Eddie, if I can be of any help.'

Eddie said, 'It's only a simple gag, but it would help me an awful lot in the act.'

Tommy said, 'Well, what do you want me to do?'

He said, 'You come on and say, "Hello, Eddie, what did you have for breakfast this morning?" I say, "Haddock" and you say, "Finnan?" and I say, "No, thick 'un."'

And Trinder thought, 'Well, that's not much of a gag, but all right, I'll please the old boy, help him a bit.' And he said, 'We'll do it tonight, shall we?'

Monsewer said, 'Oh, no, no. I'm very old and I'm very slow at learning these lines. We'll have to practise it.' So they used to rehearse every night before the show.

'What did you have for breakfast today?' – 'Haddock.' – 'Finnan?' – 'No, thick 'un.' And so it goes on. 'Tonight?' – 'No, not tonight.'

So it came to the second week. 'There's a big house out there tonight. This is my big chance. When you walk out there, Tom, they'll love it. We'll do it tonight.'

So in the middle of his act, Eddie looks in the wings and signals – 'Now, on you come.'

Trinder comes on, saying, 'Hello, Eddie.' Big round of applause. 'What did you have for breakfast today?'

'Cornflakes.'

BJ: Collapse of Trinder. He was the devil, wasn't he?

RH: They were all a great lot, you know. I worked quite a lot with Charlie Naughton.

BJ: They used to bash him about.

RH: He was the butt of the jokes. Charlie lived quite near me when I lived in Streatham, and the great story about Charlie was that he always used to go out and get stoned every night after the show. And he used to reel out of these night clubs about two o'clock in the morning, not knowing where he was. But every taxi driver in London knew him and they used to pick him up, put him in the cab and drive him home to Streatham. And the next day they'd come round to the stage door and say, 'Charlie, you owe me three quid for the taxi fare,' and he'd pay it quite happily. So that was a well-known thing.

So one day he's not so good and goes to the doctor and the doctor says, 'The main thing you've got to do, Charlie, is you've got to get to bed early. You've got to stop drinking and you've got to do some exercise. You live right next door to Streatham Common, get up early and have a walk round Streatham Common. Do yourself a bit of good.'

So Charlie knocked off the booze and he went home early three nights on the trot – straight back to Streatham. The third morning he gets up to walk round Streatham Common. It's about half past seven in the morning. He's walking round the common and a taxi driver pulls up and says, 'Don't worry,

Charlie, I'll get you home.' And he slings him in the back of the cab.

During the war they had a bomb on the Palladium when they were playing a regular season there. Just before the opening night of their new revue. This unexploded bomb lodged in the roof of the Palladium. And they said, 'What shall we do?'

And George Black, who was running their shows at that time, said, 'Put a piece of canvas underneath the bomb and we'll open. Nobody will ever know that it's there.'

So they said, 'Right, we're going to do it.' And all the band got into the pit very, very sheepish, with this bomb above their heads. And they were just going to start to rehearse, when all these bits of gravel fell on the drums. And they were up like that and ran out of the theatre.

And George said, 'I looked up to the top box and there was Charlie Naughton with a bag of gravel.'

BJ: Now you also do a marvellous impersonation of Billy Bennett – 'almost a gentleman'. Did you ever see him?

RH: Billy Bennett is one of my great heroes – no, I never saw him.

'It was a dirty night and a dirty trick
When our ship turned over in the Atlantic.'

Wonderful stuff.

BJ: Give them one of the monologues.

RH: 'It was the schooner *Hesperus*,
    We lay asleep in our bunks,
    Bound for a cruise where they don't have revues,
    With a cargo of elephants' trunks.

The sea was as smooth as a baby's … top lip,
Not even a policeman in sight
And the little sardines had gone into their tins
And pulled down the lids for the night.' Boom, boom!

BJ: Was he the original with the 'boom, boom'?

RH: Well, apparently so.

BJ: He had the drummer and he used to go 'boom, boom' at the end of the joke.

RH: That's right. My other favourite one of his was 'Christmas Day in the Cookhouse'. 'Christmas Day in the Workhouse' was a famous Victorian poem, but Billy Bennett's version was all about Christmas Day in the cookhouse in the army. And it was all about the army chef who'd manufactured this diabolical Christmas pudding that nobody wanted to eat.

'It was Christmas Day in the cookhouse.
The place was clean and tidy.
The soldiers were eating their pancakes.
I'm a liar – that was Good Friday.'

At the very end the soldier gets up and he starts calling this army chef everything under the sun and he finally throws this curse at him.

'And whatever you eat, may it always repeat,
Be it soup, fish, entrée or hors d'oeuvres.
May bluebottles and flies descend from the skies
And use your bald head for manoeuvres.'

And the tag was –

'And now that I've finished my story,

I don't care what comes to pass.
And as for your old Christmas pudding ...'

BJ: We're live on the air.

RH: 'Put that on the shelf under glass.'

BJ: Did he write them himself?

RH: I think he wrote quite a lot. A chap called Marriott Edgar wrote quite a lot for him as well, and a pair that I was a great fan of, music hall writers called Weston and Lee.

BJ: And a lot of music, too.

RH: They wrote everything from 'Goodbyee' to 'When Father Papered the Parlour', 'My Word You Do Look Queer' and all those songs. They wrote one four-line verse which I've never forgotten.

The song was called 'Epitaphs' and it's all about a bloke who was boring and fed up and whenever he was cheesed off he used to walk round the cemetery and look at the gravestones – the inscriptions – to make him laugh.

And one of these says, 'On the very next gravestone there I saw ...

'Here lies the body of William Burke,
A decent man entirely.
This stone was bought from a second hand shop
And his name's not Burke, it's Reilly.'

BJ: We must get on to the greatest of them all – Max Miller. And you do Miller marvellously. You saw him.

RH: I did indeed see Max Miller a lot, because my gran again was a great fan of Max's. All the dirty comics she was a fan of – what a terrible woman! People used to say, 'It's disgraceful you taking him to see Max Miller.'

She'd say, 'He doesn't understand what it's all about, so it doesn't really matter.'

He was one of my absolute heroes, yes.

BJ: Can you go into any of his routines on the air?

RH: Well, that's a point, isn't it? Although he did a lot of clean stuff and people forget that. I always liked this joke.

A man goes to the garage and he says, 'I've got a few bob, I want some special transport. What about that car over there?'

The salesman says, 'That is a Rolls-Royce. That's about ten thousand pounds.' This was a good few years ago!

He says, 'I can't afford that. I've got a few bob, but not that much.'

'Well,' says the salesman, 'there's a family saloon there. It's about two grand.'

He says, 'Oh, no, I can't afford that.'

'Well, what about that motorbike there? That's about five hundred pounds.'

'Oh, no,' he says.

'Well, there's a pushbike there – twenty-five pounds.'

'Oh, no,' he says. 'Too expensive.'

'A pair of roller skates? A fiver?'

'No, I can't afford that. What's that over there?'

'A hoop. You get a hoop and a stick and it's half a crown.'

'It's not a lot,' he says, 'But that'll do me. It'll get me out in the country at the weekend.'

So he buys this hoop and he goes out into the country at the weekend and he gets to a pub and thinks, 'I'll have a drink.' So he puts the hoop in the car park and goes in.

When he comes out again, the hoop's gone. And he goes raving mad at the car park attendant and says, 'What is this? I left my hoop here. I come out now and it's gone!'

The attendant says, 'What are you moaning about? It can't have cost you more than half a crown.'

'It's not the money – how am I going to get home?'

BJ: Not a typical Miller, but it's a very good one. We can't risk any of the Chihuahua jokes, can we?

RH: You don't want any of that. I always used to like his opening, when he used to say, 'Now here's a funny thing. Now here *is* a funny thing. I went home last night. Now there *is* a funny thing!'

The great story about Max was being hauled off in the middle of the Royal Variety Performance. He was a huge star in this country and he went on to do the Royal Variety Performance and Jack Benny was on that time. And they said to Jack Benny, 'You can do as long as you like.' And they said to Max, 'You can do six minutes.' And he went raving mad. And he went on and wouldn't come off.

BJ: And he went into his rude routine.

RH: That's right. And it went very well, I might tell you. He came off and Val Parnell came round and went raving mad and said, 'You'll never work for me again, Miller.'

And his reply was, 'I'm sorry, you're about twenty-five thousand pounds too late.' And of course six months later he was back at the Palladium.

BJ: You mentioned the word 'song' there. I sang 'Underneath the Arches' with Bud Flanagan. I've sung it with you at the British Music Hall Society. Do you think we might risk just one chorus?

RH: And I want you to know, listeners, that this record is not available in any shop.

*

And they sang one verse of 'Underneath the Arches' together, not just for the radio audience, but also to the crowd at the Oval who must have been alarmed to find it suddenly coming from the public address system.

Also alarmed must have been John Inverdale, to whom Brian handed directly afterwards for the start of Sport on Five. *(Test Match Special was split between Radio 5 and Radio 3 that year.)*

Brian Johnston died on 5 January 1994.

DENNIS SKINNER

interviewed by Henry Blofeld,
The Oval, 3 September 2000

It was John Major who first drew our attention to the passion for cricket of Dennis Skinner, aka 'the Beast of Bolsover'. A few years after that, at the memorial service for Denis Compton in Westminster Abbey, I was surprised to see the former miner and reputedly combative MP come in and make a bee-line to sit next to Henry Blofeld, with whom he was able to have an animated discussion. It was a surprising combination, but I felt I had to put it together again for 'A View From the Boundary' some time.

He came to us during the final Test of 2000, when the great West Indian fast-bowling pair of Courtney Walsh and Curtly Ambrose were making their farewell to England, but England were at last dominating the team that had caused them so much trouble over the previous three decades.

At this time the New Labour government under Tony Blair had been in power for three years. Our guest's political position was generally some distance to the left of that. The position of the Oval makes it the closest first-class ground to the Palace of Westminster and from our old commentary box in the pavilion, where this interview took place, you could see the tower of Big Ben.

Henry introduced Dennis Skinner as 'the last of the great parliamentarians' and also as 'a great snooker player, very considerable cyclist and extremely able tennis player' and asked if cricket had always been part of his life.

*

DENNIS SKINNER: Most sports – football, cricket, athletics, a bit of marathon running and then on to heel-and-toe road walking, with the funny gait. And my dad said to me – he was a miner as well as me – 'Hey, what the bloody hell are you doing? Tommy Lunn says to me tha'rt walking past his house, waggling thee arse!'

HENRY BLOFELD: We sat next to each other at Denis Compton's memorial service. Was he a particular favourite of yours?

DS: I once played hooky from school to see him in that great year, 1947, when he got eighteen centuries, 3,816 runs. Ask me another.

HB: How many did Bill Edrich get that year?

DS: He got twelve centuries …

HB: 3,539, wasn't it?

DS: Roughly – about that. They were a great pair. They were getting a hundred before lunch or a hundred between lunch and tea. It was remarkable. Compton got about 39,000 runs and he missed the war years. 123 centuries – he probably missed another 30.

HB: He was one of the great originals, wasn't he?

DS: Oh, without a doubt. There were no coaching manuals for him. He'd got shots that nobody else knew about.

HB: Did you know him?

DS: No, purely the fact that he was the cavalier of cricket – and everything that Geoffrey Boycott isn't.

HB: You used to play in the Bassetlaw League.

DS: I played a few times with the pit team. Every colliery had a team – cricket and football. It was part of the ritual. Remember, when you worked in a pit, if you didn't get injured you were totally and utterly fit. So fast bowling was not much of a problem and running up and down the football field wasn't either. So I played a few times with Clay Cross and Danesmoor Miners' Welfare.

HB: As a bowler – and you took plenty of wickets, I'm sure.

DS: Yes, I got a few. I used to think I was a fast bowler. Faster than Cork.

HB: And you've always been a keen supporter of Derbyshire and I'm sure you feel the same about England.

DS: Well, I do like to support the underdogs and England for a long time were underdogs. I actually supported Sri Lanka when they beat England, because they were the underdogs.

HB: By the end they were the overdogs all right, weren't they?

DS: Yes, but it was good for cricket that Sri Lanka came and managed to establish a reasonable team. *[This was Sri Lanka's ten-wicket win at the Oval two years before, in 1998, when Muralitharan took sixteen wickets in the match.]*

HB: Now, tell me about heel-and-toe walking. What took you into that?

DS: Well, I'd done a bit of marathon running. I was in the cross country when I was at school, so I was always a good long-distance runner and Roland Hardy – he was an Olympic road walking athlete for Britain – said to me, 'Why don't you go into the Sheffield Walk?' And so I went in and got second place. And I did twelve miles in just over one hour 40.

HB: But there are a lot of people out there who won't know exactly what heel-and-toe is.

DS: It's walking fast, but you've got to be in contact with the ground at all times. Occasionally people will get pulled for what they call 'lifting'. In other words, they're running.

HB: And another facet of your life – you've been quite a singer, haven't you?

DS: We used to put on road shows if a miner got injured. And we'd raise money for him, or in some cases for the widow, because you know miners get killed as well. So there were a group of us that used to put on a road show. My mate used to do Jolson. He'd got the gloves and he'd black his face and I used to try to impersonate – not all that well – the singers of that time. I go back a long way – I'm talking Guy Mitchell and Slim Whitman here. And Johnny Ray and Frankie Lane and 'I'm Gonna Live till I Die'.

HB: Then there was 'I Wonder Why', which you sang, didn't you, at a Labour Party conference to rather amusing words – well, certainly you gave Thatcher and Tebbit a bit of stick and I think Heseltine came in for it, too.

DS: It's almost unbelievable, but we had a miners' concert to raise money and I did a parody of 'Shall We Dance' and also one of the other songs from the shows – *[singing]* 'I hear Thatcher and there's no one there' – and on and on.

HB: Oh, I hoped you were going to give us the full rendering of it.

DS: We haven't got time.

HB: You've censored yourself! But do you still like to do it a bit at a party? Do you like to get up and sing an old Cole Porter song or something of that sort?

DS: Not really. I did that because it was a novelty and there were 10,000 people at the Albert Hall. You wouldn't turn down a chance to sing at the Albert Hall. I also did a parody on the SDP as well. That was 'Shall We Dance'.

HB: And of course you're a master of one-liners. You once gave David Owen of the SDP a bit of a serve, didn't you, in the Commons?

DS: I thought I'd got him absolutely bang on, because I called him a pompous sod and he is, he was and he always will be. And the place was in uproar. So the Speaker said, 'You'll have to withdraw.'

I said, 'Go on, then. I'm in a decent mood, I'll withdraw the word "pompous".'

He said, 'That's not the word I'm looking for.'

So I finished up with an early bath. I should have got a medal.

HB: You've always been a bit of a showman, haven't you? You've liked that aspect of it. And in the House you've been a consider-able figure, but you've stood up for the rights of the underdog all through your career and you've never been afraid to take anyone on.

DS: No, not really. You've got to understand I used to work in a coal mine for 21 years before I went to Parliament. And there's a lot of things wrong with society and somebody has to represent the underdog. So, yes, I'm an unadulterated class warrior. I'm not New Labour.

HB: But you're good friends with the Prime Minister, I believe.

DS: I give him advice and I wish he'd take it up.

HB: You came into Parliament in 1970 and you were telling me how you were elected on the Thursday and you were back at the pit on the Monday morning.

DS: The election was on Thursday, 18 June 1970 and I didn't know whether we got paid straight away. And I hadn't got two ha'pence to rub together, so I thought I'd better go to work on Monday. So I went to Glapwell Colliery on Monday, said goodbye to all my mates and they said, 'What the hell are you doing here? We voted for you on Thursday.'

So I rang another MP that evening and I said, 'What's the score here, Tommy, about being paid?'

He said, 'You're paid from the moment you're elected.'

So I thought, 'That's OK.'

HB: You didn't have to borrow the train fare down to London.

DS: As a matter of fact, you can travel to London free – between your constituency and Westminster, not all over Britain.

HB: When you became a Member of Parliament, you had three principles you adopted.

DS: Three basic principles, yes. There is a system in Parliament called 'pairing', which means that one MP from one side can join with another MP from the other side and play truant. And I think it's wrong, because when I went to work at Glapwell Colliery, if you didn't go to t'pit, you didn't get paid. And I thought, 'Why should you get paid if you're not there?' So I turn up every day. I put my clocking-in card in at eight o'clock in the morning.

I also decided I wasn't going to get involved in the sloppy all-party embrace in the bars. And the third thing was not to go on these junkets at taxpayers' expense.

HB: But you've really enjoyed your time in Parliament?

DS: Absolutely. It's a better job than working down a coal mine.

HB: Probably a better job than working for *Test Match Special*.

DS: I'm not so sure about that. I've been here all morning.

HB: Did you enjoy it?

DS: Yes, it was excellent. I've never had a view like this from a cricket ground. And there's no doubt at all that the England bowlers are bowling a lot straighter. The West Indian team is very brittle in my view. I picked that word up from one of your commentators this morning.

HB: But, looking back on your life as a Member over there since 1970, do you feel satisfaction in what you've achieved?

DS: Oh, yes. You'd never believe the sort of letters you get when you help somebody. They don't all thank you, but sometimes you get letters from people that you've not been able to pull the rabbit out of the hat for and they'll say, 'Thank you very much for responding, for dealing with the matter. We've just not been successful.'

It's a wonderful feeling to know that you're helping people and to be voting for things you believe in. There's not many people in Britain – there's only a few of us – that have the chance to be accountable to that extent and walk through the voting lobbies to vote for the minimum wage – I'm sounding political now, aren't I?

HB: Are there any letters you remember more than the others?

DS: I had a few letters when I've been in hospital for an operation recently. And some of the letters were from people that you'd never expect.

HB: Apart from being a very considerable parliamentarian, you are also a champion of Parliament. Does it worry you today the way things are going – how the emphasis is going more away from Parliament towards government? Parliament is perhaps no longer the place where powerful debates are heard, where indeed big decisions are not announced. Does that worry you?

DS: I think Parliament is in its element for the people on the outside when it's a close-run thing. Parliament in these last few years has had a massive majority on the Labour side. Almost unheard of. And that's why the chattering classes who write this stuff don't realise that it's not always like that and Parliament, when it's close like in 1979, when we were winning votes by one – that is real drama.

And the same was true to an extent when John Major was Prime Minister, when some of his people defected for a while.

They left the big tent and we got pretty close decisions then. And that produces a lot of drama.

And you shouldn't imagine that there were some great heroes of yesteryear. Everybody's made of clay. The reason why it's different today in many respects is because since 1989 it's been televised. So people speak – some of them – in a different way. They might be playing to the cameras, who knows?

HB: Are you suggesting that it's a bad thing that it's televised?

DS: Oh, no. I think people should see what's happening in Parliament.

HB: But you think this takes away from some of the things that happened there, the fact that Parliament was the great forum that it used to be in the old days.

DS: There used to be a lot of mystique. People didn't know too much about the Royal Family and once you strip away those layers of mystery, it becomes commonplace. There's nothing wrong in that. It's revealing. So this mystique and this mystery about the higher echelons of the establishment, when they're stripped away it produces a different image.

HB: You mentioned John Major a moment ago – another great cricket lover.

DS: I thought he was going to be an umpire.

HB: He probably is. He's probably taking his exam now. He's President of Surrey.

DS: I forecast that when he retired that's what he'd do – he'd have a white jacket on at the Oval.

HB: Do you think he'd be a good one?

DS: I suppose he would. He knows a little bit about cricket.

HB: It was John Major who was Prime Minister when you were 65 and he congratulated you in the House.

DS: Yes, he did.

HB: Did that take you by surprise? Or were you rather touched by that?

DS: Well, it did take me by surprise. That's absolutely true, but I think he was using a long-winded discussion about my age so that he didn't have to answer some other awkward question. It was very clever. Whenever you see people talking in this diversionary way in Parliament, you can bet your bottom dollar they're hiding summat.

HB: And you were well known for a remark about Colin Moynihan, who is knee-high to a grasshopper.

DS: Oh, the little fellow!

HB: The Minister for Sport.

DS: Yeah, I called him the miniature for sport. But my best line was Subbuteo.

HB: I was very nervous about interviewing you today, because you once said, 'I hate interviews. Elitist crap!'

DS: Well, I don't regard you as elitist. You went to Eton, didn't you?

HB: Yes.

DS: I've been surrounded by people in this box – they're like me. They went to a run-of-the-mill school. And anyway, some of these toffs like yourself can be pretty down-to-earth when it matters. How's that for a compliment?

HB: I take it as an enormous compliment. But in fact you've always been a hater of pomposity, haven't you?

DS: I can't stand it. I don't believe in this personality cult, either. You should stick to principles and not get carried away by people that are supposedly cleverer than yourself.

HB: Well, one of your mottos is said to be 'Don't moan, don't whine, don't whinge'.

DS: Absolutely.

HB: And you weren't talking about *Test Match Special*, either.

DS: I'm talking about the fact that some of us are lucky in life and in Parliament you get a lot of people moaning. They moan about the pay, they moan about everything. What they don't realise is they've landed on their feet. It's a good number. So I was referring to them.

They know what the score is when they get the job. It's like you taking on this role. You know you'll have to work your tripe out during summer. God knows what you do in the winter. You know that you're going to be pulled from pillar to post for all the days that Test Match cricket is on. You won't have a moment to breathe.

It's like that in Parliament. You know what the score is and nobody dragged you into Parliament and said, 'Look, you've got to do this job.' The truth is that loads of people want to do it. We're lucky to have a chance to represent people.

HB: You're 68 now. Are you going on at the next election?

DS: My party in Bolsover are demanding that I stand, because I don't think they want a yuppie from London.

HB: And you still feel that in the changing circumstances of the Commons you've got a considerable part to play?

DS: Oh, I'm not giving in. I'm a highly competitive animal. I've got no intention of finishing up going to sleep in the House of Commons. I'm going to turn up every day and when the moment comes that I'm not capable physiologically to do those things, it'll be 'Good night, Vienna'.

HB: You've been there 30 years now and in that time you must have had some very memorable incidents.

DS: One of the most important events in my view in Parliament took place not in the chamber, but in Westminster Hall a few years ago, when Nelson Mandela was introduced by the Speaker, Betty Boothroyd, on the steps of Westminster Hall. Hardly any leader from any part of the world has been allowed to speak there – but he was allowed.

He came out of gaol on 11 February 1990 and then he became President of South Africa. He was introduced and don't you know, all those Tories that said he should have been locked up for ever were on the front row.

But to see him and hear him in the knowledge that he'd been in gaol for 27 years as a class warrior and had come out and fought the good fight and stuck to his principles was something for me.

HB: Don't you think one of the most remarkable things about the Mandela story is his apparent lack of bitterness at the end of it all?

DS: Yes. And he's very much in favour of sport. I mean he's got a hinterland. He's not just political. And it's very important in politics that you should have a hinterland. You don't just do politics day in and day out.

So I'm an avid follower of cricket and of your programme. I knew all the people here before. I'd not met any of them and yet I was able to put faces to them.

HB: What about Margaret Thatcher? What did you feel about her?

DS: Well, I always said that she'd get kicked out by her own people. She went too far, you see. When I saw her the night she went to the Lord Mayor's do in the City, she'd got this Elizabethan thing on, with the collar. And I said to my mate, 'Look at her – she's gone.' She thought she was the Queen.

And only a few days later it was goodbye and the Tories kicked her out like a dog in the night. Somebody said to me, 'Fancy kicking out the Prime Minister.'

I said, 'Look, Tories are the bosses' party and when they haven't got use for any workers they shift 'em.'

She didn't just close the pits, you know. They got rid of the cricket fields, because every mine had a welfare and it had a cricket field and it had a football field. And a hell of a lot of those went in the process.

HB: How big a part should a government play in sport?

DS: Oh, they've got to be involved. They've got to set up the infrastructure in order to produce all the various sports people we need. And that's why we've got to put a stop to selling off the cricket fields in schools.

*

Ten years after this interview, Dennis Skinner was returned to Parliament again, entering his fifth decade as an MP.

STEPHEN FRY

interviewed by Jonathan Agnew,
The Oval, 7 September 2002

Stephen Fry, the multi-talented actor, writer, director and just
about everything else, was no stranger to the Test Match Special
box – only partly because he and Jonathan Agnew share the same
alma mater. So it was just a matter of time before we pinned him
down for 'A View From the Boundary'. He nearly made it in 1999
– also at the Oval – but had to pull out at the last minute, so
inevitably this was the starting point for Aggers to upbraid him,
though it was not he who made the passing reference to Stephen's
abrupt departure from the West End stage and the play Cell Mates
in 1995.

*

STEPHEN FRY: This time I couldn't find an excuse not to come.
I'm so sorry about last time. I'm beginning to get a reputation
for not turning up to things.

JONATHAN AGNEW: This is a ground you know well. You spend
a lot of time watching.

SF: I do – and I do love this ground. I always think of south
London as being London's backstage area in the same way as
you have in a theatre or in a grand country house, where the
servants' quarters have got shiny old paint flaking off. And the
Oval has got what the Americans call a 'scuzzy' atmosphere. It's
kind of down and dirty and oddly enough its heroes – the ones
the gates are named after – are players, not gentlemen.

It's the real gritty side of cricket and of course there have
been some fantastic games here – often ones where England

have won. There was the great Devon Malcolm performance against South Africa *[in 1994, when Malcolm took 9 for 57 in the second innings]*. And there was the time we beat the West Indies here, for which I sat amongst a great bevy of West Indians and it's the only time I've ever run onto the field – it was the end of the match – I got that excited. To see the Ambroses and the Walshes actually beaten was quite something then.

JA: Well, you're seeing one of the greatest here today. It's Sachin Tendulkar in his hundredth Test Match – pretty special.

SF: I'm a huge England supporter and I love cricket. Sometimes you hear connoisseurs saying, 'Oh what a pity, Tendulkar's out', and there's a part of me that says it's never a pity when he's out, because I want us to win. But in all honesty, it is marvellous to watch him on a day like this. When he started off he looked, frankly, a bit shaky. And it's always that absolute sign of class to see him weather a few overs where he is just looking a bit suspect and suddenly – he doesn't really cut loose, he's not that sort of player – it's just that the class starts to emerge. It's like a Ferrari warming up. It's a truly great sight. *[Tendulkar was playing his hundredth Test at the age of 29. He made 54.]*

JA: It's reassuring to see him nervous in a way. His life is so extraordinary.

SF: You were discussing earlier whether it's because it's his hundredth. These landmarks matter to players and it's one of the enduring pleasures of cricket that its history and its statistics are much more alive than in any other sport I know of, even baseball and boxing, which also have literature, but cricket is clearly much greater.

It's a whole cultural world and the marvellous thing is it's not just a British one. I can't bear the snobbery that says real cricket is cricket played within sight of a spire and an English field. It's wonderful, village cricket, but cricket on a coir mat or on a beach or in an alleyway in Calcutta – that's cricket as well. It's a game that's much bigger than its roots. That's what's so wonderful. Rather like the English language.

JA: Until you arrived today in that jacket – and if you're watching on the webcam, don't adjust the contrast – I imagined that you were very traditional about your cricket. Do you like the traditional all-in-whites sort of cricket, or do you like the way it's being modernised?

SF: I like the fact that the Tests are all in whites, but I have no real problem with the night/day games and the white balls and pyjamas and so on.

As I say, I think it's rather like the English language. I revere and love the English language. I love the language of Shakespeare and the Bible and Dickens. But I also love the language of South Central Los Angeles or Australia or India. It's the fact that, like a great city, it can have its tower blocks and its modern demotic efflorescence, its excrescences and be medieval. And our language is the same. And cricket still smells of Hambledon, but it also smells of Mumbai and Sydney and that's the beauty of it. People are often shocked that I am much less traditionalist.

JA: Did you play at all – or do you still play?

SF: At school cricket passed me by. I liked to lie in the long grass and make a daisy chain and be camp and foolish. But I always enjoyed watching it. I went to the same school as you were the demon bowler of – Uppingham School in Rutland – and the cricket there was very good and they had nice grounds and I used to go and watch a bit. Then, starting to watch the great days of Tony Greig's side and Ray Illingworth's side and those great girls, 'Lillian Marsh' and 'Lillian Thomson', I just became obsessed with it and also with the sort of atmosphere of it.

I grew up in Norfolk, where there's a great tradition – we provided the Edriches for England – but it is a minor county, so it was hard to get excited about county cricket. And I'm afraid – and it is one of the deep pathologies of modern cricket – that county cricket and exciting are not words often to be found close together.

It's a terrible shame. It's partly because the nature of the scoring and points allocated tends to militate against any excitement. This kind of 'shall we – shan't we' make a match of it attitude. And also it just doesn't seem to cut it in terms of its structure, whether it was three-day or four-day. I hate to say anything bad against it.

There was a little campaign in London, where they had Mark Ramprakash's picture on the end of a bus and they'd say, 'Hop on a bus and go up to St John's Wood and watch Mark Ramprakash.' I hope it worked.

It's just a kind of self-fulfilling prophecy. If you say it's dull, then nobody goes and it feels dull and there's no crowd and therefore no atmosphere. So maybe I should be saying that it's the most exciting expression of athleticism and sport in the world, is the second day of a county match.

JA: Do you worry about the future of cricket? I know you're involved in trying to prevent the selling off of school playing fields.

SF: Well, yes. It's a very sad problem that even in country schools there are no cricket grounds. But in central London it's a two-hour drive to Hertfordshire or somewhere, if you want to get a game of cricket. And at the moment they're selling off grounds faster than they can be bought by any kind of charity. So it's a real problem.

Am I pessimistic about the future of cricket? I think something like this rubber against India vindicates – as always happens – the greatness of Test cricket.

We had a fantastic triangular series, with a spectacular final against India at Lord's and everyone thought, 'Well, you can't beat that. What a great one-day match.' And then a series of Test Matches which have been absolutely wonderful and a vindication of the fact that the five-day game is truly alive. And look at how well they've sold. At almost every ground there's been a fantastic sell-out crowd, even on Mondays. And that's really good.

Though on the kind of 'talking cabbie' level I've found over the years – and goodness knows, to use a cabbie as a demographic litmus is not exactly sensible – for instance when I went to the Cheltenham and Gloucester match last week – I haven't had one yet who even knew it was on. 'Oh, so there's a match there, is there?' That was slightly depressing.

One used to imagine there was a day when you got into a cab and if you said, 'Kennington', he'd say, 'Have you heard the latest? Tendulkar's just come in', or whatever. Now it's, 'West Ham myself.'

Soccer's a great game, too, but at this time of year this is our national game and it's such a great game. So I'm not entirely pessimistic, but I do think it's a shame that somehow it's not so much in the culture. Maybe we need a hero. Maybe a Botham – or indeed Flintoff.

Since being a cricket fan I've discovered what I call the sheep syndrome. You know when you see sheep on a hillside they are the most cloud-like, fleecy, lyrical things. You go up close and they've got matted, horrible bottoms and hideous, prehistoric jaws and it's rather the same with cricket. From a distance it looks like the most gentle, lyrical game.

I remember the days I used to go and watch Gower or someone warming up in the nets and you realise that even for him – an apparently sleepy, lyrical cricketer – it's such a hard game. It's a physical game. It's really tough and more so year after year. It's a hard, fast, sharp game, where balls grind into knuckles and you dive and graze your skin. It's not this fleecy, lovely thing that everyone thinks it is.

It's a wonderful game because it's evolved – like the language. It's not a museum piece and anyone who thinks cricket is, is sadly missing out on the real joy of it.

JA: You've had an extraordinary life. You're 45 and you seem to have been virtually everywhere – up and down, up and down.

SF: I have showered in Her Majesty's prisons and broken wind in her palaces. It's sort of true. I have had a strange life, now you look at it.

I got expelled from Uppingham – not for what they used to call 'the usual thing', but from a rather bizarre thing. I was a huge fan of Sherlock Holmes when I was a boy – a really insane fan. And I was a member of the Sherlock Holmes Society of London and had been from a small age. And I got permission from my housemaster to go to London for a meeting of the Sherlock Holmes Society. This was at a weekend that was the Queen and Prince Philip's silver wedding anniversary, so the Monday was a bank holiday and I got permission to come back on the Monday morning. So I'd have two nights in London. And I just got obsessed that weekend with cinema. There were things like *Cabaret* showing and *Clockwork Orange* and I went and saw them over and over and over again. In those days you could just sit in the cinema – I think you still can, actually. And I watched one after another and got back on the Tuesday. And that wasn't a sackable offence, but I think it was the straw that broke the very weary camel's back.

So that started it off and I was unquestionably a mess, and I got involved in an awful credit card business and ended up in prison for a while on remand, while all the paperwork from different counties caught up with me. One smiles when one says all this, but it was devastating at the time.

JA: Do you know why you went off the rails?

SF: I think I was one of those people who are academically quite sharp. I've always had this remarkable memory, which I think is a very important, very useful thing. I would never wish it away. But it is not the same as an intelligence or maturity. If you can remember things you can pass exams.

I did my 'O' levels when I was fourteen. It would have meant I'd have been in the sixth form at sixteen and at university at seventeen unless I chose a gap year, I suppose. And that's far too young – at least it was for me. I was immature and I couldn't really think. So I was smarter in some very superficial ways than the other pupils round me, but not really bright in any meaningful sense. I suppose they'd call it attention deficit disorder now. I couldn't focus. I wasn't interested, so I was shifty and evasive.

Do you remember a master called Abbot? Who wrote one of the great cricket books, of course.

JA: Yes – *Three Men at the Match.*

SF: About going to watch Leicester, which may sound ridiculous, but is actually wonderful. He wrote about me: 'Fickle, flamboyant and evasive. A disappointment.' Which I think is probably about right.

So, anyway, I went from Uppingham to various other schools and then I got involved in this … and ran away. I just felt I didn't need any more education. But it was while in prison that I suddenly realised that I knew nothing.

To stay with the cricket theme, it's a bit like if a talented batsman, from the age of twelve to fifteen, suddenly has his technique taken apart and is re-taught. You can't live on just facility alone. It's essential to start from that point. And I kind of took my mind apart and I realised that I'd never really thought.

So I sat down – it sounds so swotty – and I read all the works of Shakespeare and made notes on them. A lot of them I kind of knew, because I could quote them, but I didn't really know them. My great love was literature at the time.

And then I was fortunate enough to go to Cambridge and that's where I met Emma Thompson and Hugh Laurie and Tony Slattery and got sucked into the hideous world of comedy from which I've rarely emerged since.

JA: Do you find that you have to be funny all the time? Was that part of the problem at school? Were you the school wit – the chap who could mimic Sir at the back of the class?

SF: I was a clown, yes. I'm about your height, maybe even taller – and that's tall. And, it's hard to believe, thin as a beanpole then and I was not in the least bit physically self-assured. And therefore it is a cliché, but a true one, making a fool of oneself and of others I fear – schoolmasters in particular – is the tradition out of which it all arises.

That's where characters like General Melchett in *Blackadder* come from. It's the same instinct that makes you make fun of your geography master. And that's why it's a young man's game, actually.

JA: Now, I only bring this up because you've talked about it. I don't think I've talked to someone about their sexuality before on *Test Match Special*. It's a new one. Given that that was something that was obviously going on in your mind at the time, and possibly the only person that you ever saw on television was John Inman playing that sort of part, was that also part of the problem?

SF: I think you're right. And respect – as I think you're supposed to say today – to John Inman for a very fine camp performance. But as a role model it was not exactly what you want. And if I hadn't had the good fortune to be interested in books, I wouldn't have gone to libraries and read memoirs.

There's a wonderful book which is a cricket book and an extraordinary early gay confession, if you like, by T.C. Worsley – Cuthbert Worsley – who used to be a literary editor. It's called *The Flannelled Fool*, which is a quotation from Kipling –

> Then ye returned to your trinkets; then ye contented your
> souls
> With the flannelled fools at the wicket or the muddied oafs
> at the goals.

Which is not to say that all cricketers are terrible, because he was a very natural, talented sportsman, who got introduced into the world of the mind very late in his life and felt that he'd lost out.

If you're gay when you're fourteen or fifteen now, all you've got to do is turn on Channel Four after ten o'clock and it's bizarre – there are no heterosexuals left in the world at that time according to television schedulers. And there are magazines and there's the internet and there are books and freedom of expression. In my day you either associated yourself with some unfortunate mackintoshed figure, furtively hanging round insalubrious places, or you imagined some exotic creature who'd gone off to live in Capri for the rest of his life. There wasn't much in between.

But what there was was this kind of divide between what you might call the aesthete and the athlete. It's a bit like the science/art divide in academic terms. People sometimes are astonished that I love sport as much as I do. And they think it's almost a betrayal of my sexuality and my interest in literature and art. 'How can you love Wagner and be interested in cricket?' and so on.

Well, of course there are great figures like Neville Cardus and John Arlott, who showed that it is a nonsense to suppose that there's any kind of inconsistency between loving art and sport. E.M. Forster was obsessed with it.

JA: I haven't got on to *Blackadder* yet. What a fantastic series that was. You were in two of them, weren't you?

SF: I was, yes, and I guested in the third one as the Duke of Wellington – another shouty character. It was extraordinary. The first series, just called *The Black Adder*, was written by Richard Curtis and Rowan Atkinson. And Richard Curtis was not well known then. Now, of course, he's one of the best known people in the world of entertainment, because of his films, *Notting Hill* and *Four Weddings and a Funeral* and *Bridget Jones* and so on. But he'd been the chief scriptwriter in *Not the Nine O'Clock News* and had known Rowan for ages, so they wrote the first one.

And John Lloyd, the producer, described it as looking a million dollars and costing two million. It was very expensive. It was filmed. It wasn't done in front of an audience, like a normal sitcom, and the BBC were not that keen on doing a second one.

Rowan Atkinson decided for the second one that he didn't want to be involved as a writer. He felt that Richard should write with someone else. And Richard and Ben Elton started writing it. Some people think of Ben as a snappy little Jack Russell. He's a dear-hearted, wonderful man. And his view of it was that it wasn't focused. It's a bit like a tennis match. However extravagant and athletic the gestures, if you can't see the ball, it's a meaningless charade.

He said it should all be on a few small sets. It should be in front of an audience. And the great thing was that also meant by coincidence that it would be about a tenth the price. And so the BBC consented to do a second one and this was *Blackadder 2* with the wonderful Miranda Richardson as Queen Elizabeth. I played her sort of bearded sidekick. It seemed to work really well. I think it was for the reasons that Ben said. It was that focus. And *3* was terrific, with Hugh as the Prince Regent.

JA: How do you know that something like that has run its course? People would be crying out for another *Blackadder*.

SF: That was the odd thing. The fourth one was *Blackadder Goes Forth* in the trenches. When you do it in front of the audience, they're all automatically disappointed, because you do all six of them before any of them has been broadcast. So the studio audience that comes along remember Mrs Miggins' Pie Shop and they remember the Prince and they remember the kitchens and they remember Queenie. And suddenly they've got everybody in 20th-century uniforms.

And John Lloyd and Richard Curtis would come out and explain that this is a new series and it's set in the First World War. You were always going from a rather boggy standing start, but I think it helped, because it gave it the tension that we never knew where the laughs were coming from.

For example, my only great contribution to that series was that originally the Tim McInnerny character was called Captain Cartwright and he was worrying, quite legitimately, about what his relationship was with Blackadder and with Melchett or anyone else. And it was explained. And I said, 'Suppose he had a really unfortunate name, he'd be that sort of person who was constantly being mocked because of his name – Darling, or something.'

And we tried it the first week in rehearsal and we had this vote as to whether or not we thought the joke would run dry after six weeks. And everyone voted that we should stick it in, because for some reason it is still funny. 'Darling, we're leaving.' Rowan coming and saying, 'Good morning, Darling.' It is funny and it's ridiculous that it should be, but it is. And I apologise to all Darlings listening, including Alistair Darling, the Treasury chap. They all suffer even more because of it than they already did. But it's funny how something as simple as that can allow you to build a character. So it was great fun.

JA: Let's bring you back to cricket. It strikes me that you would like the psychological aspect of this game. Here we are, planning for the Ashes, which I think people suspect there's absolutely no chance of England winning. Do you have any theories you might pass on to Duncan Fletcher and Nasser as to what they might do? [*Uncanny foresight by Aggers. England were to go on to lose that 2002/03 Ashes series in Australia 4–1.*]

SF: Well, funnily enough, you asked me this one many years ago, and I happened to be filming and we were staying in the same hotel as the Australian team. And we had breakfast together. And I said – at the time we were absolutely under the thumb of Merv the Swerve, the guy who looks like an Edwardian butcher with the huge moustache, Merv Hughes – 'Suppose the England team, when he comes on to bowl, take off their helmets. It would drive him mad.'

It's a proper use of the word 'wit'. I don't mean taking the pee out of the side, but A) to outwit and B) it's attitude. You've to look, when you're a batsman, as if this is the moment you've been waiting for. You're pleased to be out in the middle and this is your great moment.

It's obviously easier said than done – and I don't have to face him myself – and I don't have to bowl at Gilchrist.

It's the same in politics. If you look miserable and defensive, then you lose popularity points. You should look as though you've got the best job in the world and be good-humoured about things. I think a lot of it is to do with simple good humour.

JA: Just a last thought. You're made for this job in here, aren't you?

SF: I would love it more than anything. If you can't open for England on the field, then open for England on *TMS*. The trouble is I'd go, 'And it's gone to Butcher at mid-off – mid-on – what's that position called?'

JA: We do that all the time.

SF: You do it very well.

NIGEL HAVERS

interviewed by Henry Blofeld,
Edgbaston, 6 August 2005

In 2004 we received a visit in the commentary box at the Oval
from a couple of well-known actors on a day out to watch the
cricket. Their enthusiasm was infectious – they were like a pair of
schoolboys. Simon Williams was one, accompanied by his friend,
Nigel Havers.

Probably best known for his portrayal of Lord Andrew Lindsay
in Chariots of Fire, *Nigel has also been a regular on television*
going back over four decades and since this interview has even
done a stint on Coronation Street.

His arrival in the box for 'A View From the Boundary' came
during the crucial Second Test of the 2005 Ashes series, with
England, despite having taken a lead of 99 on first innings, just
looking a little wobbly in the second. Nonetheless, he was bright-
eyed as Henry Blofeld welcomed him to Edgbaston.

*

NIGEL HAVERS: I couldn't sleep last night, because I was so
excited about coming here. Every dream has now been fulfilled,
so it really is a pleasure.

HENRY BLOFELD: Well, you obviously enjoy cricket, because last
year I remember you came to visit us in the *Test Match Special*
box at the Oval. And there's always been a tie between cricket
and acting, I think.

NH: I have lots of mates in my business who adore cricket.
If they don't play, they love to watch it, and I used for years
every summer to have a sort of cricket day. And we used to hire

Chiswick playing fields and everyone brought a picnic and we'd have two sides. And I remember James Villiers was always on my side and he'd come in half cut, having had practically a bottle of kummel and say, 'Whatever you do, bowl it straight.' And put down his glass of kummel behind the stumps and you could never get him out. Which proves my point that playing cricket with a few cocktails on board is probably a very good idea.

HB: Did you play at school?

NH: I played at my prep school and went on. The first thing I learnt at my prep school – I went very young; I was six years old when I went to boarding school – and the first thing I learnt to do was play cricket. That's pretty much all I did, actually.

HB: But you must have enjoyed what you've seen this morning. Or was it a bit nerve-wracking?

NH: I'm sort of terrified about the whole thing, really, because I think this is probably the day of the series in many ways and this guy Warne … I think the only thing we can do is break his legs.

HB: This is probably right. We did fairly well, making Glenn McGrath stand on a cricket ball before play started on the first day. *[McGrath had had to withdraw from the Test an hour before the start and England had taken advantage by making over 400 on the first day. The match was to end in a two-run win for England the day after this interview, squaring the series. Shane Warne was at the heart of England's – and Nigel Havers' – anxiety, following his second-innings six wickets by making 42.]*

Now, Nigel, why acting? Because you were destined for the law, weren't you? You had a grandfather who was a High Court judge and your father was Lord Chancellor.

NH: My aunt even – she's just retired. Her name is Elizabeth Butler-Sloss. A serious judge – Justice of Appeal.

HB: What made you decide you didn't want any of this?

NH: Well, it was my dad's fault, because he was crazy about the theatre and wanted to go all the time. And so he would take me aged sort of seven or eight. My brother and my mother weren't that interested and so I went to see every show in town. And I just wanted to do it. My father was absolutely delighted. He wasn't cross with me.

HB: Your brother's followed the family trail.

NH: That did help, having my brother do all those things.

HB: I believe you first made your mark at the age of thirteen in *Mrs Dale's Diary*. I know you like to tell porkies about your age, but this does date you, doesn't it?

NH: My God, it does.

HB: What did you do in that?

NH: I played Mrs Dale's grandson.

HB: Was that a massive part?

NH: It seemed like a massive part at the time. And I remember I got a pay cheque, so it was fantastic really. I made a bit of money. *[Mrs Dale's Diary was a BBC radio soap opera that ran from 1948 to 1969.]*

HB: But what then? Where did you go to school?

NH: I went to a drama college in London, which was actually one of the best things that ever happened to me. I think there were about 30 lads and about 150 girls. So, as you can imagine, it was a good time.

HB: You've always had a reputation of being a bit of a ladies' man.

NH: Well, nothing wrong with that.

HB: No, nothing at all! I'm just deeply jealous.

NH: You've gone green.

HB: You left that drama college when?

NH: I was eighteen. I was going to follow my brother at Cambridge, which sounded like a good idea. And then I suddenly got a job working for a theatre company – Prospect Productions. Ian McKellen was the star of it. And I got this job and it lasted over a year. We toured all over England and Europe and ended up in the Piccadilly Theatre, so I was well and truly hooked by then.

HB: What was your first real break, then?

NH: My first real break was, I think, probably doing *Nicholas Nickleby* for the BBC. And I got the part of playing Nicholas, which was a big thing. Those were the days when the BBC used to do Sunday afternoon series – Dickens mostly – and on the back of that I got into the *Horseman Riding By* series, which was the Sunday evening slot. So I graduated from afternoon to evening and once you played a couple of leads like that in those days, you could pretty much guarantee getting another series. So I was really lucky.

HB: I suppose in all our jobs you need a certain element of luck, don't you – at the start?

NH: I think in my job it's about 99 per cent.

HB: It must be nerve-wracking. You come to the end of something that you're filming and you must just wonder, 'What next?'

NH: It happens all the time. You feel you've been fired twice a year, because one job does come to an end. But somehow, touching wood, one tries to keep on going.

HB: How important was *Chariots of Fire* to your career?

NH: It was pretty mega, really. It was a film you could never make again, because you can't make a film now without having some major name in it and that film didn't have any names in it at all. It was just based on a good script, with David Puttnam producing it. I don't know how they found the money. You couldn't do it today.

HB: The interesting thing about that, from your point of view, is that you had a terrible accident in rehearsals before filming began, didn't you? You were taking these hurdles and fell and in fact broke your wrist. And like many old-fashioned wicket keepers, who would break a bone in their fingers, they'd never own up to it for fear that they'd lose their place in the side and never get back in. And you actually went through the film with a broken wrist, didn't you?

NH: I did. I had to train to learn how to hurdle, because at school it was one thing I never wanted to do. It looked so uncomfortable. Anyway, I had to for this film and I was doing really well and I was showing off to Ben Cross and I clipped a hurdle and dislocated my shoulder, but I did snap my wrist and I thought, 'If I tell them about that, I'll never make the film.' So it was a very easy and economical decision to make and I just strapped it up. And it mended in a strange way, but I survived.

HB: Didn't you at one stage go over the hurdles with champagne glasses on them?

NH: Correct. They did, I'm afraid, Sellotape them down to the hurdles. Only because – I was a brilliant hurdler, let me just make this clear – but because one is travelling at such huge speed, the wind can sometimes knock the glass of champagne off its perch.

HB: Health has always been a bit of a factor in your life, because when you were nineteen, I think I'm right in saying, you had a rather nasty time with a growth or lump in your throat.

NH: I was watching Fulham play with my brother. I'm a great Fulham supporter and I was shouting and screaming and obviously we were losing and I noticed a sort of lump in my throat. And I went to see my doctor the following week and he said, 'What are you doing tomorrow?'

And I said, 'I'm meant to be rehearsing a play.'

And he said, 'Well, you won't be now. I want you in hospital tomorrow morning.'

They removed it and it was benign, thank God.

HB: But there was a worry. Did you know that it might be malignant?

NH: I did at the last minute. They didn't tell me till I was in hospital the night before and they said, 'You have to sign this form.' And the word 'malignant' sort of cropped up.

HB: And that sort of hits you.

NH: It does. But at nineteen you're invincible, aren't you? If it happened to me now I'd be shaking like a leaf.

HB: I was amused to read that you tend to tell porkies about your age.

NH: I do, but I'll tell you why. It's very simple. If I go to audition for a job, I say, 'How old is this part supposed to be?'
And they say, '38.'
And I say, 'Funnily enough, I am 38.' So it's always been the way of doing it, you see, and I've had to tell porkies about that for ever.

HB: Well, we know you're only 25.

NH: Exactly. Thank you for clearing that up.

HB: You do something that I do – when I read the obituaries I always look first at the age of the person that's died and if they're all in their eighties and nineties I heave a sigh of relief, but if I find they're younger than me I start to scratch my head a bit.

NH: Very worried, yes. I might not have that double martini in the evening.

HB: Food and wine are quite important to you, aren't they?

NH: Well I think they should be to all of us.

HB: But you're a cook too, aren't you?

NH: I love to cook. It's sort of a relaxation to me. Cooking and cutting the grass.

HB: Cutting the grass! That can be rather monotonous.

NH: I can sort of think about things.

HB: A push mower? Or do you sit on one?

NH: A push mower. Actually I haven't done it lately, because I've been away and I've had someone cut it for me.

HB: And if you were going to cook your favourite dinner, what would it be?

NH: Quite simple, really. I think some smoked salmon, which doesn't require any cooking at all. And then I might just cook a nice steak, but cooking a steak actually requires a lot of skill to get it right.

HB: Do you like your meat rare?

NH: I do actually. Heat the pan and only turn the steak once. People endlessly turn the steak round and it'll be as tough as old boots.

HB: Now, wine – do you have any great preference for that, or do you just enjoy drinking good wine?

NH: I love drinking good wine. I'm a sort of Bordeaux man.

HB: Claret rather than Burgundy.

NH: Burgundy I love, but it gives me a tremendous headache. But claret is fine and obviously a bottle of Latour '61 would be perfect.

HB: I read somewhere that you had rather a session with Latour '61.

NH: It's all gone now. And I bought a whole lot of Latour '65, which is a complete non-year. But Latour produced the wine and I found it – this is going back years – in the Majestic or Oddbins of the time and it was £1.95 a bottle. Pretty good value, I thought. I used to serve it out and people would say, 'God, this is good. What is it?'

And I'd say, 'This is Latour.' I didn't tell them the year, of course.

HB: This is often so. The big names in bad years are quite well worth buying, aren't they? Because they're better than most other things one can afford.

NH: Actually any wine now is pretty good to me.

HB: Looking back at your career, what are the favourite roles you've played?

NH: I used to have favourite roles, but every time you end a job it's sort of cast off – it's all over. But I suppose, going back, *Chariots of Fire* was a major time for me.

HB: And you really enjoyed that.

NH: I did enjoy that. I suppose it was due to the fact that I had to really train. It was a physical film to make. We had to pretend to be sportsmen and we didn't have any doubles or anyone pretending to be us. We had to do all our own stunt work, so to speak, and that was a real challenge. And then, because it was such hard work, it made the acting quite easy. It was kind of a relief to do a scene when you weren't having to run around a stadium.

HB: When you're making a film, how much are you absolutely on the script and how much do you ad lib? There must be times when you ad lib?

NH: To be honest, it's absolutely on the script and they're really tough on it and they really pull you up if you don't get it right. In a theatre, of course, no one can stop you, because you're on your own, but on a film they can shout at you and you have to do it again. And you can do it a hundred times, but they want to get it right. You just do as you're told, basically.

HB: So you've got to be calm and just carry on. Doing the same scene endlessly again and again must be one of the most exhausting things because after a certain time saying the same words repeatedly, they make no sense at all.

NH: None at all. But in the theatre the same thing applies, because you're doing the same thing every night, but you have got a different audience in front of you. But I get just as nervous filming, because there is a sort of audience of all the crew and that comes to about a hundred. People say filming must be so boring, because you only shoot so many minutes a day, but in fact waiting is nerve-wracking.

HB: Do you prefer stage to screen?

NH: I have no preference. When I'm doing one I wish I was doing the other.

HB: And you've done television series like *Dangerfield*. Was that fun? [Dangerfield *was a series in the 1990s about a doctor/police surgeon.*]

NH: It was fun. It was shot round Warwickshire and Stratford and all that area, so I actually rented a flat in the heart of Stratford and I really loved being there. And people obviously assumed I was working for the Royal Shakespeare Company. And I used to pretend I was. I didn't tell them I was doing *Dangerfield*.

HB: Have you ever done Shakespeare?

NH: I started off doing Shakespeare, but it's been a while. But I'd love to do it again. It's quite a big commitment to go and work up there – it's a year, you know.

HB: One thing that surprised me was that you played a part in *Upstairs Downstairs*.

NH: I did very, very briefly. And I don't remember doing it, to be honest. I think I was some sort of guest. Lesley-Anne Down was in it and I remember thinking how beautiful she was.

HB: But you've thought that of quite a few people. One of the people you knew quite well was Princess Diana.

NH: I did. She was a good friend. She was just a very sweet girl and it was a terrible, terrible shame – all that. She was charming.

HB: Who was your favourite director?

NH: My favourite of all was David Lean, I think. [*Nigel Havers was one of the stars of Lean's last film,* A Passage to India.] It was quite something to work with him and I didn't even audition.

I just had tea with him at the Berkeley Hotel and during tea he said, 'Would you like to play this part?'

And I said, 'I'd love to, thank you.'

And he said, 'I'm so glad. The purpose of the tea is that I always cast actors who I think I can have dinner with.'

When we were filming in India, you couldn't buy wine there in those days. Hirondelle was the only thing and it was about 25 quid a bottle. So we drank all that awful local Scotch. David knew all about awful Scotch in India, so he bought a case of Johnnie Walker Black Label and at dinner he'd have a book of *A Passage to India* on the table. And in fact it wasn't a book, it was a flask of Johnnie Walker Black Label. He just had to twist the top.

HB: You've always been cast as a bit of a toff, haven't you?

NH: I've been desperately trying to play another character, but no one seems to want to give that to me. You never know – times can change.

HB: Raffles?

NH: That was fun. The gentleman thief – yes.

HB: In so many of the films you've done, you get involved in sex scenes. Do they come easily? Do you get nervous about them?

NH: Well, no – in a word. Roger Moore said to me once that when he does a sex scene he says to the girl, 'I apologise to start with in case I get aroused – and if I don't.' So he covers every eventuality. So I've stolen that.

HB: Impeccable good manners.

NH: Is this a bit racy for cricket? I just feel so intimate with you, Henry. I feel very relaxed.

HB: My dear old thing. But I suppose your first one must have been a bit of a problem, though.

NH: No, it was fine.

HB: And who was the unlucky actress?

NH: She was very pretty and I think it was Susie Blake. I think it was in *Angels*, the TV show about nurses.

HB: How much time have you spent in Hollywood?

NH: Well, on and off. I've worked there a few times and I do like it there – it's fun – it's a good place.

HB: But it's not somewhere where you really want to make your base.

NH: Oh, I'm happy to do that any time. I haven't been able to really, with my children growing up and schools and stuff. But I'm the sort of actor who could be called up by an agent to go anywhere, so I don't mind where I go. I was there yesterday, actually. I came back last night. I had a couple of meetings to do and I just nipped over there and back in two days.

HB: Now, if at some stage the Maître d' at the Savoy Grill said to you, 'I've got a table for four for you. I want you to bring yourself and three guests.' Who would your three guests be?

NH: I've just got to get the location in my mind. I'd love my dad to come. He died twelve years ago, but I'd have loved him to be there.

And I'd like Judi Dench to be there. She just is the most wonderful girl and wonderful actress and such good fun to be with.

And I'd have to have David Niven there.

HB: I want to talk to you about David Niven, because you have the rights to film his two autobiographies.

NH: I actually don't any more. After seven years I couldn't get the script right. So the rights have gone, but they've been bought by somebody – a really nice person – and it looks as if I might be involved.

HB: What – playing David Niven?

NH: Yes. And this other person's actually got the money to make it work, which obviously I didn't.

HB: Did you know David Niven?

NH: I met him once very briefly at the bar at the Connaught Hotel, when I leant over to grab my dry martini and a voice said, 'I think you'll find that's mine.'

HB: The other actor who always stayed at the Connaught was Alec Guinness.

NH: I used to have dinner with him on and off, because I got to know him when we made *A Passage to India*. He was a wonderful guy. He didn't get on with David Lean. They never spoke. They had a terrible row years ago and yet he's in every film. So David said to me, 'We've got Alec coming in this week. Will you look after him?'

HB: So if we could get the head waiter at the Savoy to bring in an extra chair it would be for Alec Guinness, would it?

NH: Yes, it would.

HB: It would be a lively conversation.

HUGH CORNWELL

interviewed by Jonathan Agnew,
Trent Bridge, 27 August 2005

In the 2005 Ashes series we had, in close succession, Nigel Havers,
who raised the subject of sex, and Michelle Verroken, the expert
on drugs at the Olympics; and so, to complete the circle we had of
course to introduce some rock and roll. This came with the arrival
of Hugh Cornwell, formerly lead singer of the Stranglers.

The previous evening, over dinner, he had been persuaded to
perform for us and had had Mike Selvey's guitar pressed into his
hands. So the day in the commentary box started with our engi-
neers determined to place microphones perfectly to do him justice.

His autobiography, A Multitude of Sins, *had been published*
the previous year. We introduced him with a burst of two of his
best known songs – 'No More Heroes' and 'Golden Brown'.

*

JONATHAN AGNEW: I mentioned sex, drugs and rock and roll,
but I reckon, having read your book, you qualify on all three
counts yourself, don't you?

HUGH CORNWELL: It's all I could remember.

JA: It's not every punk rocker who writes about cricket on the
first page of his autobiography.

HC: And I'm made up today, because how many people get
Geoff Lawson asking for their autograph?

JA: But cricket has been very much part of your life – and
decision-making, too.

HC: Absolutely. I was thinking about leaving the band and I was watching Devon Malcolm bat and he hit a six. And I decided to hit my own six. So I left that day.

JA: What was it particularly about Devon batting and cricket? That's a huge decision for you, having been in the band for – how long?

HC: Fifteen, maybe seventeen years. Yes. It was an emotional decision. It was just him being constrained by the fielding – I think it was against India. And he made that stroke to sort of break out from it. It was just that sort of release. And his release I interpreted in my own way.

JA: That was it. In that moment of Devon hitting a six in 1990 against India. Farewell to a career.

HC: Well, hopefully not.

JA: Or entering a new one. How did your colleagues respond to that, I wonder? Did you explain it in those terms?

HC: I wasn't very brave about it. I did a gig and then phoned them all the next day and broke the news, which wasn't a very good way to do it, but I just didn't want to try to be talked out of it. I just wanted to act on what I'd decided. It's very easy to suddenly re-track and think, 'Oh no, you can't think that and shouldn't do it.' I just wanted to follow my convictions.

JA: And how much has cricket played a part in your life generally? Do you play cricket?

HC: Yeah, I play as much as I can, which isn't very much in the summer. It's getting more difficult now I'm getting busier and busier. I try to play for David English's Bunbury team, which is fantastic.

JA: For people who don't know, they're a sort of celebrity and charity team.

HC: It's brilliant. For me, being a big cricket fan, it's great. You suddenly find yourself in the slips, fielding next to Goochie. And it's like, 'I can't believe this. If a catch comes I'd better let him go for it.' So it's very exciting. People don't realise that even musicians who play the big crowds – we've got people who we idolise.

JA: Do you play with any great expectation of what you might do? Or are you just purely out there for a bit of fun?

HC: Well, I really like slip fielding and I really like batting, but I'm not very good at either. But I have caught a couple of good slip catches.

JA: Was there one in particular?

HC: Two summers ago, it was Ali Brown's benefit and he was on about 98 and he late cut and it just stuck. He wasn't very happy.

JA: You're meant to let the beneficiary get his hundred.

HC: He gave me a dirty look.

JA: What is it about slip catching that fascinates you?

HC: You have to be really concentrating. And it means you don't have to run around all over the ground after the ball.

JA: What about this current Ashes series?

HC: Cricket's the new rock and roll, I think. I'm so pleased. Obviously the one-day cricket and now Twenty20 has had an effect on the batting, but I think Troy Cooley is the real unsung hero, because now I think all international teams are going to get bowling coaches. Our attack is just superb and it's down to him, I think.

JA: He is extraordinary, the way he's taught England's bowlers to do what they do with the ball. And do you think it's England to win the Ashes? *[At this stage on the third day of the Fourth Test, with the series one-all, Australia had been forced to follow on, though they were yet to lose a second-innings wicket.]*

HC: The Aussies are on the rocks. That should be a new drink in the bars – 'Can I have an Aussie on the rocks, please?'

JA: We might have a few later on. So did you play at school?

HC: Well, I didn't play much cricket at school, because in schools, unless you're very good, you don't get much chance to play. So I ended up playing a lot of tennis, because then you can take part. But I really loved cricket. My dad was a draughtsman and he used to have a drawing board with a T square and he used to sit doing his drawings with *TMS* on, so I got into it when I was very young – when it first started in fact. And Lord's wasn't very far away, so I used to go and see a lot of Middlesex games. And Fred Titmus went to our school – William Ellis it was called.

JA: But, having sung about no more heroes in quite an angry sort of way, you've got Andrew Flintoff out there. That's quite a decent sort of hero.

HC: I think the main message is that you have to try to be your own hero.

JA: Who were your cricketing heroes early on?

HC: Parfitt was a big one and I used to love Ken McKay, the Australian all-rounder.

JA: 'Slasher'.

HC: Because he came in at six or seven and he was a bit like Gilchrist – he could transform a game. And obviously Lord Ted [Dexter] was up there as well.

And I used to score. In fact I was so into it that I even invented a game with two dice, where you threw the dice and you got 1, 2, 3, 4 and a wicket was a 5, and I used to make up games.

JA: You did organise a Stranglers match, didn't you?

HC: I did. Because we were associated with the colour black, we thought it would be a great idea to have a match against the music press and we played them at Brondesbury Cricket Club and we wore black – black pads, black bats. They all wore whites. And it was a tie – it was amazing.

JA: How common is it for punk rockers – musicians in general – to love cricket?

HC: I really don't know. Maybe it's a spectacle, so I can relate to that side of it. Because performing is a spectacle. Cricket is a performance with an all-round audience. I've never performed in the round and that's quite daunting, I think. I'm into chess and I find that cricket is like a 3D chess game. And I love the five-day games – there are so many changes that happen in a game. It can go one way or another and I love that. It's theatre.

JA: You haven't performed live on Radio 4 long wave before, have you?

HC: No, I haven't.

JA: You're about to. We heard a little bit of 'Golden Brown' there, but come on, it's a beautiful song and you're armed – not with your guitar, but this is Mike Selvey's.

HC: Yes, it's very nice. My first acoustic guitar was a Yamaha and this is one and he's kindly lent it to me and it works very well. This is a very rudimentary version of 'Golden Brown', because I'm by myself. [And he played it beautifully.]

JA: Fabulous. And Mike Selvey now knows what his guitar should sound like. You see, if all punk music sounded like that I think I'd have liked it. But it rather passed me by. Is that a common thing for someone my age to say? I'm only 45. I was in my early twenties when that was going.

HC: Well, the Stranglers were considered a punk band, but only in a very loose association. There were lots of bands – the Police, the Jam, Blondie – and they were all sort of lumped into this convenient collar of punk. And no one was going to argue, because it was a great opportunity for everyone to get famous and we weren't going to knock that. No one's going to pass that back and say, 'No, excuse me, we're not punk and we're not going to take part in this, thank you.' So there was a lot of loose association.

It really was like a sort of electric folk music, because it was trying to express the mood at the time. There was a three-day week going on. A lot of depressed things.

JA: So did you have to be angry as a twenty- or eighteen-year-old to be into punk? I actually was quite happy at the time, which is perhaps where I fell down.

HC: Yeah, maybe if you had some grievance this kind of music spoke volumes to you.

JA: And did you need the Mohican and the body piercings and that sort of thing? I mean you didn't perform like that.

HC: No, I didn't, but I met a Mohican a few weeks ago in Canada and he was very pleasant – because they look so fierce. And I said, 'I've been dying to ask you what you do at night.'
And he said, 'Well, you just sleep on your side.' I'd been dying to ask someone how they did that.

JA: And the serious side of that – 'Golden Brown' – you're singing about heroin.

HC: Yeah, but not extolling the virtues of it, just trying to tell it how it was. When I took it I suddenly realised why it was so dangerous, because it satisfies you so completely in every possible way. That is why it's so dangerous. You don't want food, you don't want sex, you don't want anything, you don't want anybody. You don't need anything because you feel so complete. And that's why it's so dangerous.

JA: Was it inevitable that somebody like you would end up taking drugs?

HC: Trying it? Well, yes, there's this sort of inherent almost job description. I play rock music, therefore I've got to take drugs, haven't I? And at that time – I don't know about now – they were rife and available and also, of course, if you've got very heavy schedules performing and touring, things that keep you awake or keep you alert for hours and hours are actually quite useful.

JA: Was it a case of starting on cannabis and then progressing through till it just got harder and harder?

HC: Well, yeah, but I just wanted to find what it was all about. I wanted to try heroin because of that song written by Velvet Underground, one of my favourite groups, which speeds up and slows down, called 'Heroin'. I thought as a songwriter I needed to try to see how that came about. It's like performing an experiment with myself.

JA: And you went to prison.

HC: Unfortunately, yeah. It was an interesting experience.

JA: How long did you have to serve?

HC: I only got two months and I ended up doing five weeks in Pentonville in London. It was interesting.

JA: Difficult time.

HC: Well, yeah. You've got to put it down as another one of life's experiences. That's the only way you can think positively about it. I couldn't write any songs, obviously. I tried to ask for a guitar and they said, 'We've got bus drivers in here, but we don't give them buses.' And I didn't quite get that.

JA: Was it prison that said to you, 'Right, I've got to stop this'?

HC: Funnily enough, no. It was ridiculous, because the weird thing was I was done for possession, but I hadn't actually tried it. Someone had given me some after a gig and I said, 'Oh, thank you very much.' And I just put it in my bag and at the end of this tour I had a complete chemist's shop in my bag. And, being responsible, I thought, 'At the end of the tour I'll try that. I don't know what effect it's going to have on me.' And I went down for having this stuff that I'd never tried.

So it was actually after I came out that I thought, 'Well, I've been done for it, I might as well try it.'

JA: What was it like being on the road? To be part of a small group like that – I suppose like we are on *Test Match Special* – but to be living at that sort of high-octane level – massive live concerts and the following that you had in those days.

HC: It's a great buzz and it's very exciting. And you grow very close to the people you're with. It's a shared experience.

JA: If you don't get on, presumably that's hopeless, is it?

HC: A lot of groups I think break down after they do a tour of America, because that's very gruelling and they end up after a tour there and they can't stand each other.

JA: I've seen some live performances – not rock and roll, necessarily – but the power that these people have on stage, singing live. You just have tens of thousands of people in the palm of your hand. I think it must be an awesome experience.

HC: It is and it plays havoc with your life patterns as well. Because you come off stage at midnight and your adrenalin's going mad. So you can't just go and have a cup of camomile tea and go to sleep. Some people try – I don't know how they do it. So you're going for another few hours and you end up going to bed very late, because you can't calm down.

JA: And how can you ever get that out of your system? There you are watching Devon Malcolm bat. He slogs a six against India. And having experienced all of that and to have held these people in the palm of your hand and everything that goes with it – I haven't touched the sex yet, we might forget that, we've done the drugs and the rock and roll – but how can you just let it go like that?

HC: Well, I didn't want to stop making music. I just wanted a more interesting challenge than the one that was happening at the time.

JA: So you're still singing and you're still writing prodigiously.

HC: Absolutely. I'm getting busier and busier and that's great. It gives me, unfortunately, less time to play with the Bunburys. It's fun – and the book's out and I've got a new record out and it's getting placed round the world, so it means you can go and play in these places. So I'll be in Oz hopefully this winter. France tonight – I've got to do a show near La Rochelle tonight. Unfortunately I can't stay and watch the rest of the day's play, which has really pissed me off. But I shall obviously have *TMS* on my radio.

JA: You can get it down there, I think.

HC: In France? Oh, great!

JA: Why don't you give us a taste of what they're going to get? This is the new Hugh Cornwell.

HC: This is a song from the new album. I'd like to dedicate it to Ashley Giles, the king of Spain – or spin or whatever – because it's about a town in Spain called Cadiz. *[And 'Cadiz' was what he sang for us, accompanying himself on Mike Selvey's guitar again.]*

JA: Thanks for all the entertainment you've given us.

HC: And thanks for all the entertainment *TMS* has given us.

SIR ELTON JOHN

interviewed by Jonathan Agnew,
Lord's, 13 May 2006

Elton John's love of cricket had been widely known about for some time, but it was the occasion of his performing for Andrew Flintoff's benefit just before the First Test of 2006 that provided the opportunity for Aggers to go along to his rehearsals in Battersea and record him for 'A View From the Boundary'.

The 'highlight' of the evening was to be 'Freddie' Flintoff joining him in a rendition of 'Rocket Man'. This had been something of a team anthem for England during the previous season – the 2005 Ashes-winning series – and, remember, this Lord's Test was the first in England since the Ashes had been regained at the Oval the previous September.

Born Reg Dwight, he became Elton Hercules John. He has sold more than 250 million records and had over 50 top 40 hits.

Sir Elton told Aggers about his early love for the game.

*

ELTON JOHN: I grew up with cricket – Brian Statham and Freddie Trueman – when I was at grammar school they were the two England fast bowlers. And there were Compton, Cowdrey and Edrich – all those people were heroes and you idolised them. Cricket commentary in those days was so exciting – the descriptions were so fantastic. The great thing about radio was that you could imagine it.

I always loved listening to cricket on the radio. I still do. I put the volume down on the telly and put the commentary up on the radio, because it's always been more magical on the radio for me.

JONATHAN AGNEW: And that sold the game to you – listening?

EJ: Oh yeah – and also being able to play it at school as well.

JA: What did you do?

EJ: A batsman rather than a bowler, definitely. I'm quite an aggressive person, so it's always fun to hit the ball I think.

JA: But presumably music took over then.

EJ: Music has always been my first love. I come from a very sporting family. My cousin was a footballer with Nottingham Forest. He scored the first goal in the 1957 Cup Final against Luton and broke his leg. His name was Roy Dwight. And my other cousin used to play for Fulham. I used to sit on the touchline at Fulham when I was a very young boy. So I came from a very big sporting family.

I loved tennis at an early age and took that up. It was extraordinary that when I was at school, tennis was the girls' sport and the boys weren't allowed to play it. And yet we always wanted to play tennis – and hockey, because hockey was such a great sport. But you weren't allowed to, so summer was always nice. Rugby was the sport in the winter and I didn't like that too much, because it was too rough. But summer was always good, because you could play cricket and I liked cricket a lot.

JA: Did you actually get to see any of these heroes? Did you go along to Lord's?

EJ: No, I didn't. I just listened to them on the radio. They became heroes through radio. It was like Peter Brough and Archie Andrews who became heroes through radio. So did all these people who became larger than life. The descriptions as they were coming in to bowl or coming in to bat were extraordinary. And then television came along and of course you saw these people actually doing it and it was even more impressive.

JA: Have there been any R. Dwight innings worth mentioning?

EJ: I don't think so, although actually I did score 24 at Lord's. I played in a couple of charity matches. I played in one at Lord's when I had green hair.

JA: I'm surprised they let you in.

EJ: I walked through the Long Room and you should have seen the looks that I got. And it was the longest walk out to the crease that I can ever remember. I thought, 'Oh please let this end.' And I got to the crease and I thought, 'Oh please, let me score one run.' And I scored 24. That was OK and I got so carried away I said, 'Yes, I'll play again next week.' It was for the Vic Lewis XI in Barnes. And Robin Jackman got me out first ball.

JA: Down to earth with a bump.
    Didn't you latch onto a tour of Australia?

EJ: The first tour I really latched onto was when we won the Ashes in '86/87. Going down to Australia and New Zealand quite a lot, as I did, I used to love hanging around with the cricketers – the Australian cricketers and the England cricketers. And they were so much fun. They're more down to earth. You can go out for a drink with them in the evening and go out for dinner. We had a lot of fun and got up to a lot of mischief together.

And then of course when we won the Ashes in Melbourne it was one of the greatest nights ever remembered. It was such a great occasion. It was so great to be part of a team that had won the Ashes. It was quite an extraordinary memory. And I must say I've always gotten on with the Aussies and always gotten on with the English cricketers.

There's something about hanging about with cricketers that I really, really like. They're very, very funny. When we did concerts in Perth, Dennis Lillee would organise – with Rodney Marsh – an Australian XI against a British XI out there. And I remember Alec Stewart was playing club cricket out there.

JA: David Gower described you as England's head groupie.

EJ: I was, yes. But he'd better be careful, because with some of the names cricketers earned during that tour, I could blackmail them easily. Allan Lamb, David Gower, Ian Botham and Bob Willis – I quite remember them in New Zealand at Auckland. They were going to Pakistan and they were not happy. They'd been away from home quite a lot and then they were going to Pakistan, so that night was quite rowdy as well.

JA: That was the infamous 'sex, drugs and rock and roll' tour.

EJ: I think that was the tour, yes.

Cricket for me has always been poetry in motion. And I love baseball in America as well, because it's that sort of game.

JA: Interesting. You can actually see the connection between the two.

EJ: Yeah, there is a connection there. It's a very poetical game – it's a very complicated game. The only way you could learn cricket is by watching it and playing it. You could never describe the rules. It's so complicated you just have to watch it.

How I learned baseball was to watch it time and time again on TV in America. But those two games are very similar in a poetical kind of way. And it's always great to watch a cricket match. I find it so relaxing. I prefer Test Matches to one-dayers, I have to say.

JA: I was going to ask you about that, because there's part of you, I'm sure, that's very traditional, although you don't see that image publicly. But you are more of a traditional cricketer.

EJ: Well, I liked one-day internationals when they first started. I just think there are too many of them now. And I think they wear out the players. Cricketers are playing too many games. I think the Test Matches are far more interesting. It's far more of a chess game. You know the format for the one-dayers. You get a lot of runs and you try to beat that lot of runs. It's interesting sometimes, but I believe that Test Match cricket is far more interesting and far more worthwhile. It's far more relaxing as well.

JA: This is the man who wore pink shoes, when you posed for the cover of your *Greatest Hits Volume II*. Not terribly traditional.

EJ: Not terribly traditional. I am a traditionalist in some ways, but I do think that you see the best cricket in Test Match cricket.

JA: Going back to that cover *[in which Elton is in cricket gear – with pink shoes – in a batting stance at the wicket]*, that was quite a brave decision of you to make, to have a photograph in cricket whites.

EJ: Yes, because America had no idea what cricket was.

JA: And it wasn't terribly sexy, was it?

EJ: I think cricket is a sexy sport. It's a very sexy sport and so is baseball. I think you just have to get into that sort of mindset. I like the fact that you can go for five days and have no one win. Americans can't get that together at all.

I've been watching the Test Matches between South Africa and New Zealand recently and it's far better than watching the one-dayers. You see more potential that way.

JA: You're here for Freddie, of course. Last summer was so special. Did you get to many of the games?

EJ: No, I didn't. I was on tour. It was probably one of the most exciting sporting occasions I've ever witnessed and the thing that really touched me more than anything else was the mutual respect that the two teams had for each other and the sporting way it was carried out. The Brett Lee innings, for example, it was astonishing, and the games were so close except for the First Test, which England got pummelled in.

And I remember watching the one we won by two runs and I couldn't bear it. I was in the south of France and I was on the phone to Michael Caine, saying, 'For God's sake!'

And he was saying, 'I can't look!' Michael Caine is a huge cricket fan.

I don't think we'll see another one like that for a long time. Two very evenly matched teams and great cricket all round. What I liked about it was the tempo in which the game was played. There were three or four hundred runs being scored all the time and it was fun and it was entertainment and yet it was great cricket. It was great bowling, great batting and two teams that really wanted to win.

JA: You mentioned the spirit. I know you like football too. Would you like to see football played in the cricketing spirit?

EJ: When you watch Spanish football on TV, when they do foul each other they pick each other up. Ronaldinho plays the game with a grin. I like that. We have a player at Watford called Marlon King, who scored 21 or 22 goals this year. He's the top scorer in the Championship. And you see him on TV – he grins and he laughs and he enjoys it and it's nice to see that element in the game.

Sport is enjoyable and it should be enjoyable to play. Whatever sport you play, you should go out there wanting to win and if you don't win you should accept it in the best way possible. I learned that when I became chairman of Watford Football Club in 1973. I wasn't a particularly good loser and you have to be gracious. And the thing that touched me last year about that Test series – yes, it was hell for leather and everyone wanted to win – but in the end of the day the mutual respect the two teams had was very touching.

JA: It's very interesting, because Steve Waugh, the former captain, has said publicly that he thought it was the friendliness the Australians showed to England that actually cost them the series.

EJ: Well, there's always been the rivalry, but they always go for a drink in the dressing room after the game. I've been there. As soon as the game's finished, it's into the other dressing room for a drink. That's the way it goes. And, yes, there was a lot of mini-sledging going on and that sort of thing.

It was terrific to see the England team competing at the level of the Australians. So often we haven't done, because the Australians have an incredible team spirit and incredible will to win and incredible professionalism in they way they do it. And I've always admired that about Australian sports teams in general. And last year, with Duncan Fletcher being the coach and with Michael Vaughan the captain and with Freddie coming on and playing such a great role – the emergence of Pietersen, the bowling of Jones, Harmison and Hoggard in different spurts – was fantastic. It was like the old days. It was so exciting.

JA: You talk so passionately about this. Are you a frustrated sportsman?

EJ: Oh, I think every singer, every musician I've ever known would like to be a sportsman and every sportsman I've ever known wants to be a musician. It's sod's law, but there's a great parallel between sport and music, because I think they're both great levellers. You could go to a park and kick a football around and people might say, 'Can we join in?' And you don't know them. And when you're on stage, playing to people you don't know and they're singing with you, it's a great feeling that you're together.

When I've played in Northern Ireland, I've played to Catholics and Protestants together. It brings people together. And sport does that too.

And some of the banter you get at sports is fantastic. Some of the crowd at Watford come out with some incredibly funny things.

For me it's my life. Music and sport are the two things that have always been anchored ever since I was a child.

You watch a county game on TV and you see new players come in you've never heard of. And you think, 'There's a name for the future.' Maybe he's being paid hardly anything, but he's playing because he loves it, and I just think that's so great to be able to do something you love.

When I first joined a band I did something I loved and we earned fifteen quid a week. We had to pay our own petrol money, our own accommodation, look after our equipment and I don't think we made any money. But we loved it and we didn't care about it, because we were so happy to do something we actually loved. And there's something beautifully romantic about being a cricketer. There's something so graceful. And I think it's camaraderie and I envy cricketers that.

JA: Do you keep yourself fresh? It's one thing for a cricketer to go out and get nought one day and 24 the next. You're singing the same songs and have been for a long time.

EJ: Every performance is different, no matter how many times you sing the songs. Every innings is different. I don't have the psychological problem, like when a player hits a bad patch – and every player's going to hit a bad patch sooner or later. It does happen to writers of songs. You write songs sometimes over a couple of years that aren't as good as you've written before.

JA: And you know that at the time, do you?

EJ: In time you know it, because you look back and think, 'That wasn't as good.' And a cricketer will go through that. Sport is psychological and being successful as a musician is psychological. You have to keep yourself fresh, you have to keep yourself on your toes. You cannot coast. I do that by listening to new music and new artists. Encouraging new artists, not listening to old things – listening to new things. It's the young people who keep you on your toes and that's how I keep myself fresh.

With cricket it's not just if you've got the talent, it's having the mental capacity to go along with it – you must agree with me. So many people have the talent that just don't have the mental capacity to couple the talent and the mental capabilities with it.

JA: Very true.

EJ: There are great performers in county cricket, like Mark Ramprakash, who's never really done it at Test Match level. It's such a shame it's never come together at a Test Match. I've always been a fan of Mark Ramprakash, ever since he was one of the youngest players to play for Middlesex.

JA: And you still keep creating yourself.

EJ: Yes, I've made a new album this year – my 42nd or 43rd, I think. You always have to create. I'm either writing musicals or film music or doing different things to keep challenging myself. You can't rest on your laurels. You can't look back. Even though you play the old standbys, because people want to hear them, you have to look forward, you have to produce new things, otherwise you'll go stale and you'll just be doing it as a machine. I could never do that.

JA: You're off on tour, doing cricket grounds this year. That's great fun, isn't it?

EJ: I've never really played a cricket ground except in Australia. I've played in Perth, Sydney and Melbourne.

JA: Do you play in the round?

EJ: No, I'll have a stage at one end.

JA: Now, you're going to sing with Freddie tonight. Are you rather surprised he chose 'Rocket Man'?

EJ: I can't wait for him to sing tonight to make an absolute fool of himself, which he will do.

JA: You'll see 1,300 people move quite quickly when he starts, I suspect.

EJ: As long as they don't move quickly when I'm singing, I don't mind. But Freddie will clear that floor quicker than anybody.

JA: Have you rehearsed?

EJ: Not a rehearsal. Jim Carrey sang it with me once unrehearsed on stage in Los Angeles and that was quite something, I can tell you. But Freddie, I think, will probably beat him.

*

We ended the programme with a recording of the duet. Happily, Elton's strong voice largely drowned Andrew Flintoff, though the 'Oh, no, no, no' came through all too clearly.

Next day Freddie confirmed that it had been 'a fantastic night'. Though he did admit, 'My singing didn't go too well. I was a bit sheepish and to begin with I froze. Luckily,' he said, 'Elton's got such a powerful voice.'

BORIS JOHNSON

interviewed by Henry Blofeld,
Old Trafford, 29 July 2006

Boris Johnson joined us in Manchester during the 2006 series with Pakistan, on the weekend that marked the 50th anniversary of Jim Laker's nineteen wickets in a Test Match to defeat Australia.

A Conservative MP, he was then the shadow minister for higher education, though in 2008 he was to leave the Commons to become the second Mayor of London.

A colourful character with his trademark shock of unruly blond hair, he has often courted and even seemed to relish controversy and he settled at the microphone with a deceptively bemused expression on his face, waiting to be quizzed by a fellow old Etonian.

*

HENRY BLOFELD: Welcome to Old Trafford. Have you been here before?

BORIS JOHNSON: Never. I've been to the football ground to give a speech for my friend, George Osborne, but never here. It's fantastic. Blissful. I love cricket and I'm very grateful to *Test Match Special* for having the most wonderful jammy day with my children.

HB: You're keeping a fatherly eye on them.

BJ: Yes, we've been watching this one and you think Monty Panesar's going to take loads of wickets. I think this guy Yousuf's going to dig in. He's digging in and he's fantastic. *[Henry had the better of the predictions here. Pakistan were 101 for 2 at lunch, still needing 241 more just to make England bat again. Mohammed*

Yousuf was out to the first ball after the interval – stumped off Panesar. They were all out that afternoon, to give England a win by an innings and 120 runs. Panesar took 5 for 72 – 8 wickets in the match, but he was slightly overshadowed by Steve Harmison – 5 for 57, to follow his first innings 6 for 19.]

HB: Did you play cricket at school, then?

BJ: I did play cricket. I was a very useless cricketer. I was in the house side. That was my point of maximum achievement.

HB: And what did you do?

BJ: I bowled quick-ish, but very inaccurately. My moment of greatest glory recently on the cricket field was in the fathers' match at some school or other, where I didn't wholly disgrace myself for the first time in a long time. But I'm the world's worst cricketer. It would be ridiculous for me to start boasting about my cricket. But I love it.

HB: We aren't modest on this programme. You've got to tell me how many runs and how many wickets you got in that fathers' match.

BJ: OK, I'll tell you. I was forced to retire on 25. I'd never reached 25 before in my life. So I thought that was it.

HB: Well, you weren't out and that was the great thing. So your average has increased.
    And what other sport do you go for?

BJ: Running around, cycling, tennis, squash – that sort of thing. The only game at which I was moderately competent was rugby.

HB: Now, Boris, it's really quite an extraordinary list – editor of the *Spectator*, *Daily Telegraph* columnist, after spending time in Brussels for the *Telegraph*, MP for Henley, shadow minister first for art and now for higher education, motoring correspondent of *GQ* magazine, novelist and briefly – for about five minutes – a management consultant.

BJ: I was a management consultant, yes. Have you ever done that?

HB: No. Tell us about it.

BJ: It was a completely pointless exercise.

HB: What did you learn in a week?

BJ: Very little. I knew that I was going to be a complete failure after I sat underground in some Mayfair hotel and watched overhead slides of growth project matrices and I simply couldn't stay awake. I knew it would be a disaster. A chap rang me from *The Times*, saying was I interested in doing that, so I went and did that instead.

HB: What did you start off doing at *The Times*?

BJ: The first thing I did was obituaries of my tutors. I thought that was a strategic move. They're all still alive – they're not meant to know that I've done this! I want you to know that they're all jolly favourable obituaries, in case they're listening. It was the only subject in which I thought I had any kind of expertise.

HB: Do you still think that?

BJ: Well, I think I've picked up a few other things, but not much, no.

HB: But you moved on from there to the *Telegraph* and you went to Brussels, didn't you, for a bit?

BJ: I did, and I had a fantastic time in Brussels and I learnt all about the doings of the European Community. I began fairly idealistic about Brussels and ended up being pretty sceptical about the way they do things.

HB: This comes across now in your writing.

BJ: Does it? I hope I'm not viscerally xenophobic or anything like that, because I'm certainly not. I think it's a wonderful and noble thing to want everyone to turn up and participate in the great partnership of nations. It would be fantastic if it worked. But it doesn't really work in the way that those who believe in political union think it should work. It simply doesn't happen like that.

HB: Is this because of the self-interest of so many of the nations?

BJ: It's because of people's deep desire to be governed by the nation to which they feel most loyal, and it's just a common fact of human nature that we want to be ruled by people who speak our language. And it's very very difficult to persuade people otherwise. And that's where it all goes wrong.

It's very deep, these loyalties. Look at all these chaps here cheering for Pakistan. Most of them were born in this country, but they feel a deep sense of kinship and affinity with Pakistan. There's a very interesting chap there, have you noticed? He's got the dome of his skull covered with the English flag and his face is painted with the Pakistani flag.

HB: Going back to Brussels, what to me is rather surprising is that our representatives go out there one hopes to represent

Britain, and one can be forgiven for feeling that at times they represent what they consider to be the greater good of Brussels and the EU.

BJ: You mean they go native. I think they get caught up in ambition and the dream of it all and they do want to create this single entity out of 25 different countries. It's a high and glorious thing to want to do and its like re-building the Roman empire – a subject on which I recently wrote a book – but it just won't work.

HB: You can get the commercial out.

BJ: I thought I'd just slip that one in.

HB: But you moved on from Brussels to what you're doing now with the *Telegraph* and you became a columnist. You enjoy that?

BJ: I do enjoy that very much, yes.

HB: You don't feel there's a conflict between that and being Member of Parliament for Henley and a politician?

BJ: I don't think the people of Henley feel that. No, I think it's quite a useful thing to be able to do – to write columns in newspapers. You can run campaigns for your constituents and that kind of thing.

HB: Of course one or two people set a precedent, like Winston Churchill and Disraeli.

BJ: That's right. And there's a lot to be said for using all avenues open to you as a journalist and as a politician. I can't see any particular conflict there. I think it would be fair to say that when

I was editor of the *Spectator* it did occasionally become tricky. And I managed to unseat myself a couple of times when the Tory party would get into a frightful rage about something that was in the *Spectator* and then I'd have to work out what to do. The answer was almost always – nothing.

HB: You had quite an interesting and lively time as editor of the *Spectator*. I must say first of all you put the circulation up enormously, didn't you? Which obviously was your primary objective.

BJ: Well, yes, I don't think I did anything to stop it going upwards, and in spite of my departure it continues to be extremely buoyant, so I don't think it was necessarily anything to do with me. I think it's just a wonderful magazine and I was privileged, as they say, to be the custodian.

HB: You had one or two moments. There was that editorial you wrote about Ken Bigley and Liverpool. Do you regret that? *[Ken Bigley was the engineer from Liverpool kidnapped and murdered in Baghdad. An editorial in the* Spectator *in 2004 suggested that this event and others had been over-sentimentalised by Liverpudlians and caused outrage. He was despatched to Liverpool to apologise by his party leader, Michael Howard.]*

BJ: I say, Blowers! I regret parts of it, but not all of it. This was the very complicated point I had to make when I went to Liverpool to talk to them all about it. There were bits in the article that I thought had been a bit too trenchant and bits that I wanted to defend and stick up for.

HB: It must have been quite an embarrassing moment, going back to Liverpool to apologise. How did you cope with that?

BJ: Stiff upper lip; keep going; soldier on. No, it was fine. If you're at the centre of any of these sorts of media firestorms, you're always much less conscious of what's going on than everybody around you. So it seems totally fine to you. My impression was that the whole Liverpool operation went rather swimmingly. Mission accomplished, I thought. I went up there. I jolly well told them that the editorial on the one hand made some good points and on the other had got a few facts wrong. And there we all are. Can I go home now? We had more readers in Liverpool than ever before in the history of the magazine. It's only chaps like you who say it's embarrassing, actually.

HB: I was just asking.

MP for Henley. You succeeded Michael Heseltine. What sort of chap is Michael Heseltine?

BJ: He was incredibly kind to me. He made absolutely no effort to stop me becoming MP for Henley and he is a charming guy and he's a seriously heavyweight figure in our party still. And quite rightly too. He's looking at the whole inner city regeneration agenda for us, which he did with some distinction back in the 1980s. And he couldn't be nicer.

HB: A slightly divisive figure when it comes to the EU?

BJ: It would be fair to say that he and I don't agree entirely about Europe. But I always feel that with these guys it's not really about Europe. They're not actually passionate Euro-federalists. What gets their goat is the idea that there's this other set of Tories – these right-wingers – who don't like it. And that's what stokes them up. People like Ken *[Clarke]* and Michael don't actually want to subsume Britain into a federal Europe, they just want to say 'snooks' to all the Euro-sceptics. It's more about factionalism than it is about ideology.

HB: And your present job as shadow minister for higher education, what does that involve?

BJ: It involves an immense amount of work and thought about universities. There's a great prejudice in this country at the moment that there are too many universities. Too many kids doing pointless degrees. There's probably a degree in *Test Match Special*. I'm sure there are people who study the moment when you say, 'I can see a seagull over the gasometer.' There probably are Blofeld studies at some university somewhere, and people think that's all wrong and crazy and there shouldn't be all this media studies and it's a great waste of people's time. And I'm a bit heterodox about that, because I'm not convinced that these degrees are such a waste of time.

And if you look at the results of people who do media studies and you look at what they go on to do in their lives, they often make very good careers and considerable sums of money. And actually the market is very often producing quite a sensible solution, which we prejudiced, stuffy people who've been to university ages ago and think it should be all about very academic, serious subjects don't understand.

And that's why I'm not in favour of hacking back universities and reducing them again, as we seemed to be before the last election. I think you should do it on a more market-based approach.

HB: But you are yourself a classicist, aren't you? You've said that you think Greek and Latin are important languages.

BJ: I do. I think they're wonderful and I'm going to fight, fight, fight to keep them on the curriculum whenever I can. I'm an out-and-out evangelist for those subjects and I have absolutely no intention of allowing the market to dictate what happens there! No, I believe in interfering morning, noon and night to try to preserve those disciplines.

HB: And you obviously enjoy this particular shadow job.

BJ: It's a wonderful job and it's engrossing. The most difficult issue we face at the moment is how to get children from the lower socio-economic groups to want to go to university. How we get them to apply and how we get them into the top universities. And everybody in the sector agrees we're running into a lot of trouble. It's very difficult to find the means of getting people from socio-economic groups C and D into the top fifteen to twenty universities in the country. And it's proving an intractable problem.

The solution I don't think is to be found in university admissions. You can't do it by obliging universities to second-guess the whole time and say this candidate's got some hidden genius. You can do a bit of that, but you've got to look at the problem in the schools, and the real problem is what's happening in secondary education and indeed in primary education.

Politicians always say this in a sort of vicar-ish way, but it would be wonderful if you could take the politics out of it. But I fear politics will creep back in.

HB: You're a novelist as well. *Seventy-Two Virgins* – how did that come about?

BJ: The publishers wanted something completely different. I sat down on a beach and I only had five or six bits of paper, so I wrote about 3,000 words per page. So I had these tiny kind of rabbinical scribblings, which I then typed up and I found it was getting quite long and it was getting towards the makings of a novel. And then I whacked it in.

HB: And you wrote it very quickly, didn't you?

BJ: Quick-ish. I don't want to minimise the artistic effort. It was the fruit of a lifetime's meditation. Every phrase licked like a bear cub.

HB: Oh, they jumped out of the pages at you.

Now, you're motoring correspondent of *GQ* magazine. How do you qualify for that?

BJ: Well, I don't know. I'm not the world's fastest driver, which was proved humiliatingly on Jeremy Clarkson's television show, where I was defeated by Tara Palmer-Tomkinson. Though I was faster than Jonathan Ross, I have to say.

HB: You drive like mad, but you also bicycle like mad. You should become the cycling correspondent of the *Daily Pedal*, shouldn't you?

BJ: I'm a great believer in cycling and I just think it's the only way to get around London. It's by far the safest way to get around London, because all the cars are going at three miles an hour thanks to Ken Livingstone's policies. It's absolutely idiotic. *[Two years after this interview, Boris Johnson defeated Ken Livingstone in the election to become Mayor of London.]*

HB: Parking at the House of Commons is easy enough – do you just chain it to a thing, or do the police look after it for you?

BJ: Well, I'm ashamed to say that several times my bicycle has been stolen from the Palace of Westminster itself under the eyes of the Metropolitan Police and assorted CCTV cameras, which is crazy. It tells you all you need to know about the concepts of property in Blair's Britain. And one time they stole my seat! To what perverted end I don't know.

HB: Do you think it's stuck up on someone's wall in a frame saying 'Boris's seat'?

BJ: I've lost my seat.

HB: Now, how do you see yourself in the future?

BJ: I can't think beyond today, actually. This is blissful.

HB: Do you want to become Prime Minister?

BJ: Well, in an ideal world. But I think it's highly unlikely that that eventuality will eventuate.

Let me give you a politician's answer. I want to do as well as I possibly can as shadow higher education spokesman and hope in the fullness of time – which I trust will not be too long delayed – to become higher education spokesman. You've got to say that in politics. It has the additional merit of being true.

HB: Is there anyone in your life who's had a great influence on you, or are you entirely your own man?

BJ: I would say my parents were pretty influential. I don't think that they'd deny it.

HB: Your father was a bit of a politician, too. And nearly was again.

BJ: Absolutely. We had a wonderful campaign in Devon, where he came within an ace of success in Teignbridge and I went down to support him several times. On one occasion he wanted me to play squash with him, which was a particularly fiendish operation, because I knew he wanted me to lose in order to bolster his credentials.

Now, here's a question. Would you have thrown a squash game and incurred all the humiliation that that involves in order to boost your father's political campaign?

HB: Lord, no.

BJ: It's a jolly tricky question. It's a bit of a moral issue. I sought advice from my political agent. I said, 'What should I do, because this is obviously a very tense moment?' Mind you, it's not beyond his powers to beat me anyway. He said, 'Don't lose.'

HB: Now, Boris, if your favourite restaurant was to say to you, when you next had a birthday, 'Here's a table for four. You can bring three guests and we'll give you the best dinner that we possibly can', who would the three guests be?

BJ: What about the Emperor Augustus? I want to find out how he talked. I'm genuinely fascinated by his accent. I want to know how he used Latin.

And I think we'd have to have one of the disciples, if not the man himself. Am I allowed that?

And what about Mary Magdelene? Let's get her along and get to the bottom of the Da Vinci code.

HB: We've got to have someone from the modern world. We'll allow you a couple of twelfth men.

BJ: What about Madonna?

HB: You wouldn't have to talk much with Madonna there. And what about a man?

BJ: Let's get Botham along.

PIERS MORGAN

interviewed by Simon Mann,
Old Trafford, 9 June 2007

The great thing about this programme has been the suggestions of names that get made to you, so that there is always a little list of names on a scrap of paper in your pocket. Piers Morgan was suggested to me by my daughter, Claire, a couple of years before we actually got him on. 'He's a genuine cricket fanatic,' she said – and so it proved.

In 1994, at the age of 28, he had become the youngest-ever editor of a national newspaper, when he took over the News of the World. *The following year he moved to the* Daily Mirror *as editor, but ten years later, that ended in ignominy when he authorised the paper's publication of pictures purporting to show British soldiers abusing Iraqi captives. They proved to be faked and the editor who had sanctioned their use was sacked. This interview, though, shows him in a fairly unrepentant mood.*

At this time Piers Morgan had already enjoyed success as a judge on US television's America's Got Talent *and this day would see the launch of* Britain's Got Talent.

*

Simon Mann: He's been described as fantastically ambitious and supremely self-confident – Piers Morgan, welcome to the *TMS* box.

Piers Morgan: Well, I'm following in the footsteps of Sir Vivian Richards, who was sitting in this chair moments ago, who was also I suspect very ambitious and very self-confident, so I will take that – as I assume it was – as a compliment, Simon.

SM: Well, I just pulled a few quotes out.

PM: That's two of the nicer things you'd have found, so I appreciate it, thank you.

SM: What's your interest in cricket?

PM: Fanatical – literally fanatical since the age of five. I've lived cricket, played it, watched it religiously and to be honest, to be sitting here at Old Trafford in the middle of a Test Match doing this with you is a dream come true.

SM: Who do you play for?

PM: I still play for a village called Newick in the East Sussex League down near Brighton. In fact I'm in pretty hot water, because they've got a big game today and they're not impressed that I'm fobbing off to be tarting myself around on the airwaves. So I'm not very popular down in my village.

SM: How often do you play?

PM: Oh, most weeks. Obviously this American adventure that I'm on has hammered my cricket schedule, but when I'm in England I play every week.

SM: What do you do?

PM: Well, what I'd like to think I do and what my colleagues would say I do are different things. I bat mainly. I used to be a fast bowler. Then as age took over and wine, women and song, I dropped to a medium-pacer, then to off-spin and now I bowl leg-spin, because it's the only way I can get any sort of control. But I'm mainly a batsman and a very poor slip fielder.

SM: Well, that happens as you get older.

PM: It does, but I'm only 42. That's a bit worrying.

I played at prep school and then I remember very vividly my first Test Match was at Lord's in 1975, watching Lillee and Thomson bowl at Dennis Amiss and Tony Greig – and David Steele was playing.

SM: That was his first game.

PM: It was. And it was amazing watching this grey-haired old guy come out and take on the two fastest bowlers in the world. And I've really just loved this sport from that moment on.

I've got three sons myself now. They're cricket mad, which is great. But I was sitting downstairs earlier with this guy who turned out to be Steve Harmison's dad. I said, 'What's it like for you at the moment?' I mean it's hard enough for me when one of my sons is going through a rough patch, but to have a son who is centre stage and having a difficult time must be very hard. He said it was very difficult.

My older boy's a left-arm medium-fast Wasim Akram model. He's nearly fourteen – Spencer. My middle son Stanley's a leg-spin bowler and opening bat. And the young one – the terror – Bertie, who's six and a half, he bowls flat out fast, so we've renamed him Bert Lee.

They're all fanatics. I'm grooming them to play for England. I don't mind which one, I've told them. And obviously this has caused a bit of competition between them.

SM: It's a good way to create competition. Give them something to aim for. Are they very talented?

PM: Well, I think they are. Every dad thinks his son's the best player he's ever seen. I think they've all got a real natural eye for a ball. Because I'm so obsessed with cricket, they've fortunately become equally obsessed. I'm very quietly optimistic.

SM: Are they more obsessed with cricket than anything else?

PM: We're all Arsenal season ticket holders, too. Don't start groaning – they're not that bad a team. But football is secondary. I always say to them, 'Look, guys, if you're ever asked if you'd rather go and watch Arsenal in the Champions League final or England at Lord's, you must always say England at Lord's.' It's just more civilised.

SM: Even if you don't mean it.

PM: Well, I don't want to be tested, put it that way.

SM: And you're a great watcher of cricket.

PM: I took them to the World Cup in Antigua. I go to the Lord's Test every year. I go on the second day with my village friends, who I've grown up with. We get drunk and misbehave in one of the stands. And the next day I go into Ian Botham's box, which is always great fun, as you can imagine. And I love it. I could watch every day of every Test.

When we won the Ashes a couple of years ago, I was there for all the last four days at the Oval. The greatest four days' sport I've ever seen.

SM: You mentioned Ian Botham – has the fact that you were editor of the *Mirror* and therefore in a powerful position given you access to the players?

PM: I know a lot of the players. I know Michael Vaughan very well. I know Kevin Pietersen very well. Freddie Flintoff – I spent the day at the races with him last week. Rather ironically, we were at Lancashire vs. Sussex, which got rained off for the day and the world's media were trying to get Freddie, because he'd just announced his new leg injury. So I helped squirrel him off to safety, which was a rather bizarre position to find myself in, dragging Freddie Flintoff away from the world's media.

But it kind of worked, and we had a disastrous afternoon at the races and it ended in particularly spectacular fashion when we put a small ransom on a horse called Flashing Floozy, which came last, which I thought summed up our day really and summed up his year.

SM: You shouldn't chase skirt, you see.

PM: Exactly. That's the lesson we learned.

SM: What's it like being a former editor of a national newspaper at such a relatively young age? You became editor of the *News of the World* at 28, which is incredibly young.

PM: That's the polite way of describing my career – the youngest editor for 50 years. There's another way of saying it – the youngest editor ever sacked. Full stop. Which is not a career ambition I was hoping to achieve. But I edited newspapers for eleven years and I had the most fantastic time. And I wrote a book when I finished, which was very cathartic. And as I wrote it I realised that I didn't have an angry or bitter or even frustrated bone in my body, because I was lucky enough to have covered some extraordinarily huge stories in that time. And as I was getting towards the end of that period I was thinking that I'd really done just about everything and you should always leave a job with yourself wanting just a little bit more, but not too much more. So I felt that I went out – for myself – on the right note really. If I could have scripted my exit it would have been on a huge story – preferably involved with Iraq, where the *Daily Mirror* took a strong anti-war position.

Now, the provenance of those particular photographs that caused my downfall remains a bit of a mystery. No one has ever found out who really took them; why they took them; what they were really of. But since then we've seen enough court martials of rogue troops, I think, for the general substance of our allegations to be proven. So I think I was marginally vindicated in that the story I was sacked over turned out to be pretty much on the money.

SM: Marginally vindicated.

PM: Well, I don't think I can claim total vindication, because I don't actually know the truth about those pictures yet. I was told by the government that those pictures were false and a hoax.

SM: Do you regret publishing them?

PM: No, because it's the same government that told us that Saddam Hussein had weapons of mass destruction, so I wouldn't necessarily take their word for anything, frankly.

SM: What about meeting Rupert Murdoch when you were 28 and him asking you to be editor of the *News of the World*?

PM: Pretty scary. I was flown to Miami and I didn't know what on earth was going on. I was the pop editor of the *Sun*.

SM: You had no inkling at all?

PM: No. The *Sun*'s then infamous editor, Kelvin McKenzie, said, 'Mr Murdoch wants to see you in Miami.' And I wondered what on earth for. And I remember this surreal moment of walking along Miami's beach with him. We both took our shoes and socks off and we were trotting through the surf, discussing world events, which for me was a very small conversation area, I can tell you, at the time. And we never mentioned anything really.

Than we went to a party that evening and I can remember he turned to another executive of his from Fox Television and introduced me as the next editor of the *News of the World*, which was certainly news to me.

SM: He was confident you were going to accept.

PM: Fairly confident, yes. It was one of those ones you weren't really going to say no to. But it was a very surreal weekend and it was a very surreal existence for the following year. To be editing the world's biggest-selling newspaper for Mr Murdoch was incredibly thrilling.

SM: What sort of reception did you get from your underlings – the people you were now head of?

PM: I think it was fair to say that there wasn't universal joy that the new editor was a spotty little geek who wrote about pop music, wore pinstriped suits and was young enough to be their grandson. So it was a baptism of fire, but we had an extraordinary run of luck and broke some huge stories and I think they realised that although I wasn't very experienced, I had that sort of fearlessness that comes with youth and just went for it. And I think that was quite exciting and empowering for all the staff. And they were a fantastic team of journalists.

SM: Did you have a feeling in your private moments then, 'I'm not really up to this – what have I landed myself in here'?

PM: I did, but – it's interesting when you compare it with cricket, for example – the younger you are, the more fearless you tend to be; the less encumbered you are by commitments, by other distractions and by self-doubt. And I think there's a lot to be said for plunging people into a big arena when they're younger rather than older because they tend to worry less.

SM: Were you up to it at the time, do you feel?

PM: Probably not. I certainly wasn't equipped in terms of experience to do the job. I did have a lot of confidence in my abilities as a journalist. I just don't think you can succeed in any profession, whether you're a cricketer or a politician or a journalist, without a level of self-confidence. Certainly in the modern media world, which is pretty ferocious. And so I didn't allow myself to show my self-doubt.

Obviously I would go home some evenings and think, 'What on earth have I got myself into?' But in terms of what I showed the staff, I always tried to be extremely self-confident, which is what I think you need from any leader of anything. And certainly an editor who's a bit twitchy about things generally tends to get the paper he deserves, which is one that's pretty inconsistent and pretty twitchy itself.

SM: There'll be some people listening to this, in fact many people, who feel that a tabloid editor is akin to the devil's son. How do you square with that? How do you cope with the fact that a lot of people despise what you've done?

PM: A lot of that is a class thing, because tabloid papers tend to be read predominantly by the working classes in this country, who are the salt and earth of Britain. And I've got no problem with pompous middle- and upper-class people taking a lofty, high view of tabloid newspapers, because what they're effectively doing is taking a lofty, high, rather pompous, privileged view of the working classes. And I will always defend tabloids and their readers for what they really are, which is a wonderful, exciting, revelatory, informative, fun way of bringing the day's news and events to life. And I've read the so-called serious newspapers all my life and been bored to tears by them most of the time. I have no problem in having edited papers which at least gave people a laugh in the morning.

SM: Did you say that most journalists are morally bankrupt?

PM: Yes.

SM: That's true, is it?

PM: Well, you know it is. You're one of them. I do think journalists work themselves into the most hilarious moral indignation about stuff when, given what I know about most journalists' private lives, there would not be enough trees in the Amazon rainforests to detail them .

I've been out of newspapers for three years now, so, even though I still get introduced as the former *Mirror* editor, I don't actually see myself any more as part of that world necessarily, although I remain very proud of a lot of stuff we did. But you look at it from the outside and it's fairly absurd, the moral piety that comes with working for newspapers and television and radio. We do collectively as media whip ourselves into the most hilarious moral frenzies about stuff.

And it's interesting, working abroad, the different ways that these things play in different countries. Because in America they treat people in public life very differently from how they do in England. In England there's what I think is quite a healthy 'build them up, knock them down' atmosphere that pervades about people.

SM: Some people hate that, though, don't they?

PM: They do, but I think – having worked in America – that it's actually quite healthy. Because in America it's the other way. There's universal adulation for anyone in public life. And you do feel that that collective adulation for celebrity and famous people is pretty corrosive to a society and to a country. And I quite like the way that in England you have the media to keep people on their toes when they're in public life and celebrities who get above their station. At least we have a media that's quite fearless and aggressive, who will prick the balloon from time to time.

SM: So what you're saying is that the media will make mistakes, but overall it does a good job, because in a democracy you need those checks and balances.

PM: Well, there are very few countries for example where I, as editor of the *Daily Mirror*, could have launched such an aggressive, sustained campaign against the Iraq war. If you go somewhere like America, the media were pretty neutered over the Iraq war. And you do wonder, if they had papers like the *Daily Mirror*, doing what we did, if perhaps George Bush could have been reined in a bit. The media there only turned round when it was far too late.

So the free press in Britain gets a bit of a bad rap and they do go too far. They do sensationalise and they do make big mistakes and when they do they get pretty severely punished. But overall I'd much rather have a free and quite anarchic press than to have a neutered one.

SM: Have you made more friends than enemies, or more enemies than friends?

PM: Probably half and half, if you embrace the media as I have. I've made no problem of doing that. When I was on the *Mirror* we didn't have much money to spend on promotion and I always thought if I could think of wheezes to get on TV then, yes. It was, I suppose, a bit self-promoting and I didn't mind that, because I've always quite enjoyed the limelight, but also it got my paper talked about and that can be predominantly a good thing.

Occasionally it would get you into trouble, I'm sure, but I've got no problem with that. I like the media world. I like doing interviews. I like having time to go on things like *Question Time* and having rows with people. I'm aware if you do that and you're quite provocative and opinionated, then half the people that hear you are going to disagree with you and probably hate your guts. But the other half are always fine about it and agree with you. So it's swings and roundabouts, really.

SM: Who have you fallen out with most spectacularly? Ian Hislop? Jeremy Clarkson?

PM: I wouldn't have them round to dinner tomorrow, no. Hislop punched me … no, he couldn't reach. Clarkson hit me three times in the head.

SM: Did you deserve it?

PM: I probably deserved it. We kept running pictures of him with someone who wasn't Mrs Clarkson in compromising positions. I suppose in a funny way it ought to have been his fault, but it rapidly in his eyes became my fault. So when he saw me at the British Press Awards, he whacked me three times.

I was trying to conjure up the sporting metaphor to deploy as the third punch rained in, and I remembered the words of Muhammad Ali to George Foreman in the 'Rumble in the Jungle', 'Is that all you've got, George?'

And I turned and said, 'Is that all you've got, Jeremy?' Which he was quite sporting enough to put in his *Sunday Times* column.

It was a bit like a scene from *Bridget Jones*, when Hugh Grant and Colin Firth are in the fountain. Handbags at dawn. All rather unedifying and quite embarrassing.

SM: You took revenge on him in the book, though, didn't you?

PM: I did, yes.

SM: You can tell the story – as long as you're careful.

PM: Well, he came up with the best excuse ever as the reason that he wasn't having an affair. He basically inferred impotence, which struck me as a pretty good excuse, I must say – but slightly unlikely.

SM: And not true?

PM: Well, I don't know. You'd have to ask him.

We actually made up recently. I won't say completely made up. We met in a bar at four o'clock in the morning. It was one of those scenes where we might have been going to hit each other again. My family were quite army-orientated and they were pretty depressed that I'd been hit three times without retaliating. But I thought you've got to be civilised about things and so I walked over and shook his hand and we had a bottle of wine. And he actually revealed that he had broken the little finger on his hand, punching me. And I showed him the scar on my head and it was sort of showing off our war wounds. It was quite a proud moment for both of us, actually. Very embarrassing for anybody else.

SM: How do you get on with Tony Blair?

PM: I quite liked Tony Blair. He's a very charming guy when you meet him. I met him many, many times on the *Mirror* one-to-one and got on very well with him. My big problem was that I always thought he ran the country as if he was still a QC or a lawyer, in that he would basically argue anything if the money was right.

You look at Iraq and you do believe that if Tony Blair had refused to support George Bush on Iraq that war may never have happened, and it's been one of the most catastrophic foreign policy disasters not just of a lifetime, but of many lifetimes. So I always had huge problems with what he did with the country's foreign policy and the effect it's now having on us domestically. Even getting a flight up here today, the security that we have to endure is all a direct result of this nonsense.

I also had a bit of a problem with Mrs Blair, who I never saw eye-to-eye with.

SM: Did she try to get you sacked?

PM: She did try to get me sacked, which many of your listeners might think was a very good idea and might actually redeem her in their eyes. No, I never really got on with Cherie. It was a bit like two matchsticks in a dry field. It didn't take a lot to go off.

SM: Did it make you feel powerful when you got to meet the Prime Minister? Is it 56 times that you've met him one-on-one?

PM: Yes.

SM: Well, that's a powerful position to be in, isn't it?

PM: I guess so. I didn't really think about that at the time. Towards the end, to be honest – this will sound really weird – it used to get rather boring. I would go down to meeting number 52 with Blair one-to-one and he'd say, 'Hi. The paper's looking great', which he always said – lying. And then we'd talk about football and the weather and a little bit about Iraq. And he'd say, 'Are you going to rein back?'

And I'd say, 'No.'

And he'd say, 'OK.' And he'd shake my hand and I'd go back to my office.

Like anything, if you meet anyone enough times, you just get rather bored with each other. So it's probably good for me and him that I departed. Though he did have this memorable dinner when I left.

I went to have dinner with just Cherie and Tony for two hours in the flat at Number Ten. And that was very amusing, because he was getting drunk with me, drinking lots of bottles of wine, and Cherie was drinking water and stony-faced. And there was this great moment – a bit like *The Good Life* – Margot and Jerry – when I said, 'Come on, Cherie, why do you hate me so much?'

And Tony said, 'No, she doesn't', trying to calm things down.

And she said, 'I do, actually.' And it all turned out to be something about me writing a story about her having bad skin, which apparently she was mortified by. And for that reason she needed my head on a plate.

SM: Well, people hate it when newspapers are really personal.

PM: The odd thing was the *Mirror* was never personal about Cherie. The *Daily Mail* used to crucify her, but the *Mirror* actually was never that bad about Cherie. She just didn't like me personally. She said I had a dodgy moral compass. I wasn't quite sure what she meant by that. But anyway, I'm sure she was right.

SM: What's life been like since leaving the *Mirror*?

PM: Well, I've ended up judging dancing cows with David Hasselhoff in Hollywood, which I must say wasn't on my checklist of future jobs. So it's all rather surreal. Tonight we start *Britain's Got Talent*, to which I've tried to add the question mark to the title to make it more balanced. But I didn't honestly think I'd be judging things with Simon Cowell like blokes who put clothes pegs on their heads or piano-dancing pigs. But that's what I've ended up doing and it's very entertaining.

SM: How did that come about, then?

PM: Well, I've known Simon Cowell a very long time and he just rang me up and said he needed someone fairly obnoxious to go to America and be rude to Americans on a talent show. And he couldn't think of anyone better equipped than me to do the job.

SM: We've had an e-mail saying that 'Piers Morgan on *America's Got Talent* excels at being very rude to poor wretches who compete each week. All these shows seem to have a rude British judge.'

PM: I think it's obligatory in America now. They call us 'snarky'. I never quite found out what 'snarky' means. But I assume it means fairly obnoxious. It's a bit like playing a pantomime villain. The Americans get the joke, because of Simon Cowell being so successful out there.

It's all a bit tongue-in-cheek. They expect us to be amusingly rude – not too personally rude, just about their acts. You've got to remember you are seeing some extremely deluded people who genuinely think their act's worth a million dollars, when it probably wouldn't be worth a subway ride home. So I think it's a duty and a responsibility to put them back on the straight and narrow.

SM: Is this show huge out there?

PM: The second season started on Tuesday to record ratings, you'll be appalled to hear. It's the number one show in America – and it's coming here.

SM: It's on tonight on ITV. *Casualty*'s on BBC1, I should say.

It's three years since you were sacked. Do you feel that in a way you've done the best thing you're ever going to do in your life, or the most satisfying thing?

PM: Certainly my ambition was to be a journalist and then to work on a national newspaper and then it was absolutely to be the editor of a national newspaper, and I got incredibly lucky to achieve my ambition at 28 and do it for eleven years. So I really achieved my ambition very young and I've had a wonderful time doing it. I've got no regrets. I think I got out when I was getting bored and that's a good time for me and the paper.

My energy was beginning to be diverted towards other things like television and stuff, which I've really enjoyed, too. And also I'd never have written the books I've done if I hadn't left the paper and left editing.

Being a talent show judge is great fun. Other people have always had this weird insistence that I ought to do something more serious, but I've never felt the need to be any great *homme serieux*. I just like having a good time.

SM: Would you like to go back to newspaper editing?

PM: Well, I think newspapers are changing very fast, so I think the nature of what you would be doing is really evolving by the day and all newspaper sales are going through the floor. Everything's migrating to the internet. I think there might be excitement in perhaps being the first editor of an online newspaper, but whether you would actually want to put yourself in to run a national newspaper now in the current market conditions, which are extremely difficult – I think I'd find it very tiring.

Also I'd think, like a cricketer who gave up and went back three or four years later, 'Why have I done this? I've already been through this mill and I've thoroughly enjoyed it.' Why go back into something when you've quit really at the right time? Because psychologically I think I quit when I felt ready to move on. So it would take an awful lot to persuade me to go back to newspapers.

SM: Is it a really demanding life?

PM: It's incredibly demanding. I've got so much more free time now. The ability to go to bed and turn your phone off cannot be over-rated after eleven years of being woken at three in the morning and changing front pages. All incredibly exciting, but inevitably draining on your body. They say that for every editor who goes past 50 still editing, it's about five years off your life and I can understand why, because it's relentless. It's seven days a week.

I'd come to a cricket match and spend most of the day fielding calls, planning things. And also when you're in that world everything seems so incredibly magnified in its importance. When you come out you realise that most people don't read newspapers like it's the end of the world. They read it for a quick resumé of world events, bit of a laugh, bit of entertainment, do the crossword, and when you're on the other side of it, preparing these things, it seems like you are absolutely consumed with the vitality of every word that comes out. And that is not how most people on the outside view it.

SM: What's going on in your private life?

PM: All sorts of mayhem. You really don't want to go there on *Test Match Special.*

SM: Well, I asked that question because I've seen some recent clippings that we've dug out. How have you reacted to the fact that people have got interested in your private life?

PM: Simon, let's cut to the chase. If you wish to invade my privacy on *Test Match Special*, you're going to have to just be brave about it and pile in. Come on, now's your chance. Don't hold back. I wouldn't.

SM: OK, who are you seeing now?

PM: Celia Walden. A lovely girl.

SM: How long's that been going on for?

PM: Quite a while.

SM: And have you been seeing anyone else while that's been going on?

PM: Absolutely not. You're quite good at this. You could be a tabloid journalist. You shouldn't ease off, though. You've got me on the rack. Come on.

SM: Where's it going?

PM: Hopefully very far. I can think of a lot worse places to be going.

SM: And the kids get on with her?

PM: They're all very friendly.

SM: What's interesting is that this interview's been bowling along and your answers have been lasting for about a minute or so, and now it's your private life, you're clamming up.

PM: Well, I'm more than happy to start asking you about yours.

SM: Happily married.

PM: Come on, let's get back to more serious matters, Simon.

SM: Well, that's instructive.

PM: Like all tabloid journalists, you have to understand, we're rank hypocrites and the last thing we ever want are the turrets turned on us. The only fortunate position I have is that most of my friends now edit other tabloid newspapers and I know where all the bodies are buried. So I'm sort of fairly protected. You, however, are in a more difficult position, Simon.

SM: Have the papers been after you?

PM: They have, actually. I had the absolute joy of being pursued by two car-loads of paparazzi through the streets of London. Terribly exciting I have to say. And we got to Chelsea Harbour and they didn't realise that only black cabs can get through, not ordinary cars. And they tried to get through and were stopped. And then two of them got out and were running after our cab, which I thought was heroic in that we were going 40 miles an hour and they were both in their fifties.

But they did get a couple of sneaky snaps, which then appeared in the *Mail on Sunday*. And I was delighted, to be honest. I thoroughly enjoyed being pursued. I thoroughly enjoyed being papped – loved having my privacy invaded and don't really see what the problem is.

SM: You really mean that, do you?

PM: I do mean that. In America I remember being in a make-up room with David Hasselhoff, my co-judge, and one morning the *National Enquirer* out there – the real scandal sheet – exposed me. 'Dark past of talent star.' And it was all stuff I'd put in my own book. 'He was dodgy share tipper. He faked Iraqi photos' – all this kind of nonsense.

And Hasselhoff was waiting for me with this huge grin, saying, 'They got you, man. They got you, you tabloid scumbag.'

I said, 'Yeah, they did. They gave me all of page eight. Can you believe it?'

He said, 'Are you pleased?'

I said, 'Pleased? I'm delighted. And, by the way, did you notice what they called me, David? They didn't just call me *a* star judge on *America's Got Talent*, they called me *the* star judge.' At which point you've never seen a man move faster to his agent. Furious! So it was all fair in love and war.

SM: So that's the way to play it. That's the way you'd advise. Just to go with it.

PM: I've spent years listening to celebrities squealing about invasion of privacy and paparazzi and all that kind of nonsense. And I hear Hugh Grant every few weeks about how he hates fame and doesn't want to make any more movies. And then he forces himself to make another one and forces himself to go to premieres and forces himself to pose for pictures. And you think, 'Look, mate, if it's really that gruelling, why don't you just stop making them and go and live in a shack in India?'

And Keira Knightley last week said she'd had to go on a retreat to recover from the stresses of fame. Well, I wouldn't worry too much, love. You're in *Pirates of the Caribbean*. You got lucky. Enjoy it.

Honestly, it's very depressing hearing celebrities whining about fame. Look at most of the audience here today, watching at Old Trafford. Most of them work damn hard for their lives, don't earn vast amounts of money, don't have limousines, body-guards and wonderful, glamorous lives and yet they're probably very cheerful with their lot – not miserable and whining all the time.

SM: One final thing. We've had an e-mail from the cricket correspondent for your local village side in Sussex. 'Piers Morgan's a really competent cricketer and being falsely modest. Bowls tidily and sets intelligent fields.'

PM: Well, there you are. Modesty was always my byword.

DANIEL RADCLIFFE

interviewed by Jonathan Agnew,
Lord's, 23 July 2007

If I have not given Shilpa Patel enough praise for her talents in tracking down interview victims, this one was certainly one of her crowning achievements. A little bird had told her that the star of the Harry Potter films, Daniel Radcliffe, was attending all five days of the First Test with India in 2007, just sitting in the stands as an almost anonymous fan.

As chance would have it, the match coincided with the publication of the seventh and last in J.K. Rowling's series of books about the schoolboy wizard, so Harry Potter fever was heightened. At that stage five of the films had been released.

It was on the final day of the Test Match that Shilpa pinned down her target on what was already a very special day for Daniel, being his eighteenth birthday. Shilpa, being all-powerful, secured him a perch in the MCC President's box and that's where Aggers found him.

*

JONATHAN AGNEW: You haven't been sitting in a posh box. Where have you been?

DANIEL RADCLIFFE: We've spent a lot of time in the Compton Stand and a little bit in the Edrich Stand. It's been fantastic. The best time we've had is when we were surrounded by the Indian fans on day two, because the competition and the banter was so much more exciting.

JA: Did they know who you were? Were they Harry Potter fans?

DR: I think they guessed when a little kid came up to me and asked me to sign his book. That was the big giveaway.

JA: You must be signing hundreds of those at the moment – although directly I suppose that's nothing to do with you. That's all J.K. Rowling's. You're swept into it, aren't you?

DR: Absolutely. Every other pace you take here you see another copy of the seventh book, obviously just released, so Potter fever's at fever pitch at the moment.

JA: Actually, without the glasses I wouldn't necessarily have got you, you know. The owlish glasses are a bit of a giveaway with Harry Potter, aren't they?

DR: That's why I tend not to wear them when I'm out and about. That and the cape tend to tip people the wink.

JA: And the broomstick, no doubt.

DR: Exactly.

JA: Not many eighteen-year-olds get to spend a day at Lord's for their birthdays, I suppose.

DR: Everyone – tabloids especially – is expecting me to have some massive bash with lots of other celebrities. That's so not my thing, so just to come here for a day was a bit of a dream, really. I've never been to a cricket match before.

JA: You've been following cricket, though, haven't you?

DR: Most people got into it with the Ashes we won *[in 2005]* and I got into it with the Ashes we were whitewashed *[2006/07]*, just simply because of Paul Collingwood's double hundred in

Adelaide, which is also the reason he is my favourite player. Unfortunately, he hasn't done so well in this Test, but he did take a very good catch.

JA: Maybe I could conjure up a bit of magic and get you to meet him.

DR: That would be amazing. So far I've got Andrew Strauss's autograph and Sachin Tendulkar's.

JA: Were they aware who was asking for their autographs?

DR: No, they weren't. They were doing the thing that I do when I'm in a crowd of people, which is just keep your head down and keep moving as you sign. So I don't think any of them saw me.

JA: This is rather odd, because I have behind me, I have to confess, a book from Andrew Strauss for you to sign for his child.

DR: Excellent!

JA: If this is the first game you've been to, and you got into the game by watching England get so thrashed, how did it happen?

DR: There was something about being in Australia. I love Australia and I love Australians, apart from when they talk about cricket, because they love to gloat. And something in the patriotic side of me was stirred. I suddenly became this obsessive cricket fan and wanted us to beat them, which we didn't, but we will next time. *[As 'next time' was the 2009 Ashes series, which England did indeed win 2–1, some of Harry Potter's prophetic powers have evidently rubbed off on Daniel.]*

JA: And Collingwood's innings in particular. You were watching it on telly, presumably – in Australia?

DR: I was in Melbourne, but I was watching it from Adelaide.

JA: So what was it about that?

DR: It was the celebration. First of all it was the elation that started between him and K.P. that was lovely, because they were spurring each other on. And that final celebration, when he got his double hundred, was just so impassioned that it was really inspirational.

JA: He gave that great cry, didn't he?

DR: Yes, it was quite primeval and scary in a way, but I liked it all the same.

JA: Apart from Paul Collingwood, which other players are grabbing your attention – Pietersen, presumably?

DR: Pietersen obviously – and Ryan Sidebottom – I just think he's great.

JA: With his hair – he could almost be in a Harry Potter film, couldn't he?

DR: He could absolutely. And then I rather like Ravi Bopara. I think he's really good for the future. And Matt Prior – I really like him.

JA: This is your first live game then, Daniel. How have you taken to the way that people behave at cricket grounds? Has it surprised you? Is there a certain etiquette? What have you learned about watching cricket in the various stands that you've been in?

DR: I've learned that the Edrich Stand is encumbered by children. So that was a mistake we didn't make again. And then today we had to move because we were in a very, very rowdy crowd and I didn't want the England players to think I was part of that.

JA: You've just met Charles Fry here and you made the connection with C.B. Fry, didn't you? *[Charles Fry, at that time Chairman of MCC, is the grandson of C.B. Fry, the pre-First World War England captain and accomplished all-round sportsman.]*

DR: I was really pleased with myself. But I like John Betjeman poems and C.B. Fry's mentioned in one of them. Fry's quite a distinctive name – and an easy one to remember.

JA: It's a good knowledge. What about the game itself, is it doing it for you?

DR: I love the fact that it's a very specific sport. It's not like football, where everybody seems to be into it. It's also the fact that there are so many rules and complications. Some of them aren't really necessary, but I just enjoy them. I enjoy the pedantry of cricket as much as the play.

JA: But your game is Quidditch, isn't it? That seems quite complicated.

DR: I don't know the rules fully. I was asked the other day on television some technicality and I didn't know and I got laughed at by the presenter. It was horrible.

JA: It's sort of football and hockey on broomsticks, isn't it?

DR: It's a combination of that and basketball. Apparently, in a sort of Harry Potter convention they had in America, they worked out a way of doing a sort of grounded version of Quidditch, which I would not pay to see. I just don't know how it could possibly work.

JA: How do you film it?

DR: I couldn't possibly reveal that information. It's very, very, very clever computer-generated stuff. They put me on a pole, on a broom. To be honest, it's incredibly painful to film. If anybody has ever sat on a bicycle and have their feet taken off the pedals and leant forward.

JA: Very nasty.

DR: It is, quite.

JA: And it happens quite often, does it?

DR: Not so much now, because she's stopped writing it. I think I'm probably the only child in the whole of the UK who is pleased not to have Quidditch in the Harry Potter books.

JA: You're eighteen now – you can stop saying 'child'.

DR: You're right. I forgot I was eighteen when I woke up this morning and then I opened the presents, which was great!

JA: Are you quite an obsessive sort of fellow, to have got so quickly into cricket? Are you someone who Googles a lot? Would you be interested in the history of cricket?

DR: Absolutely. That's the other great thing about cricket is it's a pretty old sport and there is so much history to it and so many long-standing rivalries and the history between the various players, let alone the teams. And that's another thing that attracts me to it.

JA: How do you feel about the one-day stuff and Twenty20?

DR: I'd love to go to a Twenty20 match. I think you hear a lot of people saying it's not right and it's not proper and I don't understand that, because I just think it's incredibly exciting. It's not just smash it and run. There are a lot of tactics in it as well. Particularly Leicestershire is the team I like watching, because they've got Paul Nixon.

JA: Well done. That's my old county.

DR: Oh, really?

JA: What on earth sort of life do you have? Is it constantly like this? *[Photographers had found him and there were lenses pointed at him by now.]* Are you still at school?

DR: I've actually left school last year.

JA: You've obviously been acting for a long time. Has the schooling been difficult?

DR: It was. When I was at school my marks were all right, but they weren't great. But when I was filming, because I was tutored one-to-one on set, my grades got so much better. It was never that hard to juggle in a way, because for a long time it's all I've known. So you get used to it after the first few months.

JA: I'm always amazed by the kids that you see in *Les Miserables* or any West End show where these young kids are coming on. It's quite late at night. What sort of life do they have? How do they juggle all of that?

DR: I can't really speak from experience of that, because by the time I did the play earlier in the year, I was no longer in school. So I don't know. There's a lot made of the child star thing, but I think if you've got good people around you who are going to be honest with you and treat you as a kid rather than an actor, then you'll be all right. No one ever talks about people like Christian Bale and Jodie Foster, who started acting really young and have made it and done really brilliantly. They always focus on the negatives. It's possibly just a tougher time for some people than it is for others.

JA: I guess it means you've got to grow up pretty quickly, though.

DR: I think it's something that just happens when you're on set and you're surrounded by adults. When you're a kid I think the only relationships you have with adults are as teachers or parents, whereas suddenly you're working alongside them. So I suppose you do tend to mature slightly faster.

JA: Was it something you always wanted to do? What fired you up? Your parents are involved in theatricals.

DR: They were both actors when they were younger and my dad was a literary agent. He looked after writers and directors. He now chaperones me on set. And my mum's a casting director. I hasten to add that she's never cast me in anything. That's not how I got the role!

JA: Presumably when you first auditioned for this role you were so young you possibly didn't know what it was all about at the time.

DR: I didn't. I had no idea of the significance of it to be honest. It was only on the third film that I thought, 'Wow! I'm really enjoying this.' I was always enjoying it, but it was the first time I thought, 'This is something I want to pursue and go on to do when I'm older.' So hopefully, if people still work with me, then I will be able to do that.

JA: Can you remember that first audition? How old were you?

DR: I think I was just eleven and I remember it very, very vaguely. Actually I remember being quite nervous, but more about meeting the people than about not getting the part, because you walk into a room and it's full of adults and directors and producers and you're a little bit intimidated. But that was the great thing about Chris Columbus, who directed the first two movies. He was so easy to get on with and he made everybody feel very relaxed as soon as he met them.

JA: What did you have to do? Sit on a broomstick?

DR: I think I had to do one of the scenes with Hagrid and luckily I have these freakishly large eyes, which apparently looked mournful, so that was essentially how I got it, I think. Also I think they only had a month before they started filming, so it was probably a case of desperation amongst other things.

JA: But presumably if you'd known what a huge chance this was going to be, your nerves would have been going.

DR: That's the brilliant thing about being eleven. Nothing like that fazes you. You're unnaturally confident, because it's harder to take in the bigger picture of something. So you just go into it all guns blazing. And you're a lot less inhibited then because you haven't done the whole puberty thing.

JA: Indeed. In fact you'd have done it on set, probably.

DR: Yes, I have grown up on set.

JA: Take us onto the set, Daniel. Obviously they're all different, but what's it like for a really young kid, as you were for that first film? Were you prepared for it?

DR: I think I was, just because my parents have always been absolutely fantastic. Because they were both in the business, they were very good at preparing me for what I had to do when I got on set and to be focused but also have a good time.

I remember the first day we were on set, on the call sheets, which we get every day, there were only four people on it. It was myself, Emma *[Watson]* who plays Hermione, Rupert *[Grint]* who plays Ron and Robbie Coltrane, playing Hagrid. And I thought, 'That's not too bad. That's hardly anybody. I can do that.' And the next page it told you how many extras were going to be there and it was about 350. So it was mildly intimidating, but again Chris Columbus was so good with all the kids on the set.

He did the films for two years. It's ten months we do to film one, so it's quite a long haul and he was brilliant at getting us enthusiastic every day we came onto the set.

JA: Literally – ten months non-stop working?

DR: Pretty much. The second film was actually longer. It was eleven months. They're saying the next one's going to be about eight or nine, but I don't believe that for a moment.

JA: But where are you living when you're on set?

DR: We film it at Watford Leavesden studios, so I live at home all the time. I never have to go very far each day, unlike poor old Emma. I think she comes from Oxford every day.

JA: And who of the other characters have been really good to you?

DR: I suppose Matt Lewis, who plays Neville in the films, is just great. To be honest I get on really well with everybody. My best friend on set is a guy called Will, who works in costume and he's been there since the very beginning. We're great mates. And obviously Rupert and Emma – we've been together so long now we all get on really well.

JA: Almost like a family.

DR: Pretty much. The whole set is, though, because the crew's barely changed over the last five movies. So we're all really close to be honest. There's not too much tension at all, which you would probably expect on a shoot that long.

JA: Mistakes? There must have been a few laughs, weren't there?

DR: I think every one assumes that because the films are quite big-budget they must be just foolproof to work on and that there are never any cock-ups of any kind. And of course they happen constantly. I've got a lot better at not laughing mid-take.

JA: You're a giggler, are you?

DR: Oh – I used to be terrible. Me and Rupert Grint used to be absolutely appalling together, just laughing all the time. To be fair to us, we have got a lot better. We're managing to control ourselves a lot more now.

JA: When I make a mistake on the radio or television, it doesn't really matter – it's gone. But if you make a mistake on this huge-budget film, do you think, 'There's another million dollars down the pan and we'll have to re-shoot the whole thing'?

DR: I try not to think about that. But also I try not to make mistakes any more. But, yes, that is a terrifying thought, isn't it?

JA: What about J.K. herself? What's your relationship with her?

DR: Really good. Jo's lovely and we get on really well. She hasn't given me any hints as to any of the books ever. I still haven't read the seventh one, because I've been here. I have got it at home and I started it last night. But she's lovely to us and to everybody on set and if you ever do have a question about a particular choice you've made with the character, she can either say, 'Yes, that's good', or, 'No, never do that again.'

JA: So she's very hands on, in fact?

DR: She'll never come in and criticise. She views the films as totally separate things from the books, which they are. So she totally understands that things do have to be cut and things do have to be lost in order to make a two-and-a-half-hour film, because if you filmed the whole book it would be about six hours long.

JA: How did you create the character? I know it's largely written down for you, but it's the actor's job to make the person, isn't it?

DR: When I started out, because I was so young, I wasn't thinking so much about the character as just saying the lines and saying them well and remembering them. So I was probably playing me at eleven in the first two films, really. But then, after I started to get into the technical side, I got into acting as a way of expressing myself. That sounds really pretentious, but I guess that's what I'm trying to say. I then started to think more deeply about what the differences between myself and Harry are, so I don't just end up playing myself in all the films. And also, as you say, most of it's written down. It's so detailed a character in the book. But the character still remains very, very separate from who I am.

JA: Enough Harry Potter for now. What about taking your kit off on stage, Daniel? That caused a bit of a stir, didn't it? *[Earlier in the year Daniel had starred on the West End stage in* Equus.*]*

DR: It did a bit, yeah. I found all that quite funny. I expected there to be a bit of shock. But most of the people who were criticising – and there were more than a few of them – generally hadn't read the play. Because if they'd read the play, they'd know it was important. It wasn't just gratuitous nudity. It wasn't really a surprise, but I did find it rather funny.

JA: And what sort of nudity was it? Just sort of lying there quietly and just keeping out of the way sort of nudity, or was it parading round full frontal nudity?

DR: I was blinding horses naked. So it was quite physical nudity.

I was quite nervous the first two times I did it, but after that you actually stop caring.

JA: Was that something that you felt you had to do just to break away? A lot of shock horror factor, wasn't there?

DR: I didn't just do it for the sake of shocking people. It was the fact that it's an amazing play and it's the first revival in the West End for 30 years and it's such an honour to be involved. That was the reason for doing it. But also it did have that added bonus that it started to make people see me as an actor, rather than just Harry Potter.

JA: And that's got to be the big goal in your life, hasn't it? You've been part of something really special and will continue to be for a while. It's what comes next for you, isn't it?

DR: There will always be a certain number of people who will view me as Harry Potter, but that's more their problem than mine, because that won't stop me doing other things. I'm just going to continue working, hopefully, and doing other hopefully interesting jobs. And it's up to them whether they want to see me as an actor or they want to see me as just Harry.

JA: But you're young enough to shake Harry off, aren't you?

DR: Time's on my side for a little while – touch wood.

JA: And cricket-wise, this is the start, hopefully, of a long love affair.

DR: Absolutely. I can't see it changing.

[At that point Aggers presented Daniel with a birthday present from Test Match Special *– the book* Test Match Special: 50 Not Out, *signed by the commentary team.]*

JA: Read that, rather than Harry Potter, tonight.

DR: I shall do.

JA: And Shilpa's got a cake.

*

A rare instance of TMS *presenting someone else with a cake.*

DAVID CAMERON

interviewed by Jonathan Agnew,
Lord's, 11 July 2008

Shortly after David Cameron became Leader of the Conservative Party in 2005, Jonathan Agnew told me that he'd met him at some function and discovered that he was a bit of a cricket fan. That is the sort of news we like to hear and so his name was added to our 'hit list'.

He came to the commentary box on the second day of the First Test against South Africa in 2008, enjoying a morning in which Kevin Pietersen and Ian Bell took their partnership to 286 for the fourth wicket. Pietersen, by the time rain brought an early lunch, had gone for a glorious 152, but Bell was to fall later for 199. Eventually, despite following on, South Africa were able to bat out the draw comfortably.

An issue at the time was the impending return to the England side of Andrew Flintoff, after an eighteen-month lay-off for injury, and who would be the one to make way for him.

Within two years David Cameron would become the youngest British Prime Minister for nearly 200 years, but on this day, even surveying a wet Lord's, his youthful enthusiasm was more immediate.

*

DAVID CAMERON: I feel I've arrived in the temple of cricket. I've listened to *Test Match Special* for a long time and it's great to be here. I've even found the cake! I'm depressed to see you've eaten half of it already and it's only lunchtime.

From this view you can really see the ball – how straight it is – which way it's swinging. You get an incredible view, which anywhere else on the ground – and I love coming to Lord's – it's not quite like this.

JONATHAN AGNEW: You have followed cricket? You've played cricket?

DC: Yes, I used to play quite a bit at school and then played a little bit for my village, where I was brought up. Then I stopped for a long time and then last year, weirdly, I played a game for my brother, who has a team every year and I got the highest score. I got 65 – the highest score I've ever had in my life. And that was having not played for a couple of years. So, total fluke – very aggressive – dropped about three times, but everything seemed to go the right way. I was more of a tennis player than a cricket player, but played quite a bit. And I always liked coming to Lord's to watch some cricket. Some happy memories here.

JA: Village cricket! It's the bedrock of all of society, isn't it?

DC: It's very competitive, with a lot of cut-throat competition. The trouble is I've now got young kids. And cricket and children don't really go together, because it's the whole day. Cricket and politics and children really don't go together, so this is a bit of a treat. I've bunked off work for a morning to come and watch.

JA: Any memories of watching cricket in years gone by?

DC: The first time I came to Lord's I watched Bob Woolmer make a century against the Australians and I think it was about 1977. *[It was indeed 1977 in the Jubilee Test Match that Bob Woolmer made 120 in the second innings of a drawn match, having made 79 in the first.]* I remember that and a really exciting memory coming to watch Botham bowling them out in the morning. He got 8 for 30-something, I'd had the day off school and the whole thing was over by lunchtime. *[A good memory again of 1978, when Pakistan were bowled out for 139, losing their last eight wickets on the Monday morning for 43. Ian Botham took 8 for 34, following a century, and England won by an innings and 120 runs.]*

JA: Was he one of your childhood sporting heroes?

DC: Definitely. It's corny to say so, but it's definitely true. For that 1981 Ashes series I was just the age of cricket obsession and I remember particularly the Headingley Test, switching on the TV and thinking they're not going to get anywhere and seeing that incredible 149 and Graham Dilley and then Bob Willis's incredible bowling. That Test Match I suppose will always be the one I'll think of and remember the most. More so than when we got the Ashes back in 2005 – just because I think I was so alert and excited about cricket at that stage and Botham just seemed to be doing the completely impossible.

JA: And a nation needs sporting heroes, doesn't it?

DC: Yes. They cheer us up when things are a bit grim, as they are at the moment. We need heroes and I think Kevin Pietersen has been great for English cricket. That great Ashes innings a couple of years ago. I was actually visiting a school next to the Oval at the time and these huge cheers were going up. So we need our heroes and cricket's provided a few.

JA: To slip into politics – the selectors are trying to get Andrew Flintoff back into the side and you've got your own Andrew Flintoff – you're trying to get David Davis back into your team. *[The shadow home secretary, David Davis, a month before had resigned his parliamentary seat to force a by-election on the single issue of civil liberties and the extension of detention without trial for terrorism suspects. Mr Davis had won back his seat the day before this interview.]*

DC: Well, cricket and politics are similar in that it is a team game and you've got to play as a team. David is a star.

JA: So you can feel a bit how Geoff Miller does.

DC: Cricket is different in that you've got really to look at who is playing the best cricket at any one moment and they earn their place back in the team. I suppose if anything politics is even more of a team game than cricket in that way.

JA: It doesn't strike one as being that, does it?

DC: No, everyone thinks it's kill or be killed and knives in the back, but it isn't actually. You succeed in politics when the team plays together and thinks as a team and has its disasters as a team and recovers as a team and wins as a team.

JA: Do you select entirely on merit? Here we have Ian Bell having scored a hundred.

DC: Do you think he'd like a place in the shadow cabinet? It is on merit. You need a parliamentary party where people are competing for jobs and that's now happening. We've got enough Tory MPs now that they are genuinely competing to get onto the front bench – to get into the shadow cabinet.

I think, though, there is a role in making sure you are representing some different views and some different voices. I appointed the first Muslim woman to any Cabinet or shadow cabinet – Sayeeda Warsi from Yorkshire. She's there on merit, but I think it's a good thing to turn round and say to British

Muslims, 'Look, you can go all the way to the top. You can be part of this country. You can succeed in whatever field you want to.' I think it's important that we are a collection of all the talents and all the voices.

JA: What about sportsmanship in politics? Again, something that we're very keen on up here in *Test Match Special*. Sportsmanship is everything, I think, as far as cricket is concerned. Is there much sportsmanship in politics?

DC: There is. When your opponents do something good, I think it's right to say well done. I think the Prime Minister's done very well over Zimbabwe. He really pushed it to the top of the agenda at the G8. He showed those pictures of the opposition politicians beaten up. And I said, 'Congratulations. You really played an important role.'

And I think that a bit of sportsmanship of saying that I like that idea – that's your idea, but I'd like to do it too – that's good. We should have more of that. But, as in cricket, there should be some time for robust exchanges as well. We have our own umpire, if you like – the Speaker, who tries to keep order. Not always easy.

JA: He gives the occasional one out.

DC: Sometimes he lets one through as well. But you never criticise the Speaker, because otherwise you don't get called, so he has an added advantage.

JA: You mentioned Zimbabwe and that's something I really must talk to you about. How did you feel the ICC handled that issue? Should you mix politics with sport? *[A week before, Zimbabwe had withdrawn from the 2009 Twenty20 World Cup to be held in England.]*

DC: I think it's inevitable that the two do get mixed. I think it's right that we're saying Zimbabwe shouldn't come and that we shouldn't tour. I think that is right. You try and keep them separate when you can, but there are times when it does get mixed and particularly in a country like Zimbabwe, where Mugabe is in charge – effectively – of everything. And I think that to pretend that you could go ahead and have a sporting relationship – you know that Mugabe would use that massively to try and enforce his own position. And we've got to do everything we can as a country and as a European Union and as a developed world to say that what Mugabe is doing is unacceptable.

JA: Is it a realistic view, do you think, for the ICC to take the stance that we have nothing to do with politics? Which is their view. And many people were of the view that Zimbabwe should have been suspended anyway from the ICC. But they weren't, they voluntarily stepped down. They'll still receive their appearance money for this thing that they're not actually appearing in. Are you comfortable with the way sporting bodies do this?

DC: It's a difficult one. I'm not sure that I want to dive into this great row on a day like this, but I think they've got to show some awareness, if I can put it like that. Obviously they're a sporting body – they're responsible for the sporting side, but they have to show a wider responsibility – a wider awareness.

JA: And what needs to change in Zimbabwe in your view for us to play sport against them again? Is it simply that Mugabe has to go – full stop?

DC: Right now it is very hard to see any way that the country is going to recover with Mugabe and his henchmen being there. This guy has terrorised his own people, has stolen an election and has turned the breadbasket of Africa into a complete basket case. I think it's impossible to envisage how Mugabe can stay and Zimbabwe be all right. He has to go. I think he's got to be out of the picture. I think the way he's behaved is so appalling he has to be out of the picture. I can't see some sort of middle way.

And I think the key is obviously South Africa. They have such an influence over Zimbabwe as a trading partner, as a neighbour, as the power of the region, I think they could do a lot more just to say this is unacceptable.

JA: Back to cricket. Twenty20. We're talking about it lots up here. Have you seen much of that?

DC: I haven't. I'm enthusiastic. I want to go and see some games. I love one-day internationals and I remember going to a day/night game first in South Africa years ago and having a fantastic evening. You know they have these sort of *braais* – the barbecues round the edge of the ground. You could hardly see the cricket there was so much smoke. But it was fantastic. And the climate is so much more suited to it than ours is.

Cricket is exciting. I think five-day Tests are incredibly exciting and the subtlety for those of us who love cricket – the endless subtle changes between who's ahead and who's behind. But we've got to have the really fast, exciting end of cricket too and I don't think there's a conflict. I think there was a time when you had the old guard saying, 'We can't have too much of this new stuff.' I think you do both. I don't see a conflict.

JA: But with your background – Eton and Oxford – it suggests traditionalist.

DC: Well, I've been a bit of a moderniser. I've said to the Tory party, look, some things have got to change round here. More women candidates – emphasis on the environment and the NHS. But I'm a traditionalist in some ways.

JA: Coloured clothing and Twenty20 sounds your sort of thing, then.

DC: Don't lose what you've got – it's the same with the Conservative Party – don't lose the tradition and the under-standing of British history and traditions. But add on the new. I call it the politics of 'and'. And I think we need the cricket of 'and'. I'd hate it if suddenly we lost Lord's and players dressed in white clothing and all of that. But I don't think there's a conflict between having that and also having the new, exciting edge of cricket.

JA: Because we need to get kids playing, don't we? That really is the important thing that Twenty20 is doing. We've got to get kids playing sport – full stop.

DC: Absolutely. I think the move there was against competitive sport in some parts of our country – people go to a sports day and you can't have a race that anyone might win – is pathetic – it's ridiculous. We've got to kick that sort of political correctness out completely.

I went to a small prep school. We were beaten by everyone – it was a good preparation for being a Conservative politician, actually, losing often. But in life you do win and you do lose. And I think trying to wrap kids in cotton wool and say competi-tion is a bad thing is crazy, and I think it's bad for them too. So sport in schools is absolutely vital.

I think actually the cricketing authorities, with some of their programmes, are doing quite a good job.

JA: Chance to Shine and that sort of thing?

DC: Yes. I went to the Oval to talk to them about it and hear about their plans. I think it's quite impressive actually.

JA: Do you think it's a shame that it comes down to charities to try to get cricket operating in schools? Is it too late for cricket in schools? I remember John Major giving a speech at a Cricket Writers' do a few years ago. He said that his biggest regret as a politician was the selling of playing fields in his time. Is it too late?

DC: We've said there ought to be a moratorium on so-called D1 land, which includes playing fields. We shouldn't lose any more playing fields. I think the problem is that on the one hand you want to harness the enthusiasm of the voluntary bodies and the clubs which bring an enormous amount to sport and at the same time sport will really only thrive if it's got a key part in the school day. So I think you've got to do both.

We came up with a policy at the previous election of giving all kids a kind of voucher to spend with local sports clubs, like the rowing clubs and the bowling clubs and the cricket clubs involved with the school. I think that was a good policy and we should look at that again. But you can't ignore what happens in the main school day. You've got to have the playing fields, you've got to have the teachers who are enthusiastic about sport and you've got to have the time.

JA: Teachers always get a bit of stick in conversations like this.

DC: I feel sorry for them, because the government is always asking – 'This week you've got to do cooking lessons', then it's citizenship lessons, then it's health lessons. Politicians are always throwing more stuff at teachers. No wonder they turn round and say, 'Well, I'm completely knackered. I've got an enormous curriculum. All these extra things you've asked me to do – and now you wonder why I won't do the sport.' So we've got to back off a bit and trust the head teacher and the teachers who run the school to do more and lead by example, that sport should be a big part of that.

JA: People reckon, David, that I've got the best job in the world.

DC: I think you have.

JA: Well, I reckon yours can't be bad. You can govern without responsibility. You can ambush the poor old Prime Minister there at question time. Up he gets every week and you've been swotting away for a week with the questions you're going to ask him. The poor old fellow gets harpooned, because he doesn't know what you're going to ask him.

DC: He gets the final say, though, that's the thing. I get the advantage. I pick the subject and I can think of what I want to ask, but he gets the last say. And Blair was always very good at this. No matter how good your question was. No matter how you'd tried to make a strong argument. In the end you'd sit down when you'd finished and he'd carry on harpooning you. So that's the disadvantage.

Look, I love my job. It's an incredible opportunity to lead a political party, to set out the ideas of the alternative government, to say how I think we can do things differently. I really enjoy it. There are some pressures. You may have noticed there have been a few Conservative leaders along the last few years. I'm trying to reduce the turnover.

JA: Is it fun?

DC: There are fun elements to it. There's some hard work involved. There's a lot of policy development work. There's a lot of team leadership. There are a lot of fascinating conversations, but also tragic ones. I was talking to the head teacher of a school yesterday where a boy had been stabbed actually on his way to go and play sport, 30 yards from his home, just going off to the football pitch. And when you hear about things like that, it makes you burn with desire to get something done about it. But it is tragic that not far away from this beautiful ground there are some terrible things happening on our streets.

JA: I love the theatre of Prime Minister's Questions.

DC: It is theatre.

JA: Does that achieve anything?

DC: Yes. I've worked now on both sides of the fence. I worked for John Major briefly when he was Prime Minister and I helped him prepare for question time. There is a purpose. If you're Prime Minister you've got to know absolutely everything that's going on in your government. Your tentacles have got to stretch out into every department and you've got to be happy with every answer to every potential question.

So it brings the government together. They've got to work out, 'Are we right about this car tax thing? Are we right about our plans on Zimbabwe?' It's a very important moment to make the government accountable.

I think the other thing is – yes, it's theatrical, yes, it's noisy – but I think there's something at the heart of it. To be a Prime Minister and to go through question time, you've got to show you're on top of your game and I think that's an important thing.

JA: Is it possible to flannel your way through it?

DC: You have good days and bad days. You definitely have days when you think, 'That was a good set of questions. I got a good point across', and other days when you think, 'Well, that didn't really work.'

I'd hate it if people thought that's all Parliament was about. The select committees do a vital job, scrutinising departments. The debates we have about legislation – hopefully we get those right. We do all sorts of things to call the government to account. This is just one bit of theatre.

When I started being Leader of the Opposition, I wanted to try and take some of the Punch and Judy out of it and make it a bit more reasonable.

JA: How long did that last?

DC: About five minutes. I accept – I failed. I put my hand up. Because it's the time when all the MPs who've been busy signing letters and working, crowd into the chamber and it's like the Circus Maximus. They're going to see Christians fed to the lions and either you're a Christian or you're a lion. Some weeks you're one and other weeks you're the other.

JA: It looks quite hostile at times. When you're watching on telly, you only get the person who's speaking, you don't see what's happening yards in front of you on the other bench.

DC: It is quite hostile. It's also very noisy. The TV drowns out a lot of the noise. The things they shout at you, you couldn't repeat on a family programme like this – particularly Dennis Skinner.

JA: Big cricket fan, Dennis.

DC: Is he? I didn't know that. I've got something nicer to talk about.

JA: How much time does go into the preparation?

DC: I have a think about it on Tuesday night before Wednesday. Then I get up on Wednesday morning – that's the day I cycle into work, get a bit of blood coursing through the veins – and sometimes I change my plans completely and I chat with a few people about it. It takes a morning of preparation. Always a relief when it's over. At about ten minutes to twelve you think, 'I would rather be anywhere – even facing Ntini – than doing this.'

JA: I just have a feeling that it doesn't matter how good you are, it's the people's view of the government that matters. If people are happy with the government, they'll vote them in next time and if they're not happy with the government they'll vote against them, rather than for the opposition.

DC: Up to a point. The Conservative Party is doing well at the moment, partly because the government is doing badly. But I would argue for some of the changes we've made in terms of modernising the party, in terms of talking about the issues people care about, whether it's the state of our health service or the breakdown we see in society. I think part of the success is because we've got our act together. We've sharpened up. We've got good people in the shadow cabinet. We've changed the way we select candidates. We've presented a more modern face. So some of the success is down to us. But I confess that Gordon Brown has helped a bit.

JA: That's the only one of those you're allowed, David.

DC: You started it!

JA: But the fact is that whatever you do in politics, it always ends in tears. There's always a sad ending.

DC: That's true. It was Enoch Powell who said, 'All political careers end in failure.' I take the view that it is, as David Davis said, a noble cause. I think public service is important. If you think you can contribute, you should try. And I think it's enormously satisfying.

As a constituency MP – later today, after a bit of cricket, I'm going on down to my constituency – all the time you feel you are achieving some things on behalf of the people you represent.

Look, if it all goes wrong and you fail in your bigger ambitions, the fact is that actually being a Member of Parliament, serving your constituency, progressing those sorts of issues you care about – that is a good thing.

JA: It's very noble, but wouldn't you love an ovation like Kevin Pietersen – 29,000 people saying 'Well done'? Bat raised – that was fantastic. Politicians don't get that.

DC: No, that's very true. You often get 29,000 people shouting at you. But if you believe in what you're doing, if you think it's worthwhile and if you think you have the chance to make the changes you'd like to see, then do it. But be yourself, give it your best shot and others will judge you. As long as you're happy in what you're doing and you feel you're being true to yourself, I think then you can achieve good things and not be miserably unhappy at the same time. If you are miserably unhappy, go and do something else.

JA: Sportsmen have to be a model for society. What do you think about the scrutiny that politicians face? Does it matter if you lit a dodgy one up at university? Does it really matter?

DC: I thought this was going to be one of those nice, gentle interviews!

I've laid out my credo on this. If you're in public life, people have a perfect right to dig around at you and your life. But I think you are entitled to say, 'Before I came into public life I had a past, which is private. The past can remain the past.' I think that's a reasonable line to draw.

JA: I do agree with that entirely. Which is why I make the point – the scrutiny is still there. Is it not frightening off decent people?

DC: That is a worry. I worry that the scrutiny does frighten off some good people. I'm very keen on city mayors. I think all our big cities should have mayors and I think people like Mayor Bloomberg in New York, coming out of business into politics – that's great. I'd love to encourage a generation of business people to do that, but I think they do worry about the scrutiny.

Personally, I think I'm asking people to make a big decision to make me their Prime Minister and I think they're perfectly entitled to know a bit about you and your life – likes and dislikes – what makes you tick. And so a certain amount of scrutiny is inevitable.

JA: Has your life changed massively over the last couple of years?

DC: Recently I had the *Daily Mirror* following me to work on my bicycle – by car and bike for four weeks, without me knowing. So I do get a bit of sometimes unknown scrutiny. But it's nice to know they were looking over me. They caught me going through some red lights, which is terrible and no one should ever go through a red light.

No, life hasn't changed that much. I can still go shopping and I don't get too harassed. I can live a pretty normal life at the weekends.

JA: But you can't do anything wrong, can you? You have to be an absolute goody two-shoes from now on. You can't say naughty words. You can't speed – no one wants you to speed, of course.

DC: Whenever I make a speech saying that in order to solve the problems of the age, we need everyone to be responsible and to take responsibility, I always say, 'Look, by the way, politicians are human. We screw up. Our marriages break down. We fail frequently as citizens. We go through red lights sometimes on a bicycle.' To say that responsibility is important, doesn't mean we're perfect, that we're lecturing you. We're not. We are flawed and failing too, but we have to accept that responsibility is an important thing in life. Does that make sense?

JA: I think it does.

Isn't this the most amazing place, in that you have all the history and tradition and yet you have cutting-edge technology like the hover cover out there.

DC: The big change I notice from coming years ago is the big screens, showing the replays. That has changed the way the crowd react. We used to be crowded over the radio, 'What the hell happened there?' Now you're all watching it.

JA: Have you any views on technology in cricket?

DC: I've heard the debates you sometimes have and people take strong views. I favour generally trying to use the technology. I think at Wimbledon the system of challenges did work quite well this year. When you're sitting there watching the television, saying it clearly wasn't out and yet the guy was given out, I think it is worth – just as a fan and not as a politician, I hasten to add – asking, 'Could we use the technology a bit more?' The third umpire's been a big success, hasn't it?

JA: There is a possibility that you might be Prime Minister when the Olympics happens here. Does that excite you?

DC: It excites me hugely. I think it'll be fantastic for the country. It frightens me too, because it is an enormous undertaking. Your whole country is on show and it is so important that it's a success. And you've got so many moving parts, getting everything finished on time, making sure the security's right, making sure you secure the legacy for the future. It's an enormous undertaking and whoever wins the election, it's absolutely vital we make the right decisions.

JA: Were you for it from the start – the money and the whole debate about where it should be?

DC: Yes. I think there have been some problems over the budget in that not enough was said early enough about how big it was going to be. It's been drawn out slowly about how big the budget is. When you go to the site it is inspiring what is going to be achieved in terms of transforming that part of the east of London. Most of the decisions have now been made and the main thing is to make a success of it.

JA: How do I, sitting in Melton Mowbray, think that this Olympics is going to belong to me?

DC: That's what the whole legacy programme is about. It's about making every school feel that they are doing things in the run-up to 2012 that make sure they feel they get a benefit from it. And also it's making the games themselves accessible – particularly by public transport.

JA: Have you got a view on drugs and sport?

DC: I think the sort of zero tolerance approach has got to be right in sport. Because it can so poison sport. The approach the government and the authorities have taken I think is right.

JA: You can't be a successful sportsman without being ambitious, I think. Is it possible to be a successful politician without ambition?

DC: I think it's a myth to think that everyone who goes into politics wants to be Prime Minister. They don't. When I first became an MP I did not think, 'Right, I want to lead the Conservative Party.'

JA: Honestly?

DC: Honestly. And most people who go into politics don't think that either. They believe in public service. They care about the area they represent. They have some things they care passionately about. There are lots of people in Parliament who aren't wildly ambitious, but they care very deeply about a particular issue and they push it and fight for it.

JA: Characters. We're always bemoaning the lack of characters up here. Can you be a character in modern politics? Without stepping on people's toes? Without being off message?

DC: Look at Boris. A year ago people said to me, 'No one will beat Ken Livingstone. He's got London in his pocket for ever.' Boris is a character and I think that probably helped him get his message across. And Ken Livingstone was a character, too. I hope that modern politics doesn't squeeze out any non-conformity and difference. *[Boris Johnson had just recently defeated Ken Livingstone in the election for Mayor of London.]*

Character is important. In the end a lot of people want to know not just what your policies are, but what's your character like. How will you react to different situations? What's your judgement like? I think there's room for characters. We've got some on our side and they've got a few on theirs.

JA: Our visitors' book here has John Major signing in various roles and then as Prime Minister. So perhaps if you sign now, in years to come you might be able to update it.

LILY ALLEN

interviewed by Jonathan Agnew,
The Oval, 22 August 2009

It is no secret to regular Test Match Special *listeners that Aggers has discovered Twitter. In fact he has become something of a Twitter addict. Whatever the pros and cons of this might be, it did throw up one bonus with the surprise revelation that the young singer/songwriter, Lily Allen, was a cricket fan.*

The final Test of 2009, in which England recaptured the Ashes, brought her in whenever concert commitments permitted. The afternoon session of the day before this interview had seen Stuart Broad provide the final turning point in the match and the series, ripping out the heart of Australia's first-innings batting with four quick wickets.

In putting this book together, I have always tried as faithfully as possible to capture the speaking style of the interviewee in each case. A great feature, though, of this session was Lily's frequent delightful chuckle and that, I am afraid, I could not capture. Please imagine it for yourself.

*

JONATHAN AGNEW: We've been looking forward to this.

LILY ALLEN: Not as much as I have.

JA: You've made quite a journey to come here. You're a busy girl.

LA: Yeah, I am. I was here on Thursday and then at eleven o'clock on Thursday evening we went to Holland. I played there yesterday evening and got on the bus overnight and then drove here from the M25 this morning.

JA: I was speculating earlier that this wasn't the old National Express bus, was it?

LA: No. It's a sleeper bus. It's got my own bedroom in the back, but actually I didn't get much sleep. Nerves, Aggers – you've got me nervous.

JA: What I did hear yesterday was that you were trying to listen to the cricket from Amsterdam and you went to some pretty decent lengths.

LA: Well, on my bus they had a radio, but they didn't have long wave, so we managed to get one of the sparks to literally weld a mobile phone to some speakers and we got you that way. And when I did the walk to the stage it was just when Broad started bowling everyone out and we got to the side of the stage and I was looking on the BBC Sport website and refreshing, refreshing, refreshing. And I was screaming, 'Australia are all out!' and I was really, really happy and really excited.

And everyone's saying, 'What are you going on about?'

I just like cricket – obviously!

JA: It was an exciting day.

LA: When we left on Thursday it was a bit deflating, but yesterday it was really, really exciting. But I guess that's cricket.

JA: Now, when did all this start?

LA: I guess about the same time that I heard that Freddie Flintoff had a wee at Downing Street. That was when I got interested in cricket. No, I followed the 2005 Ashes and my boyfriend's very into it. So we've been watching it for the whole summer. But I personally think it should be seven or nine Test Matches, rather than just five. I think it should be all-out war over the summer.

JA: Just play them all the time? It's OK if we're winning.

It's an unusual inspiration, Lily. I look back at the way I got interested in cricket – Peter Lever bowling at Lord's, or whatever it was. Andrew Flintoff relieving himself in the Prime Minister's garden – that must be an unusual way of getting involved in the game.

LA: Yeah, maybe.

JA: He got in trouble for that.

LA: Did he?

JA: I've been reading some of your messages. I think you thought he was a bit of all right, didn't you – Freddie?

LA: I think he's quite attractive. Not as attractive as Graham Onions and not as attractive as Stuart Broad. Lots of girls seem to fancy Broad. I personally don't. He's not my type. I like a bit more rough round the edges. He's kind of a bit of a pretty boy, isn't he? Very good at cricket.

JA: Very good at cricket. This Onions thing is strange, isn't it? Onions was a bit surprised by it. He's a very quiet lad, you know.

LA: Oh, poor Onions. I'm sorry, Onions. It's all right, I'm over you now.

JA: Well, that didn't last long.

LA: Players come and go.

JA: So, like many, you were drawn into cricket in 2005. That was great, wasn't it? Were you actually following it and were you caught up in the cricketing bandwagon?

LA: My dad's really into cricket and so's my brother, so I'm forced to sit and watch sport all weekend. But I'm happy to – especially when things are exciting as they were then and are now.

JA: But did you start as a kid? Did your dad go off and play cricket?

LA: Yeah, he used to play. They had sort of pub teams and we'd go every weekend over the summer and the girls would sit up in the pavilion, making sandwiches, and the boys would play cricket. I'm just getting to grips with the scoring and stuff. It completely went over my head when I was a kid. Now I'm trying to figure it out. I'm not very sure about the extras thing.

JA: Well, they're runs that don't come off the bat.
    How are you getting on with the umpiring signals?

LA: That one's good! *[Holding up one bent index finger.]*

JA: Oh, the crooked finger – Billy Bowden.

LA: I've now got my own thing for a four.

JA: Sort of paddling. Why that?

LA: I don't know. We just came up with it on Thursday and it caught on. Everyone was doing it in our stand after a while.

JA: Umpiring signals are essentially designed so that everyone can understand what they are. But they do have their own quirks, like umpire Bowden.

LA: This doesn't come across very well on radio, does it?

JA: To a 24-year-old singer, what's the appeal of cricket?

LA: I'm an entertainer and my shows last an hour and it's all very quick and life in the fast lane. I'm not into Twenty20 at all. I'm into Test Matches, because I like the whole five-day slog.

JA: You are a traditionalist.

LA: Yes, I'm a traditionalist and I like the kind of beauty of the game – the whites against the green and the pace of it. And the fact you're allowed to drink in the stands is great, which you're not allowed to do at football. I like so many things. I like the fact that umpires have to be able to hear as well as see everything. Because I often hear you say that something has come off padding rather than wood. You have to hear the noises, don't you?

I really like cricket. I love football as well – I support Fulham and I go down there as often as I can. But cricket is a new thing for me and I sort of am obsessed with it. I Twitter about it all the time.

JA: Well, this is how it started. I was sitting, minding my own business at Edgbaston – I'm new to this Twitter. I looked at how many followers you have and it's obscene. Over a million.

LA: Just beating Bumble.

JA: He is a Twitter cheat – he's massaging his figures. But messages started to come through that you were stuck somewhere on the motorway.

LA: I was on my way down to Somerset and you guys dropped out and I couldn't hear you and everyone kept Twittering to listen to 198 long wave instead of 720 AM.

JA: That's the London frequency.

LA: So that was my first run-in with *TMS*. I was panicking that we'd lost you. But we found you again, thanks to the Twitterers.

JA: We keep plugging the Twitter, because it's good fun actually. I get a lot out of it – including following you, because you've been really busy. Over the last few weeks you've been all over the place.

LA: I've done 33 festivals this summer, which is a lot. I'm going to a festival this afternoon. At 4:50 I'll be on stage. And then I'm playing tomorrow again in Stafford.

JA: Festivals being one night and on you go?

LA: Well, they tend to happen over the weekends. They start everywhere in Europe on a Thursday and then they end on Sunday. Obviously you can't play the same festival every day, so we travel from festival to festival – on a bus usually. And we try to do perhaps Eastern Europe in one block weekend and then the rest of Europe. That's how it works.

JA: It sounds exhausting.

LA: It's tiring, but I'm young.

JA: Well, what a colourful life you have. But it's interesting that you have that traditional side of you. Isn't cricket an extraordinary contrast with what you do?

Now, thirteen schools. How do you get through thirteen schools? Were you expelled from all of them?

LA: No, I was asked to leave a couple of them.

JA: Is that different?

LA: I won't go into what for. Yeah, I went to a lot of schools, but that was also because we moved around a lot. We lived in Ireland for a bit and we lived in Los Angeles for a bit when I was a kid. We moved all over London and you have to be in the catchment area for certain state schools and we'd move out of them, so it just made sense.

JA: It wasn't just for bad behaviour.

LA: Some of it was for bad behaviour.

JA: You've always been a bit wild, have you? Are you a party girl?

LA: Who wouldn't be in my position? Having fun. Come on, Aggers!

JA: Well, that's great, but don't you get a lot of negative stuff as well, though, because you're out there and having fun?

LA: Yes, but I try just to ignore it. Most of what you read in the newspapers is absolute rubbish. In fact today in the *Sun* it said that I was here on Thursday, writing on programmes that I fancied all the cricketers and that we went for a drink with the players in the bar afterwards. In fact I was out of here as soon as the last ball was bowled.

JA: But you do have this spotlight on you a lot of the time, don't you? Photographs being taken here, there and everywhere.

LA: That's the thing, really – the photographs. So long as they have a photograph, they'll make up a story to go with it. The key is just to try and stop the photographs. That's what I'm working on presently.

JA: But can you?

LA: I can, yeah. I've taken them to court and I've just got a harassment order against them, so they're not allowed to come near me really.

JA: I put your name in the computer to do a bit of research and found a new term to me – 'wardrobe malfunction'. It seems there has been a photographer around at times, just when things have happened.

LA: About six months ago it was like a red carpet outside my house. Every time I walked out of the door there would be twenty guys with cameras and they'd all get in cars and follow me across the whole of London, wherever I was going. And then they'd get out and clamber all over my car, scratching it up. Occasionally during the day, if you bend forward, something might hang out and there are guys with cameras there to catch it all the time. That's the 'wardrobe malfunction'.

JA: But do you mind? You get publicity out of it.

LA: I'm not shy. If there's one thing I do not need, it's publicity. But I'm not embarrassed about things like that. I get annoyed when people make things up that hurt other people. When it starts to get my family or boyfriends involved, that starts to be upsetting. But I put myself in this position, so I'm willing to take some flak. But it's when other people get hurt that it upsets me.

JA: They're quite brave to take you on – boyfriends and things. Because that opens up their lives too.

LA: Let's not go there, Aggers. Let's move on.

JA: Let's talk about your music, because I'm just getting into that. Do you write a lot of your music?

LA: Yes, I write all my lyrics and the top lines that I sing. I write everything. I kind of have a little bit of help from producers as far as background music goes, but everything else is mine.

JA: Really? From start more or less to finish. I looked at iTunes and after every song of yours there was, written in red, 'Explicit'.

LA: Yeah, I do swear quite a lot in my songs.

JA: Why?

LA: Because I feel it's the right way to express how I'm feeling at that particular time. If I'm trying to be angry, a swearword might help.

JA: The other day I'd got the lyrics for one of your songs that I'm not going to go into. I was reading the words aloud off the screen – quite loudly.

LA: Are you sure you weren't looking at one of my wardrobe malfunctions?

JA: I think I had the split screen. I was reading out the title to this song quite loudly, when, to my absolute horror, I looked just here to my left and three yards away there was a lovely woman, bearing a cake and she said, 'Aggers, I've brought this for you.' And she heard me saying the most appalling language. That was quite embarrassing.

LA: That is truly awful. Talking of appalling language, I think we should be able to hear more of the sledging. I think that's how you're going to get more young people into cricket. We've got to get more microphones down onto those wickets. You can see it on the TV, but you can't hear it. I want to be able to hear what they're saying – I think some pretty horrible things to each other, to try to wind each other up – no?

JA: Well they do sometimes. I think it's a bit over-rated.

LA: Oh, don't say that.

JA: Sledging, as I remember it, was more mickey-taking. It wasn't terribly nasty.

LA: You mean bullying, Aggers.

JA: I couldn't bully somebody. In a way it's eating away at your confidence. Shane Warne was a brilliant sledger.

LA: And he had a good googly, I hear. That's what I know about Warnie.

JA: Back to your music and the lyrics. Is there much of a message? Are you writing seriously about things?

LA: I try to keep things light-hearted and funny. I do definitely touch on serious subjects. But I think that's more like me as a person. If I've got something serious to say, I'll try and kind of 'funny it up' a little bit, so that it doesn't look like I'm being too earnest. It's all fun and games.

JA: I think the song I was referring to was about racism and you make a message there about the BNP and the elections and that sort of thing. So that's something you do feel strongly about and you've got a great platform for expressing your views, haven't you?

LA: I think it's important for everyone to be interested in society and what's going on politically. And it's obviously really great for me to be able to communicate with my peers in a way that other people wouldn't be able to. That's what I enjoy.

JA: It's quite a responsible position – or am I getting too old-fashioned and serious?

LA: It's all fun and games. I try not to take things too seriously and I try not to come across as being too serious. It's just fun.
  [At this stage, the approaching end of the lunch interval was indicated by the sound of the singing of 'Jerusalem' coming through the window.]

JA: Do you like all this side of it – 'Jerusalem' and 'Land of Hope and Glory' and all that sort of thing?

LA: Yeah, I do like that. I like all the Barmy Army and the trumpet-playing. It's a really good atmosphere down here. Better than it is at a lot of football matches I've been to.

JA: And how does it compare with what you do? When you go out on stage, is it like a cricketer going out in front of this?

LA: I don't know, because I've never played cricket.

JA: No, but you've sat and watched. What sort of mood do you have to be in to go out and do it? How do you prepare for it? How many people turn up for these things?

LA: Yesterday was 35,000. I think today will probably be about the same. Glastonbury was about 60 to 70,000. Sometimes it'll be 10,000 and sometimes it'll be 5,000. It rather depends where you are and which territory you're in and how well the record is doing in that place. It's a very different thing. I go on stage for an hour. If you're Stuart Broad you'll be on here for hours. If you're Freddie, maybe not.

JA: Well, we hope he is. You're obviously not fazed by it. How do you get used to going on stage and performing in front of so many people?

LA: I have a kind of ritual. I like to turn up to a concert two hours or so before and get a feel for where I am and what the crowd's going to be like. I never go anywhere near the stage, because that scares me. The first time I'll see the stage is when I walk out. I might have a little snoop round the front of the stage, trying to be as inconspicuous as possible. I do have rituals. I do all my own hair and make-up. I sit there and put music on in my dressing room and decide what I'm going to wear on that day.

JA: Can you tell straight away how you're going down?

LA: If it's going badly you need to step up your game, so it's a challenge and that's probably what I enjoy about it. When you do feel things are going a little bit flat, you really have to try to pull it out of the bag. Because people have paid good money to be there, so you've got to try to give them entertainment.

JA: I found an interview you gave, where something went rather horribly wrong at an encore.

LA: Oh, let's not talk about this, Aggers, please.

JA: Well, I'd like to, because it amused me at the time. It had obviously been quite a successful one, hadn't it?

LA: I was ill. And I went to the toilet between the last song and the encore and as you can imagine it was a bit of a stressful situation. And it wouldn't end – this stressful situation. And I could just hear the crowd going, 'Li-ly, Li-ly, Li-ly, Li-ly', while I was sitting on the toilet. And it was just the worst thing – really, really awful. So it did take a little while for me to get back out there. But I explained to them what had happened and they found it very funny.

JA: One question from a Twitterer. 'Any plans for a cricket song?' says Johnny from Shropshire, 'Now you're into the game?'

LA: Maybe. We'll see.

JA: It's good for the game to have people like you turning up, though. It is seen, don't you think, as a traditional old thing by a lot of people. It's great for cricket that there are young people like you, who've got a profile, who are going to come along and support Test cricket. Because people do talk about Twenty20 taking over the world.

LA: I'm not into Twenty20 at all. I don't like it. Sorry. I've only just started getting into Test cricket properly this year, really. What I like about it is that it's so much the polar opposite of what I do. It's so relaxing sitting here, watching the whole slog for five days. It's brilliant. You can get on with doing other things and then come back to it. My life is so fast, fast, fast – next, next, next – so it's nice to have that contrast.

Before I go, can I just say I'd really like the cricket whites to be a little more cream if possible. *[The previous year England had switched their kit to a whiter-than-white version, doing away at the same time with the traditional cable-stitch sweaters.]*

JA: Ah! That has been one of my beefs as well. I feel exactly the same way and I've gone on about these clothes that England wear.

LA: I just think they're a little bit too football.

JA: You're the first person I've had here who's brought notes. Is that you? You've got quite an organised mind.

LA: Very. I'm a complete control freak.

*

And at this point Aggers was able to present Lily with a cricket book signed by that target of her admiration, Graham Onions. And with a last giggle she was gone.

BILL WYMAN

interviewed by Jim Maxwell,
Lord's, 15 July 2010

The former Rolling Stone, Bill Wyman, found his way to Lord's during Test Match Special's *first-ever commentary on a Test not involving England – Pakistan playing Australia. (We were not doing commentary during the Triangular series in 1912, you see.)*

Since leaving the Stones in the early nineties, Bill has had his own band, Bill Wyman's Rhythm Kings. He is a successful writer, photographer and restaurateur, but it was his passion for cricket that brought him to the commentary box, and Jim Maxwell started by asking him if he'd been a regular at Lord's along with those other great Rolling Stone cricket watchers, Mick Jagger and Charlie Watts.

*

BILL WYMAN: Yeah, they're watchers. I'm a player as well. I played for about twelve years for the Bunburys and I still do the occasional game. So I've had the privilege of playing with all the greats, which has been fantastic. Batting twenty yards away from David Gower and watching him play – Viv Richards I've played with, and Brian Lara and all the England players. It's been fantastic. They're all my idols. To be actually there on the soil with them has been a wonderful experience. So I still do it occasionally.

JIM MAXWELL: It's been said a few times with other guests that musicians' great thing is that they want to play cricket – they want to play sport – while every cricketer would love to be a brilliant bass guitarist.

BW: John McEnroe got me in New York once – we'd watched the tennis – he came to my hotel room and he said, 'I want you to show me how to play bass in an hour.'

I said, 'Do you want to take me out and show me how to play tennis in an hour? It ain't on.' They think it is and it's quite amusing, actually.

JM: He's got some music ability, McEnroe.

BW: Yes, they got a band together eventually, with Vitas Gerulaitis, who was a great friend of mine, and Jimmy Connors. It was a bit heavy metal, which is not my cup of tea, but they did a good job.

JM: We'll just talk a bit about this cricket career of yours, because I think I was reading that you're probably the first person who's been on Sky TV taking a hat-trick at the Oval.

BW: I was playing with the Bunburys against an Old England team which had all kinds of people playing. Gower was playing, Derek Underwood, Foxy Fowler. Bob Willis was umpiring – a whole host of people. And the great thing was that two days before I'd had lunch with Keith Miller, who was one of my idols as a kid in the fifties – him and Neil Harvey. It was great to meet Harvey a few years ago as well. So I had lunch with Keith Miller and when we got to the Oval, Keith was in the stand with my other god, Denis Compton, and they watched me take a hat-trick, which was fantastic. Instead of me watching them score these amazing hundreds or taking wickets, it was the other way round. It was extraordinary – it was just a magic moment.

Trevor Macdonald was my first – he plays a lot of charity cricket. Gary Lineker was my second and he wasn't pleased, because he used to play for the Bunburys a lot and he always gets 60s and 80s, because he's very co-ordinated. So he wasn't very pleased at getting out first ball, and then Charles Colvile came in and he was going to tell us what to do. And I got him as well. Then we were getting phone calls at lunchtime from all the cricket grounds, saying, 'Well done, Wyman, we don't like him.'

JM: What do you bowl, Bill?

BW: Leg breaks and googlies.

JM: A good googly?

BW: Yeah. When I was playing quite a lot, I could pitch it quite well and it always confused people, because they didn't expect me to bowl googlies. So over the years I bowled Graeme Hick once, I bowled Michael Holding round his legs – he got his revenge on me in that game later – and in my last game I bowled Mark Ramprakash – he was done with a leg break and he came and gave me a big hug, so it was all quite nice.

Things just sort of happen, I don't know why, every time I play the game. I carried my bat on the hottest day in England, I've played with Botham and Flintoff and I'm in two *Wisdens* – God knows why. Someone told me and sent me the copies. 'Bill Wyman, fielding at gully, caught the ex-England captain, Brian Close, one-handed, with a cigarette in the other hand.' And when I took the hat-trick at the Oval I was smoking.

Me and Eric Clapton used to smoke all the time in the slips. It was our mark. We knew where to go. We went up the other end and when we came back we knew where to stand. When I took the hat-trick, I got this phone call and a voice says, 'Bill?'

I said, 'Who is it?'

'Charlie.'

I said, 'Charlie, where are you?'

He said, 'Somewhere … Buenos Aires or somewhere.' He's a bit vague, Charlie. He said, 'I've just heard that you took a hat-trick at the Oval.'

I said, 'Yeah.'

He said, 'You didn't stub your cigarettes out on the hallowed turf, did you?'

He's a lover of cricket.

JM: He's a collector, too, isn't he?

BW: He's got Bradman's jackets and caps and all kinds of stuff.

JM: Does your fascination run to that? Are you a collector?

BW: I do have some things. I've got a photograph of the England touring team 1932/33 and it's all signed. But I don't have many things.

I was talking just now to someone else about the nineteen wickets and Jim Laker. And I went to a special thing a couple of years ago, where they celebrated that, which was fantastic. But I remember a few years before that, when they used to play games of England Probables against the Possibles before the Test Matches. And in this game, Laker took 8 for 2 and no one talks about that. He bowled about fourteen overs, 8 for 2, which is extraordinary. But then they didn't have covers. You dealt with the weather, which I think is much more interesting, actually. *[The match Bill is recalling was the Test trial of 1950, played at Bradford. It was England vs. the Rest, and the Rest were put in on a drying pitch and dismissed for 27 in an hour and 50 minutes – Laker fourteen overs, twelve maidens, 8 for 2. England won by an innings and 89 runs before lunch on the second day.]*

JM: Where did your interest in cricket stem from? How did you get interested in the game?

BW: When I was at school I used to come to Lord's and the Oval when I was about twelve or thirteen. And my grandmother and I used to watch it on her little six-inch black-and-white television screen. She was mad on cricket, because she worked next door to where W.G. Grace was living in Lower Sydenham at one time, when she was in service, and she became a cricket fan. And she got me into it. Then I scored for Lloyds Bank for two years when I was a kid in Beckenham and they used to go on trips. I'd go to matches and I used to read a lot about it – about the history.

I was talking just now to someone about Spofforth.

JM: The Demon.

BW: There's an amazing story about how he bowled a ball so fast once that it knocked the stumps out, the wicket keeper completely missed it and a guy on the boundary tried to stop it with a coat. It tore through the coat and hit a dog and killed it. Is it true?

JM: Even if it's not true, it's a good story – like most of these stories.

BW: And wonderful things about George Gunn, who used to play with Grace. He batted with a broken bat. He wouldn't change it – just papered over it and made 50-odd. Amazing things. So I know a lot about the early history, which makes it much more interesting.

I didn't really play cricket after school until I played for the fathers against my son and I suddenly realised I could still play and bowl, though we had to play with a shaved down bat.

JM: Did someone teach you to bowl?

BW: No, I just learnt with a tennis ball in the street and it held me in good stead. Then I started to play for the Bunburys. Eric Clapton asked me to play and I think in the first game I got about 40 and took a couple of wickets. And I thought, 'Oh, I can still do it.' So I played for the next twelve years. I do the occasional match when it's a 20th or a 25th anniversary.

JM: So you're still getting asked.

BW: David English is still trying to talk me into playing for the Bunburys. I was with Jeff Thomson last year near Newmarket. It was a charity match and we kind of messed around a bit. That's where I bowled Mark Ramprakash with a leg break.

JM: In your days of touring with the Rolling Stones, did you take little side trips to go to cricket matches?

BW: Never time.

JM: Because I know you went to Australia a number of times. No Ashes matches?

BW: No, unfortunately – because we played on cricket grounds. In '73 the Stones played on all the main Australian grounds, which was kind of nice. Just to see all that stuff on the walls – the old pictures and things. It was great.

JM: Is there an opportunity to play concerts here at Lord's?

BW: No, they always go to football grounds.

JM: This place is very quiet in winter. Maybe it's not encouraged, but you'd think it would be a wonderful venue for that. You could do a Twenty20 game and a concert.

BW: The trouble is I think the seats are too far away. Where are you going to play? Are you just going to play near the stand and have that stand full? You can't play in the middle and have the whole thing full, because you're too far away. In a football ground you're nearer. I think this is twice the width of a football field, isn't it?

JM: What was the biggest audience you've played in front of?

BW: Probably Hyde Park, when we did the open-air free concert in 1969. Between a quarter and half a million people. Then we played Altamont in America in '69 and we played to about 300 to 400,000 there. But in a concert situation, it was in Prague, when we went there in 1990. We played to 119,000 in a stadium.

JM: It's one of my earliest memories as a youngster in Australia, going to a shop and paying in those days I think it was about ten shillings for a 45 – and I've still got it – 'I Can't Get No Satisfaction'. And I've been reading that it was a near thing about that actually being released as a single. It was almost a split vote.

BW: It was, yeah. When we cut all the tracks in the RCA studios in Los Angeles, we were talking to Andrew Oldham, Ian Stewart, our keyboard player and Dave Passenger, who was the engineer who did it all. And we were trying to sort out which would be the next single. And Dave and Andrew said, 'How about "Satisfaction"?'

And two people said 'No.' And the two people who said 'No' were Keith Richards and Mick Jagger, and the rest of us said 'Yes.' And so it was released on a majority vote. But of course in recent years Mick has always denied that and said it was Keith who said 'No.' But they do like re-writing history. They have a convenient memory sometimes.

JM: Going back to all the wickets you've taken, what was the best dismissal?

BW: Michael Holding. Round his legs with a googly. Because I'd bowled him two leg breaks which he'd played and then I bowled the googly, which went round his legs and hit his leg stump. And he walked up to me. And he got an inch from my face and he said, 'You wait till you bat, man. I'm going to sort you out.'

I went, 'Oh yeah' – big laugh.

So we go into the lunch interval and the Bunburys are saying, 'He's in the dressing room and he's fuming and saying what he's going to do to you when you bat.'

And I said, 'Get out of it and stop winding me up.'

And he comes and walks right behind me and says, 'I haven't forgotten. I'm going to get you when you bat.'

And I said, 'Stop winding me up.'

I was second wicket down and we lost two quick wickets to this fast bowler, and as I stepped onto the grass from the pavilion, there was an ambulance on the boundary, way over there and the siren's on, with the lights flashing. And I thought, 'That's a funny coincidence.' But they had one because there were a lot of international players there.

So, as I walked out, Michael Holding took the ball from the bowler and decided he was going to bowl. So I got there and asked for middle and leg. I'm a left-hander. And Holding is walking to the sight screen and I'm going, 'He's winding me up. Ha, ha, ha. He's been doing that ever since I got him out.' So I take middle and leg and look round at the field. There's not a person in front of me. They're all 30 or 40 yards behind – wicket keeper, seven slips, deep fine leg, deep third man. They're all way back there.

And Holding starts to come towards me at full pace. And I thought, 'No, he's still winding me up.' And he got ten yards from the stumps and the umpire and I thought, 'He's serious!'

JM: Did you have a helmet on?

BW: No, I didn't have anything.

He swung his arm and I didn't see a thing. There was a kind of 'whoosh' and 'Howzat!' and I looked round and the wicket keeper's throwing the ball in the air. They're all going, 'Yes!' And the umpire says, 'Out.'

I said, 'Out? How can I be out? I didn't even see it, let alone touch it.'

And Michael Holding comes right the way up to me, about an inch from my face again, and says, 'Of course you didn't see it, Bill. Because the wicket keeper had the ball all the time!'

It was quite a sigh of relief, because I have batted against Wayne Daniel and been hit on the thigh and had a bruise that big for weeks.

JM: You wear some protection.

BW: Oh, well, the box, that's all, just the little box, that's the only thing. So you did get injured sometimes.

JM: I would have thought those fellows would give you a nice little half volley, just to get off the mark.

BW: Some of them did. Viv Richards used to bowl sort of half pace and he was all right. But even Wayne Daniel bowling at half pace is still pretty fast for us amateurs. And I batted against all those great bowlers – Muralitharan as well.

JM: Did you pick him?

BW: No.

Nick Cook was bowling against me in one match. I was batting for Allan Lamb's lot at Northants. I'm batting away and I've got about 24 or so and Muralitharan comes and stands a yard away from me at silly point there. And I said, 'What are you doing there?'

And he said, 'We're going to get you out – next ball. You've got enough runs. We're going to get you out.'

I said, 'How?'

And he said, 'I'm going to catch you next ball.'

I said, 'I'm not going to give you a catch. You're right there – I know you're there. I'm not going to give the ball to you, am I?'

'You're out next ball.'

Nick Cook comes in – straight at my legs. Being a leftie I tried the leg sweep – off the top edge of the bat, straight into his hands. He said, 'I told you.'

And then you realise just how far ahead of you they are.

JM: You mentioned that you'd played as a band at a lot of famous venues, but you've also played cricket here at Lord's.

BW: I don't think I did anything special here at Lord's. I remember David English and me at Edgbaston went out and we were told to get as many runs as we could in four overs. And we got 62 runs. He got 49, I got thirteen. It was amazing. It was a charity thing where everybody had to try to get the most runs in four overs and we won it.

You did have those days. You just had fun. It was a great thing to do, playing charity cricket with all the greats – all the people you've admired.